GREAT SOFTWARE DEBATES

Wiley/IEEE Computer Society Publications
The world-renowned IEEE Computer Society publishes, promotes, and distributes a wide variety of authoritative computer science and engineering books. These books are available from most retail outlets. To buy our books visit *http:/wiley.com/ieeecs*

For information on the IEEE Computer Society books, please e-mail to csbooks@computer.org or write to CS Press Books, IEEE Computer Society, P.O. Box 3014, 10662 Los Vaqueros Circle, Los Alamitos, and CA 90720-1314. Telephone +1-714-821-8380. Fax +1-714-761-1784.

Additional information regarding the Computer Society Books: *http://computer.org/cspress*

GREAT SOFTWARE DEBATES

ALAN M. DAVIS

A JOHN WILEY & SONS, INC., PUBLICATION

For general information on our other products and services please contact our Customer Care
Department within the U.S. at 877-762-2974, outside the U.S. at 317-572-3993 or fax 317-572-4002.

Wiley also publishes its books in a variety of electronic formats. Some content that appears in print,
however, may not be available in electronic format.

Library of Congress Cataloging-in-Publication Data is available.

ISBN 0-471-67523-7

Printed in the United States of America.

10 9 8 7 6 5 4 3 2 1

In Memory of My Father
Barney Davis
1910–2003

Contents

List of Figures and Tables

■■■■ Preface

My purpose for assembling these essays is to make you think about the things that you may have been taking for granted up to now about software. The "right" things to do in this field are not so obvious. These essays are designed to shake you up, and perhaps make the hair on the back of your neck stand up (from anger, hopefully not fear!). I think that our industry suffers from too many people who just go along with the flow, and choose not to question what we do and why we do it. This collection of essays captures insights gained during 25 years of experience in the software industry. Many of them are controversial, and you may find you do not agree with all of them. That is the intent.

When you find an essay you particularly agree with, talk with your colleagues, and see if you can do your part to change the current course of the industry—or at least your little corner of it. After all, the industry is nothing other than the sum of all these little corners, just like yours. So change it!

And when you find an essay that you strongly disagree with, send me an email (A.M.Davis@IEEE.org), discuss it with your colleagues, tell them how misguided I am (and my essay is). I don't ask you to agree with me; I just want you to take an active role in making things change for the better in the software industry.

I wrote many of the essays included here during the past decade in my role as editor-in-chief and co-columnist (with the late and great Winston Royce) of Manager of *IEEE Software*. When appropriate, I have updated the original essay with new comments to bring it up-to-date, but most stand on their own and still apply today. The fact that most of these essays apply as much today as they did when first written bears testimony to my claim that the industry is making relatively little progress with respect to its practices. I have of course also added numerous new essays to capture my recent thoughts.

I envision two types of readers of this book: practitioners and students.

- For practitioners, this book serves as an agent of change. When you are frustrated by the lack of progress in your organization, you will likely find an essay or two here that supports your claim that something must be done. Feel free to use them to support your case. Do not feel like you are unable to make changes because of your specific role in the organization. As an executive, a middle manager, a first-line manager, or an individual contributor, you have that same frustration with the inability to make things happen, to change the way the organization "has always done something." Regardless of your role or title, talk to others, find colleagues who also want to see change happen, and then make it happen.

- In academe, most of these essays make great starting points for debates in graduate or advanced undergraduate courses. Have two students each take opposite viewpoints on the issue described in an essay. Have them debate their respective positions in front of the class. Or have them write their own essays taking both perspectives. I have on occasion asked individual students to take both positions by themselves. The exercise helps reinforce objectivity, and the usual lack of absolute truths. To assist this, I have added "seeds for debate" to the end of every essay.

Section 1 provides essays that address the state of the software industry as a whole. I spent most of my industry career as a manager, so Section II presents a series of essays dealing with the challenges facing most managers in the software industry. Most of the practical research that I have done (I have also done my share of impractical research!) has been in the area of requirements, i.e., the field devoted to ensuring that software is built to address real needs of real customers. And, thus, Section III is a collection of essays on requirements. After spending around half my career in industry and half in academe, I have developed somewhat of a curmudgeon's view of the value of research as performed at most academic institutions. It is with that attitude that I present the essays of Section IV. Finally, in Section V, I view software development from a more philosophical perspective.

Just a final reminder: You *can* make a difference!

ACKNOWLEDGMENTS

I wish to thank the staff of the IEEE Computer Society for many years of working together happily and productively and for helping me help the software profession. Among them, I especially wish to thank Angela Burgess, a friend who taught me how effective an essay (or column or editorial) can be in a magazine; Dale Strok, who served as managing editor during most of my tenure as editor-in-chief of *IEEE Software;* and Deborah Plummer, who served as my primary interface during the creation of this book. I also wish to thank Ann Zweig and Ann Hickey for their support and friendship.

I also would like to thank two universities for their contributions to this work: the University of Colorado of Colorado Springs for granting me a sabbatical so I could devote time to writing, and the University of the Western Cape, South Africa, for providing me with a stimulating environment during my sabbatical.

My parents (Hannah and Barney Davis of Freehold, New Jersey), and my children (Marsha of Boulder, Colorado, and Michael of Colorado Springs) have been instrumental in shaping me into the person I am. But, more important than anybody else is my wife and best friend for 28 years, Ginny, who has supported me through good times and bad, who gives me the strength to keep trying to make a difference in this complex world (as she tries to do the same), who gives me support when I am downtrodden, and who gives me love all the time. Thank you, dear!

About the Author

Al Davis is professor of information systems at the University of Colorado at Colorado Springs and president of The Davis Company. He has consulted for many corporations over the past 25+ years, including Boeing, British Telecom, Cadence Design Systems. Cigna Insurance, Federal Express, Flight Dynamics, Fujitsu, General Electric, Great Plains Software, IBM, Loral, McDonald's, MCI, Mitsubishi Electric, NEC, NTT, Rational Software, Rockwell, Schlumberger, Sharp, Software Productivity Consortium, Storage Tek, and Sumitomo.

Previously, he was

- Chairman and CEO of Omni-Vista, Inc., a software company in Colorado Springs that assisted companies in selecting the right features to include in products in order to maximize ROI.
- Member of the board of directors of Requisite, Inc., acquired by Rational Software in 1997, and by IBM in 2003.
- Vice President of Engineering Services at BTG, Inc., a Virginia-based defense contractor that went public in 1995, and was acquired by Titan in 2001.
- A Director of R&D at GTE Communication Systems in Phoenix, Arizona.
- Director of the Software Technology Center at GTE Laboratories in Waltham, Massachusetts.

He has held academic positions at George Mason University, University of Tennessee, University of Illinois at Champaign-Urbana, and the University of the Western Cape, South Africa.

Dr. Davis is the author or co-author of 100+ papers on software and requirements engineering. He received the Core Member Award in 1999, the Meritorious Service Award in 1999, and Certificate of Appreciation Awards in 1984 and 1998, all from the IEEE Computer Society. He received Recognition of Service Awards in 1990 and 1992 from the Association of Computing Machinery. He was also an IEEE International Distinguished Lecturer in 1983.

He was Editor-in-Chief of *IEEE Software* from 1994 to 1998, and co-columnist for the Manager Column for IEEE Software from 1992 to 1994. He is an editor for the *Journal of Systems and Software* (1987–present) and was an editor for *Communications of the ACM* (1981–1991). He is the author of *Software Requirements, Objects, Functions and States* (Prentice Hall, 1990 and 1993) the best-selling *201 Principles of Software Development* (McGraw Hill, 1995), and *Just Enough Requirements Management* (Dorset House, 2004). He is the founder of the IEEE International Conferences of Requirements Engineering, and served as general chair of its first conference in 1994. He has been a fellow of the IEEE since 1994, and earned his B.S. in mathematics from the State University of New York at Albany in 1970, and his M.S. and Ph.D. in Computer Science from the University of Illinois in 1973 and 1975, respectively.

THE SOFTWARE INDUSTRY

On one hand, the software industry has made great strides since its inception 50 years ago. Programming languages are more sophisticated. Our development processes are more mature. The applications we are constructing are more complex. The problems that we tackle increase in complexity, size, criticality, and range every year.

On the other hand, when compared to any other mature discipline (e.g., medicine, building construction, any engineering discipline except so called "software engineering"), we find major differences in the degree of satisfaction by intended users. These other disciplines seem to produce solution after solution that work as expected. And although the software industry is tackling increasingly more complex problems, it seems to create more useless systems than useful solutions. The data from many studies supports this observation.

This section explores various aspects of the software industry as a whole. The first essay, *Software Lemmings*, chastises the professionals within our industry for acting just like lemmings. Rather than making sound decisions, we regularly take a course that "everybody" is taking. After all, there is safety in numbers. In the case of giant herds of wildebeest marching across the plains of Africa, an individual animal's safety is increased because a lion attack will devour the weakest members of the herd. Our safety in numbers is a bit different. When software professionals do the same thing that everybody else is doing, they cannot be blamed for failure; all that has to be said is "but everybody is doing it!" On the other hand, if a software professional chooses to do something unique, he or she *can* be blamed. This latter argument is further explored in the next essay, *Recovering from Method Abuse*.

In *Tomorrow's Blacksmiths*, I take a much larger look at the future of the software industry. It asks, "Is software really the future?" Or are we so blinded by our own local achievements that we are failing to see a bigger solution?

Politics and religion have always attracted a wide range of disciples ranging from fundamentalists to moderates to liberals. And each religion and each country has experienced power shifts among these various players. Thus for example, in the early 2000's, Iraq was controlled by the power of Islamic fundamentalists, United States Jewry by liberal (reform) Judaism, and the South African federal government by liberalism. In the next essay, *On Software Development Strategies, Politics, and Religion,*

Great Software Debates. By Alan M. Davis
ISBN 0-471-649880 © 2004 Institute of Electrical and Electronics Engineers.

I explore the roles of conservative and liberal movements in the history of the software industry, with emphasis on power shifts.

The next essay, *Art or Engineering, One More Time,* places software development on a scale measured by engineering on one extreme and the visual arts on the other. The verdict: somewhere in between, in a position similar to home construction.

Many naïve individuals in the software industry develop metrics to measure this or that aspect of a software product or the process used to develop it. The essay, *Why Build Software?,* reminds us all that such metrics are of little significance relative to the "ultimate measure," i.e., that of whether the software solves the problem for which it was intended.

Yogi Berra said, *It Feels Like Déjà vu All Over Again.* And this brief essay describes how we could conclude that our industry is making great strides if you wear rose colored glasses, and how we could conclude quite the opposite opinion if we remove those glasses.

The essay titled *Eras of Software Technology Transfer* describes how empiricism replaced rational thought in the late 1980's, and how rationalism is slowly creeping back into vogue.

Fifteen Principles of Software Engineering is just what it says it is. I explore the 15 most important principles that software practitioners should follow.

I admit it. I have become discouraged by the way our industry uses software cost schedule estimation technology. I think it is great that folks like Barry Boehm, Capers Jones, and Larry Putnam have collected and analyzed reams of data about past projects. But I think that what people have done with this data tells only half the story. The essay called *Thoughts on Software Estimation* explores my seven biggest frustrations with the practices of software managers as they attempt to determine how long it will take to complete a software project.

Software Lemmings*

In the summer of 1958, I sat in front of my parents' bungalow at Rockaway Beach, armed with a pencil and a pad of paper. Day and evening, I collected data on the never-ending parade of subway trains that stopped at the station at the end of the block.

Every day I collected long columns of data. The neighbors were in awe. The neighbors' children were jealous every time I shouted out a new all-time record.

Obviously, the Davis boy had great talent with numbers. Obviously, he was going to be a great mathematician. Obviously, he was on the path to wisdom, truth, knowledge. I was encouraged to continue. If I was collecting data, it must be good.

What data was I collecting that entire summer 35 years ago? Arrival time, departure time, train number, number of passengers who got on board, and the number of passengers who got off. Then I added all these together to get a grand total for that train, gleefully announcing each new high. Very valuable stuff.

I was not doing anything more worthwhile, positive, or smart than the next kid. But I had a lot of people thinking otherwise for awhile.

It seems to me that software developers, in their search for the Holy Grail, are like all those who were convinced I was doing something meaningful that summer. Like children, we envy others who seem to know something we don't know. Like lemmings, we tend to follow the leader, without ever asking ourselves if we want to go where the leader is taking us. We tell ourselves that if everybody else is taking a certain path, it must be the right way to go.

I would like to play the devil's advocate for a moment and examine some software-engineering paths that have led to cliffs or box canyons in the past, paths we now believe will lead to the Promised Land, and those that have not yet been blazed. My goal is to get us all to think more about our chosen path so that we can make an intelligent decision to remain on it or perhaps to take a road less traveled.

Table 1 summarizes the lemming paths explored in this column and gives you an idea of their popularity, goals, risks and payoffs.

---

*Originally published as "Software Lemmingineering" in *IEEE Software*, 10, 5 (September 1993), pp. 79–81, 84.

Great Software Debates. By Alan M. Davis
ISBN 0-471-649880 © 2004 Institute of Electrical and Electronics Engineers.

TABLE 1.1   Lemming Trails

Trail	Active years	Goals	Time to achieve consistent results	Risk	Payoff
Structured	1965–1986	Reduce development cost	1975	Low	Low
		Increase documentation quality	1975	Low	Low
		Increase user satisfaction	1975	Low	Low
Object	1980–2000 (OOD and OOP)	Reduce development cost	1990	Low	Medium
		Increase reliability	1990	Low	Medium
		Increase maintainability	1990	Low	Medium to High
	1988–2000 (OOA)	Reduce development cost	1993	High	Low
		Improve user satisfaction	1993	High	Low
Process maturity	1990–2005	Improve process	1993	Low	Medium
		Increase user satisfaction	1993	High	Low
		Increase quality	1993	High	High
		Reduce development cost	1993	High	Medium
C	1980–2000+	Reduce development cost	1980	Medium	Medium
		Increase portability	1985	Low	High
		Increase quality	Never	High	None
		Increase maintainability	Never	High	None
Prototyping	1985–2000+	Increase user satisfaction	1993	Low	High
		Reduce development cost (by delivering throwaway prototypes to customers)	Never	High	None
CASE	1988–2000+	Moderately increase productivity	1993	Low	Medium
		Dramatically increase productivity	2013+	High	High
		Increase documentation quality	1993	Low	Medium
		Increase quality	1993	Low	Low
Reuse	1988–	Reduce development cost	1996–2003	High	Application-dependent
		Increase quality	1996–2003	High	Application-dependent
Comquats	1988–	Reduce development cost	1996–2003	High	Application-dependent
		Increase quality	1996–2003	High	Application-dependent

STRUCTURED PATH

In the 1970s, structured techniques were sold as a solution to the software industry's apparently escalating costs and growing customer dissatisfaction. First it was structured programming, then structured analysis and structured design. For a decade, we blindly marched in formation to the beat of a structured drum. By the end of the '70s, "structured" had become synonymous with "good." We were barraged with the adjective "structured."

In retrospect, the collection of widely disparate programming practices that have at various times been called "structured" has clearly been infused into our professional culture. Today, we no longer say "structured programming," we simply say "programming."

Structured analysis and structured design have not fared as well. The original structured analysis paralyzed us through overanalysis and was found unsuitable for complex real-time systems. Later versions, proposed by Paul Ward, Derek Hatley, and Edward Yourdon solved the overanalysis problems and added control mechanisms to more easily model real-time systems.

But no one stopped to ask why we were doing structured analysis in the first place. If we had, we may have realized that the goal of the requirements phase—a document that describes the system as a black box—cannot be described with hierarchical dataflow (or control-flow) diagrams.

And structured design, a simple set of practices to transform a structured analysis into a calling hierarchy, is only as effective as structured analysis.

Still, the lemmings that stampeded down the structured path had little choice. There was nowhere else to run! Now, many survivors have joined new herds heading down various other paths.

OBJECT PATH

In the late 1980s and early 1990s, object-oriented techniques were sold as a solution to the software industry's cost and customer-satisfaction problems. First it was object-oriented programming, then object-oriented design, and now object-oriented analysis. Now, "object-oriented" has become synonymous with "good," and we are barraged with this adjective.

Object-oriented programming is based on very sound principles of quality programming discovered 20 to 30 years ago: data abstraction, information hiding, encapsulation, inheritance, and so on. It is great to see these proven principles become popular. By the year 2000, they will be so infused into our culture that we'll no longer say "object-oriented programming," we'll just say "programming."

Object-oriented design (most schools of it, anyway) is based on the same solid foundations. Object-oriented designs exhibit a trait Michael Jackson preached 20 years ago: A design that fails to mimic the real world's structure is not just bad, it is wrong!

So what's at the end of the paths marked OOP and OOD? Improved maintainability and reliability, and probably reduced development costs. These are certainly sufficient reasons to stay on this track. But don't believe the road signs that promise dramatic increases in productivity and incredible success at reuse. Both might be true, but then again they might not be! Most who have chosen this path have unrealistic expectations.

Object-oriented analysis is another story. Keeping in mind the goal of the requirements phase—a specification—let's ask ourselves if we can achieve that by performing OOA. The answer is no—no OOA technique helps you achieve that goal. Even when we augment objects with state and behavioral descriptions, the problem we encountered with structured analysis remains: How can we ascertain the black-box behavior of the overall system by examining the individual behavior of a set of objects?

The claim that OOA is great because the transition to OOD is so easy is almost insane. No engineering discipline claims to have techniques that make transitioning from requirements to design easy. That very transition is 90 percent of what engineering is!

Claims of increased maintainability and reliability from object-oriented techniques make little sense in the context of requirements. The unproved (though possible) claims of dramatic improvements in productivity and reuse from using object-oriented programming and design techniques are less justified at requirements time.

PROCESS-MATURITY PATH

I got the impression at this year's International Conference on Software Engineering that everybody has at least one foot in this stampede. The goal should be to consistently produce high-quality (reliable, maintainable, usable . . .) software that satisfies customer and user needs within schedule and on budget. This calls for engineers with the right background, training, and skills; managers with the right background, training, and skills: the ability to select the correct development process for the project at hand; and enough resources (time, money, tools . . .) to get the job done. Many are following the process-maturity-model path, trying to achieve this goal.

Such models emphasize the importance of a repeatable, measurable development process. These are certainly two very important aspects of achieving the goal, but they are definitely not sufficient alone, and they may not even be necessary. With the right people, you can succeed without process repeatability or measurability. With the wrong people, you can't succeed even *with* process repeatability and measurability.

For example, hospitals routinely collect data on the success rates of surgeons, to compare and contrast physicians. However, good surgeons are good even without data. And extremely difficult operations yield very poor data regardless of how good the physicians are. Furthermore, having hard data doesn't help the surgeons get better; it simply enables the medical profession to more accurately inform the patient of the prognosis.

At this point in the industry's development, it is more important to select an appropriate process model for each project than to expect a tailored version of a generic process model to work for all projects in an organization. In short, the process-maturity path is only the first leg of a very long journey on the path to quality software, but it is just that and nothing more.

C LANGUAGE PATH

Here is another incredibly popular path. And a very dangerous one, because it leads us away from proven quality-instilling programming practices toward hacking.

That is not to say it's impossible to produce quality programs in C. Certainly it is possible. But programmers who prefer C are probably more interested in producing software fast. They'd rather not take the time to avoid error-prone constructs; they don't mind playing around at the bit or pointer level. (Programmers who prefer Ada, on the other hand, tend to avoid tricks in favor of producing error-free, fail-safe software.)

Why is the C path so crowded? The reason is simple: Unix has become a de facto standard across many hardware platforms, so writing code in C gives companies maximum flexibility in response to evolving hardware.

There is no real reason to leave this path right now, but don't deceive yourself as to your reasons for taking it. It is for market share; it is for portability; it is for short-term revenue (all very good reasons). It is not to produce a quality product, it is not for long-term market penetration; it is not for long-term profit.

PROTOTYPING PATH

Software prototyping started to become popular in the mid to late 1980s. As originally conceived, prototypes provide an early version of a system to a user, helping to uncover things like necessary or unnecessary functions and effective or ineffective interfaces. Because so many software systems built today fail to solve the users' problems, prototyping helps ensure that requirements are known before we build a full-scale system.

Prototypes are helpful only if they are built quickly, so a plethora of techniques and tools appeared to help us rapidly build prototypes. However, by 1990 the quick-and-dirty prototype was also seen as a solution to escalating software costs and slipping schedules. The logic was, "If we can produce software prototypes quickly, then we can deliver all software quickly simply by calling the prototype a product."

Think about it. If we are ineffective at producing quality software when we try, how awful will our products be if we don't try? If we don't know how to build in quality at reasonable cost, how can we expect to build in quality at negligible cost? And we certainly don't know how to retrofit quality into a prototype.

In typical lemmingineering fashion, we have taken a great idea and misapplied it.

Prototyping is a great way to help ensure user satisfaction and thus reduce cost. It is a terrible way to reduce development costs by eliminating all the techniques we know ensure quality.

The lemmings on the prototyping path have suddenly veered toward a cliff.

CASE PATH

Originally, most CASE tools were graphical editors that had rudimentary syntax-checking capability. If you are using structured analysis (or any other graphical technique) intelligently, CASE tools offer considerable improvement in productivity but only superficial improvement in quality.

CASE tools help a software engineer in the same way a word processor helps an author. A word processor does not make a poor novelist a good one, but it will make every author more efficient and their material more grammatical. A CASE tool does not make a poor engineer a good one, but it will make every engineer more efficient and their product prettier.

Don't get me wrong. CASE tools have considerable value, as do word processors. Unfortunately because it is such a competitive market, CASE tools are being sold not for their primary value, but for a whole variety of other features: automatic code generation, automatic prototype generation, automatic test generation. In evaluating CASE technology, let's try to keep in mind that there's no such thing as a free lunch.

The lemmings are (and should be) stampeding on this path, but, once again, many are not aware that what lies at the end of the path has been oversold.

REUSE PATH

All engineering disciplines encourage synthesis through the use of building blocks. Home builders use prefabricated doors and windows; bridge builders use prefabricated steel beams; circuit-board makers use off-the-shelf integrated circuits; IC makers use standard cells. In these disciplines, this practice is called "use" or "engineering," never "reuse." Only in our discipline is "reuse" such a buzzword.

Clearly, if we could use prefabricated software components (that are larger than statements) in producing new systems, development costs and schedules would be reduced and product quality should be enhanced. We are now busily populating repositories of potentially reusable components and constructing new components for systems with an eye toward their eventual reuse. An amazing amount of effort is being expended on such an immature technology.

Do we really know what a prefabricated, reusable component should look like? Of course, the marketers of repositories will say yes. Clearly, we will have to experiment with many components and many repositories before we learn what such components should look like and how best to store, retrieve, and compose them. I fully endorse vast experimentation by researchers and practitioners alike. However, the technology is still very new.

Unlike many other paths, the goals here are quite realistic and will eventually be achieved. But the path is not yet paved. Step carefully and don't be overconfident in the short term.

COMQUATS [SIC] PATH

Superimposed on our efforts to reduce cost and increase quality is our repeated disappointment with the degree of user satisfaction we have achieved with custom-built software systems. One branch of the reuse path is the commercial off-the shelf path. COTS is the ultimate in reuse. We take an existing, complete "system" and add custom software to build a new application, thus greatly reducing costs.

The resulting system may not be perfect, but then neither are fully custom systems. Increased quality (in terms of satisfying user needs) is fully dependent on the degree to which the COTS software is suitable and how easy it is to customize. Increased quality (in terms of reliability, safety, and availability) is dependent on the quality in the COTS software, hence the name Comquat, or commercial off-the-shelf quality software.

LOOK BEFORE YOU LEAP

Just because everybody's doing it doesn't make it right. On the other hand, just because everybody's doing it doesn't make it wrong. In conclusion, I offer this advice.

- Set realistic goals and be realistic about the likelihood of success.
- Don't believe the hype. Determine for yourself if a path makes sense for you and your organization. Pick a path after clearly understanding its potential risks and rewards, in both degree and probability.
- Be cautious, but don't ignore every path. You can't afford to.
- Don't forget your goal—to solve user needs with a reliable, maintainable, usable, safe system within schedule and budget. Your goal is not to "reuse maximally" or "use object-oriented analysis."
- When you achieve your goal after 17 steps of a 25-step recipe, stop!
- Whatever you do, do not follow any path just because everybody's doing it.

EPILOGUE

Since I wrote this article, a few of the fads I discussed have disappeared; software reuse and COTS have now taken on their proper roles: as useful techniques that no longer are treated with so many hullabaloos. In the mean time, the industry's love affair with dot-com's has come and gone, along with a significant redistribution of wealth. And new fads have arrived to take the places of those now gone: xml, .net, C#, Java, the search for a single notation to represent all concepts, and so on. These will all absorb huge amounts of energy and money, will make some contribution for future generations (but nothing in proportion to the energy expended to perpetrate their use), and will then gently disappear.

SEEDS FOR DEBATE

1. Select any of the items described in this paper as a fad, and present a case for why it is not so. That is, argue for why the fundamental bases of that item are so critical to the future of software, that it will remain forever.

2. Develop and document an argument that the fads I discuss in this essay have been misrepresented. In actuality, only the words to describe those concepts behave like fads; the concepts themselves live forever.

3. Select some software concept that is popular today (i.e., when you are reading this book, not when I am writing it). Present an argument for why it is but a fad. Also present the opposite argument: that it is a major step in evolution and its concepts and practices will endure.

Recovering from Method Abuse*

In his *The Logic of Failure* (Addison-Wesley Longman, 1996), Dietrich Dörner describes a recurring syndrome among both managers and engineers: the performance of actions that lead to (project) failure while preserving the actors' egos. This syndrome is alive and prospering in our industry. It goes like this:

1. You develop and follow a well-defined procedure for accomplishing some task.

2. If the task succeeds, you take the credit.

3. If the task fails, you blame the procedure, thereby preserving your ego because, after all, you were just following the procedure.

METHOD ABUSE

We over-methodize our activities not because it feels good or right but because it's safer. Most organizations institutionalize this practice in any of several ways, making it even harder to kick our procedure dependence.

Costing. The project follows any of the many software cost estimation algorithms or tools. For example, say a project's estimated cost, using the company's standard cost-estimation tool, is $1 million. In the manager's heart, she believes the real number is closer to $2 million. Yet $1 million becomes the estimate of record. After all, if the project manager contradicts the tool and is wrong, we can only blame her! If she concurs with the tool's $1 million estimate and it turns out wrong, she can blame the tool.

Quality Metrics. Imagine this scenario: a corporation has focused on a half-dozen or so measures of product quality. A project manager is getting close to product delivery, having achieved the quality goals as defined by the metrics. Yet in his heart, he believes real quality has not been achieved and that the customer will probably not be satisfied. He decides to ship anyway. If the customers are dissatisfied with the product, he can blame the corporation's quality metrics. On the

*Original published in *IEEE Software, 15,* 1 (January/February 1998), pp. 4–7.

other hand, if the project manager delays shipment, he risks personal attack by his management and the customers for being overly cautious or untrusting of company standards.

Process Improvement. A corporation decides to embrace any of the popular process improvement models, such as CMM, Spice, or ISO. Some are prescriptive; they tell you what you should do and should not do. Although others tell you to define your own ways of doing things, those models then demand that only the defined methods be used. In either case, a manager ends up with the same ultimatum: If I do these things the approved way, I am following the corporate edict. If I don't, I am on my own. What choice does the manager have? If she follows the rules, even if they are not appropriate for her project she has a higher probability of personal success than if she does what she thinks is right, as shown in Table 2.1's outcome analysis.

Architectural Selection. Suppose the company has "always done it one way," that is, all products have had the identical underlying architecture. The company begins developing a new product. The designers could adopt the usual architecture, or they could do a trade-off analysis among alternative architectures to select the one that affords the optimal combination of performance, maintainability, resilience, elegance, and functionality. If they follow the corporate way, they will not be blamed for failure; after all, they followed the prescribed method. If they employ an alternative architecture, they put themselves at severe risk and will be blamed personally if their product is flawed.

Design Method. The design method *du jour* (or should I say *de l'an*) is object-oriented. Here it is not so much the corporation that drives the method as it is our industry peers. If we follow the OO method (ignoring for now that there are many OO methods), we preserve our own egos. But if we demonstrate guts and decision-making skills by selecting the method we most believe in, we place ourselves at risk. Sure, if we succeed, we'll take the credit; but if we fail, we will take the blame.

Performance Evaluation and Hiring Decisions. We develop a set of criteria for determining if an employee is doing a good job or if a prospective employee will do so. For each criterion we assign the individual a score from 0 to 5. We add the scores, perhaps weighted, and assign each individual a number that presumably captures his or her value. We use the resultant ranking to hire, fire, and give raises

Table 2.1.   Outcome Analysis

	Project succeeds	Project fails
Follow the "corporate way"	Manager gets the credit	Blame the company
Follow the "manager's way"	Manager gets the credit	Blame the manager

and bonuses. We hide behind this method. If an employee complains about unfair treatment, we explain "Sorry, but that's how you fared based on our objective evaluation method." Once again, we preserve our egos behind a method.

STEPS TO RECOVERY

My name is Al Davis and I am an over methodizer. I have relied on methods and procedures too often—and so have most of you.

If we continue down this path, we will inevitably become builders of cookie-cutter, low-risk, low-payoff, mediocre systems. Sure, such systems fill the need for uniform products. However, glory and success come to those who take risk, who put their own careers on the line by embracing big, hairy, audacious goals, or BHAGs (see James C. Collins and Jerry I. Porras, *Built to Last*, Harper Collins, New York, 1994). Remember that low risk inevitably results in low payoff. By "just following the method" you will keep a low profile but receive little reward for your efforts.

The next 20 years will be crucial for our industry. We may develop into an industry of tract-house builders, or we may reach for new challenges, new hopes, and new solutions.

SEEDS FOR DEBATE

1. In this essay, I describe how sticking with an estimate provided by a software estimation tool will help you "cover your rear." In the essay "Thoughts on Software Estimation" starting on page 49, I propose some significant changes to how software efforts should be estimated. Will taking the advice of the "Thoughts" essay help solve the "cover you rear" problem? Take both sides in answering this question, and present your case.

2. Take the position that Dietrich Dörner is overly pessimistic, and now reanalyze our industry's current practices with respect to costing, quality metrics, process improvement, architectural selection, design method, performance evaluation, and hiring decisions.

3. I assume that the "cover your rear" behaviors I described in this essay are subconscious (as I believe are all of Dörner's behavioral claims). Have you met anybody in your life who does these kinds of things consciously? If so, put forth an argument for whether conscious or subconscious actions of this type are healthier? More repairable?

4. Develop a plan for how you are going to make a difference on your next team (at school or work) project by doing things with your "brain in gear," rather than just taking the easiest conformist path.

Tomorrow's Blacksmiths?*

As the turn of this century approaches, it is helpful to look back at an event that occurred at the turn of the last century. At that time, blacksmithing was one of the most essential occupations. The blacksmith's job was to keep horses running, and was thus central to the communication and transportation systems of the day. For thousands of years, the energy of the horse had been harnessed and transformed to serve people efficiently. The horse allowed our ancestors to do things they could not have otherwise done. By about 1910, however, the horseless carriage had made major inroads. The horse—and the blacksmith—were displaced.

DIGITAL HORSEPOWER

We have now found ways to harness the energy of electronic calculating machines. Like the horse in previous centuries, these wonderful computers allow us to do things we could not otherwise do. Not only are they the very hearts and brains of our communication and transportation systems, they are central to our health care, entertainment, national defense, and countless other aspects of life. And at the core of all these computers is software. Software is even more critical to the computer than the horseshoe was to the horse.

As softwaresmiths, we seem content with our crucial role in enhancing everyday life. Perhaps we have good reason for this contentment. After all, blacksmithing was around for centuries before it became obsolete within the span of 20 years. Perhaps we should not start to worry about obsolescence until our profession is at least that old. Then again, perhaps we should start worrying—or at least thinking about it—now.

UNHITCHING THE CARRIAGE

The horseless carriage effectively replaced the horse for two primary reasons: increased reliability and increased efficiency. Of course, until the advent of the automobile, horses seemed suitably reliable and efficient; only when the alternative ap-

*Originally published in *IEEE Software*, 12, 3 (May 1995), p. 4.

peared did horses suddenly seem lacking. We should also note that the demise of the horse's role in society (and by extension, that of the blacksmith) was brought about not by insiders (the blacksmiths themselves) but by the folks who invented the automobile (Daimler, Benz, Olds, and Packard). Similarly, when a replacement for the computer (and software engineers) is found, it is not likely to be by an electrical or software engineer.

This raises many questions. What will replace computers and software? Will it be electrical or electronic? Biological or chemical? What attributes might it exhibit? When will it appear? How soon after it appears will the software engineer be displaced?

Even if they had anticipated the threat to their profession, the blacksmiths could not have remedied the basic weakness of the horse. It may also be true that no amount of research by software engineers will overcome the basic weakness of the computer. Still, we are perhaps too smug. We acknowledge that our products are less reliable and our processes less efficient than they could or should be. We see our weaknesses where the blacksmiths did not. The opportunity and the challenge of improving the efficiency and reliability of software lies before us. Are we doing enough to forestall our perhaps inevitable demise? Are there other things we could be doing? Your letters and comments are welcome.

EPILOGUE

Nine years have passed since I wrote this warning. I am happy to announce that the end is not here yet.

SEEDS FOR DEBATE

1. Create an argument for why software developers are not the blacksmiths of the future.
2. One could argue that the arrival of the horseless carriage did not destroy the livelihoods of all blacksmiths. In fact, what it did was to enable those few blacksmiths that remained in the trade to become even more valuable to those who still needed them. Might that become the future for software developers?
3. Characterize the types of revolutions that might occur that could unseat the preeminence of software.
4. Instead of disappearing like blacksmiths, perhaps software development personnel will become so infused into other industries that they will no longer be considered members of a single "software community." Thus, when you ask an individual what they do, they would say, "Oh, I work in the plastics industry." And if you ask what they do, then they'll tell you that they happen to do software development within that company. If this becomes reality, what are the implications for software education? For software societies? For the future of software breakthroughs?

On Software Development Strategies, Politics, and Religion

After 30+ years in the software development industry, I have finally started to understand the pulse of the industry. I see the industry pulled in this direction for a dozen or so years, and then that direction for a similar number of years, with seemingly little overall direction. I believe that drawing an analogy to phenomena in the worlds of politics and religion may help improve our common understanding of what is happening.

The first programs written for computers tended to be treated like toys. As software became embedded in more and more aspects of society, and we relied on it more, and applications became increasingly complex, we of course needed to increase software's inherent reliability. This desire in turn has driven us toward increasing levels of control of the software development process. But the trend has not been uniform. As shown in Figure 4.1, industry practices have moved generally toward increasing amounts of control, but every few years, control regresses to earlier lower levels.

The purpose of this paper is to improve our understanding of the forces that create such a saw-toothed trend.

THE TREND

The trend of an industry is nothing other than a collection of the trends in every company within that industry, and those trends are nothing other than the composite of the trends occurring on individual projects within those companies. Let us examine a typical software development project. That project has embarked upon software development and is following a specific set of practices that it considers to be appropriate. If the project is successful[1], then the team is likely to use the identi-

---

[1]Most research defines *successful* as on time, within budget, and satisfying all the documented requirements [1]. I disagree strongly with such a definition. Even though I have spent much of my career in the requirements domain, I do not believe that satisfying the documented requirements is as important as solving a real business need or leveraging a real business opportunity. Thus, if the documented require-

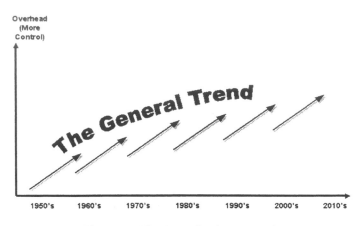

Figure 4.1. The General Industry Trend.

cal practices the next time it is assembled for a new project. If the project is unsuccessful, project management is generally "punished" by instituting increased management controls the next time. Thus each success results in little or no change to process, while each failure results in increasing controls. So, it seems logical that in the long term, controls should increase through time. This is the reason that the arrows in Figure 4.1 generally move toward the upper right corner.

Languages

Let's see if this has been the case. At the dawn of computers, software was seen as just a chore necessary to make computing machines do their jobs. They were hacked together in assembly language with little or no discipline. Within a few years, programmers noticed that they were being asked to make changes to existing programs in order to perform additional tasks. They found themselves unable to comprehend what their own programs were trying to do, and so they added a discipline to make it easier to modify their programs: comments.

By the late 1950's and early 1960's, assembly language programs were getting larger, and more difficult to maintain. Also, experience showed that certain kinds of control structures and data structures were being used repeatedly. The result was the creation of many so-called high-level programming languages, which enabled

---

ments correctly capture a real business need or opportunity, then it is in fact sufficient to satisfy those requirements. But if the documented requirements fail to capture the essence of the business need or opportunity, then the project is a failure if it meets the documented requirements! Similarly, delivery dates are often chosen arbitrarily. Meeting the deadline but missing a market window is a failure, not a success. And delivering 2 months late to a hungry and excited market is a success! So, for me, a successful project is one that correctly addresses the business need or opportunity, in a timeframe acceptable to the market, the users and the customers.

programmers to use those structures more easily, in fact forcing the programmers to use only a predefined set of such structures [2].

There was an immediate and vocal backlash from some programmers. These programmers objected to the control placed upon them by the new languages [3]. They expressed their resentment by arguing that programs resulting from use of such languages were not as efficient as those resulting from assembly language. Their argument was valid (the programs *were* less efficient), but managers were willing to accept the reduction in program efficiency in return for an increase in system reliability, and a decrease in the cost to maintain the software. This argument lasted at least a decade (some might say it is still being fought today). This bifurcation of the industry moderated the trend toward increased control.

Software Design

By the early 1970's, increasing system failures drove managers to find ways of increasing the likelihood that software products would satisfy customer needs, and could be maintained within reasonable budgets. Structured design [4] was introduced. Structured design demanded that programmers actually think about how their software programs should be organized before starting to write code. The next 15 years showed increasing attention being given to design, structured as well as many other, but historically less significant, approaches. Structured design clearly introduced more control over the software development process.

The outcry against design could have been predicted. Soon after structured design was introduced, software developers began to argue that they were wasting their precious time producing stupid design documentation instead of producing useful code. Many programmers and organizations refused to introduce design principles into their practices. And this created a moderating force against the absolute trend toward increased control.

Requirements and Design

Structured design had the effect of increasing efficiency and decreasing maintenance costs, but did little to increase the likelihood that the resulting systems would satisfy actual needs of the users and customers. So, soon after the introduction of structured design, structured analysis was introduced [5] [6]. Structured analysis added discipline to the process of understanding the needs of the users. Once again, this represented additional control over the software development process, and there was much backlash from programmers and designers who wanted to spend their time building systems instead of "wasting their time" talking to customers.

In the mid-1980's, object-oriented design (OOD) was introduced as a more logical, less costly, more straightforward, and more easily maintained way of designing software [8]. OOD became an approach even more widely used than structured design of the previous decade. Some even argued in writing that OOD was universally applicable. This wide scale use of assembling systems from objects introduced yet more control over development personnel. And once again the backlash was significant [9]. The most outspoken opponents to OOD argued that the additional levels of control over their practice decreased their productivity and ability to innovate, and resulted in decreased efficiency of the system. Proponents argued that the increased control resulted in increased quality and productivity, and that any resulting decrease in efficiency would be more than acceptable.

The popularity of structured design made people aware of the absence of a way to get from user problems to the initiation of design activities. Similarly, the growing popularity of OOD made its practitioners similarly aware. Thus, a series of object-oriented analysis (OOA) techniques [8] [10] was developed to bridge that gap. OOA became extremely popular among OOD fans because it required them to do little more than OOD, but at a slightly more abstract level. Of course, the followers of object-orientation demanded that everything must be done in an object-oriented way, and therefore OOA had to be "correct."

The outcry against OOA was loud but short-lived [11]. It came from two camps. The first camp was composed of those who objected to anything that controlled the process. But the other camp was composed of the individuals who actually used OOA and OOD. They themselves realized that OOA made little sense. It did not aid in understanding user problems: it had nothing to do with either requirements or analysis. It was simply a first step of the design process, conveniently termed object-oriented analysis to appease the software engineering community. Given both backlashes, it was predictable that the object-oriented community would turn to an alternative: the user scenario.

Scenarios

The user scenario, more recently termed the use case [12] [13], has become so popular in the object-oriented community, most of its followers (and perhaps even its leaders) are not even aware that it has been a well-established, proven, standard tool used by analysts for many decades prior to the rise of object-orientation [14] [15]. Many of the recent use case fanatics proclaimed that they had found the universal means to express requirements, ignorant of the fact that (a) the most challenging types of requirements (e.g., the non-behavioral requirements, although see [16] for a counter-argument) are not easily expressible in scenarios, and (b) the most difficult part of the requirements process is elicitation, and eliciting requirements from users and customers is all about communication, not about notations. Thus, many started writing papers concerning the lack of universality of use cases, and the fact that elicitation is primarily a right-brained (about thinking and feeling), not left-brained (about notations and formalisms) activity [17].

Capability Maturity Model

The capability maturity model (CMM) [18] was originally developed for the U.S. Department of Defense as a means of ensuring that government contractors would be capable of delivering quality products in a predictable and repeatable manner.

The CMM and CMMI [19], its more recent successor, have attracted a large base of extremists who have taken a laudable goal and created an industry-wide obsession with measuring everything. Some measurement is good and practical; other aspects of software development just make no sense to attempt to measure.

The counterrevolution to CMM started soon after CMM became popular [20], and extends to this day [21].

Agile Development

In response to the series of ever more encompassing and controlling approaches to building software, a new movement surfaced: Agile development [22]. Agile development, and its most popular instance, eXtreme Programming (XP) [23], is one of the few times that an antiestablishment movement developed a name to place on its banner. In the past, those against major software development initiatives were labeled simply as anti-this or anti-that. The effects of such a label were twofold: (a) an immediate rise in popularity because followers could identify themselves by name, (b) the immediate creation of an antiantiestablishment movement. Notice that in the 1960's, one could be pro- or con-structured programming. It made no sense to be against those who were against something; such people simply considered themselves to be pro. But because the agile movement now had a name other than con-control, the antiestablishment became the establishment, and thus it developed its own opponents [24]. Of course there are also those who want to be seen as moderates by accepting both extremes! [25]

We can now all see the reality of the saw toothed curve shown in Figure 4.1.

THE FUNDAMENTALIST FORCES

Fundamentalism is defined as a ". . . movement or point of view characterized by a return to fundamental principles, by rigid adherence to those principles, and often by intolerance of other views . . ." [26].

Throughout history, fundamentalist politicians and religious leaders have argued vehemently for positions deemed extreme by a majority of the population. They take a law (whether documented in any of the great books of the world's religions or a country's constitution), and demand that it is *the* law, not to be compromised under any circumstances. Contrast this position with that of moderates. Moderates take the position that a law captures the spirit of what a society (whether political or religious) believes is right or wrong, but that reason must be introduced when applied; in particular, special circumstances could cause us to reconsider whether the law is absolute. Thus, the original drafters of the United States Constitution believed that individuals of African descent should not have the right to vote. Political fundamentalists in America argued for two hundred years that this "law" should be upheld because it was stated as a basic precept of the United States. A similar argument is being put forth today by fundamentalists who claim that every U.S. citizen should have the right to carry a concealed handgun. Examples of similarly extreme fundamentalist views with respect to every major religion in the world today are all too common.

Fundamentalist movements in software development have been vocal since the dawn of computers. Our industry is mature enough to understand a set of far-reaching basic principles [27]. Thus, for example, we all generally believe that measuring the software development process is a good thing. After all, how will we know if we are improving unless we measure? But fundamentalists interpret the basic principle "measurement is good" to an extreme position: "To not measure is bad," or its contrapositive, "You must always measure." Similarly, we all generally believe that designing software in terms of objects is a good thing. After all, how can you argue against a principle that says, "Encapsulate data with the procedures that modify it, so that it is protected from other programs"? But fundamentalists interpret the basic principle "objects are good" to an extreme position: "To not design using objects is bad," or its contrapositive, "You must always use object-oriented design."

The role of these fundamentalist forces is shown in Figure 4.2. Notice that their primary effect is to place upward pressure on the trend.

THE LIBERTARIAN FORCES

Libertarianism is defined as a movement or point of view characterized by "maximizing individual rights and minimizing the role of the state" [26].

Throughout history, libertarian politicians and religious leaders have argued vehemently for positions deemed extreme by a majority of the population. They take the position that religious and constitutional laws should be minimized; and that individuals when left to their own free will make correct choices without "interference" from such laws.

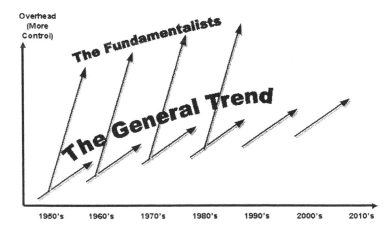

Figure 4.2. The Effect of Fundamentalism on the General Industry Trend.

Libertarian movements in software development have been vocal since the dawn of computers as well. Each time a new wave of "guidance," "best practices," or "controls" are introduced into our industry, libertarians declare that such controls are unnecessary; that by leaving software developers alone, they will naturally behave in responsible ways, and will produce the best product in the least amount of time. This is evident in the anti-structured programming, anti-structured design, anti-structured analysis, anti-OOD, anti-OOA, anti-CMM, and the agile movements.

The role of these libertarian forces is shown in Figure 4.3. Notice that their primary effect is to place downward pressure on the trend.

THE DYNAMIC

The two forces, that of fundamentalism and libertarianism, interact in time in a series of phases, as shown in Figure 4.4.

At some point in the evolution of our industry, we are in the doldrums. Productivity is high, but our quality, repeatability, predictability are relatively low. We are however all blissfully happy in our ignorance and innocence. One or more events awaken us to the potential danger of our situation. Somebody gets the idea that institutionalizing some new technology, tool, concept, or principle can increase our ability to deliver quality software. The idea catches on, and initial results seem positive. Overzealous fundamentalists proclaim the arrival of *the* solution to the industry's woes. We enter a period of self-aggrandizement in which we are so proud of what we have accomplished, we no longer have our real goals in focus. The phenomenon of goals displacement causes us to replace the goal of solving real user problems with trying to achieve some measurable level of quality, controllability, and/or repeatability. However, positive results are sporadic because the idea does not and cannot possibly work in all situations. Productivity is eventually brought to

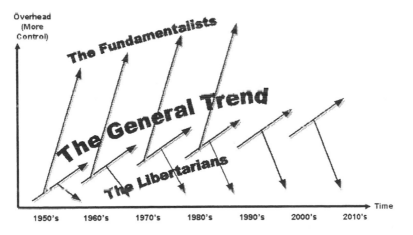

Figure 4.3. The Effect of Libertarianism on the General Industry Trend.

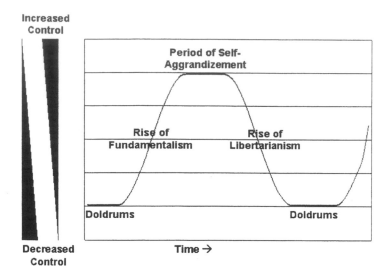

Figure 4.4. The Cycle of Software Processes.

its knees, making us all vulnerable to the libertarians. During the rise of libertarian popularity, productivity once again returns, at the expense of those principles we held so dear during the period of self-aggrandizement. And this returns us to the state of the doldrums.

SUMMARY

In summary, our industry is extremely young. Although basic techniques of building software are known, our best practices are not. As in the case of all nascent industries, we are vulnerable to wide swings in practice, to the whims of most eloquent (but not necessarily the wisest) spokespeople, and to constant change. It takes most disciplines fifty to a hundred years to become mature enough that the truly best practices become commonplace and standardized. And when this happens, neither the fundamentalists nor the libertarians garner much credibility among the masses.

REFERENCES

[1] The Standish Group, *The Chaos Report,* 1995, www.standishgroup.com.

[2] Sebesta, R., *Concepts of Programming Languages,* 5th Edition, Reading, Massachusetts: Addison-Wesley, 2001.

[3] Reilly, E., and F. Federighi, *The Elements of Digital Computer Programming,* San Francisco: Holden-Day, 1968.

[4] Stevens, W., et al., "Structured Design," *IBM Systems Journal, 13,* 2 (February 1974), pp. 115–139.

[5] DeMarco, T., *Structured Analysis and System Specification,* New York: Yourdon Press, 1978.

[6] Gane, C., and T. Sarson, *Structured Systems Analysis: Tools and Techniques,* Upper Saddle River, New Jersey: Prentice Hall, 1979.

[7] Booch, G., "Object-Oriented Development," *IEEE Transactions on Software Engineering, 12,* 2 (February 1986), pp. 211–221.

[8] Booch, G., *Object Oriented Analysis and Design with Applications,* Reading, Massachusetts: Addison-Wesley, 1993.

[9] Rosenberg, D., "UML Applied: Nine Tips to Incorporating UML into Your Project," *http://www.umlchina.com/Indepth/9tips.htm.*

[10] Coad, P., and E. Yourdon, *Object-Oriented Analysis,* New York: Yourdon Press. 1990.

[11] Davis, A., "Object Oriented Analysis to Object Oriented Design: An Easy Transformation?" *Journal of Systems and Software, 30,* 1 & 2 (July–August 1995), pp. 151–159; reprinted in current book on page 129.

[12] Jacobson, I., et al., *Object-Oriented Software Engineering: A Use Case Driven Approach,* Reading, Massachusetts: Addison-Wesley, 1992.

[13] Cockburn, A., *Writing Effective Use Cases,* Reading, Massachusetts: Addison-Wesley. 2000.

[14] Taylor, B., "A Method for Expressing Functional Requirements of Real-Time Systems," *IFAC/IFIP Workshop on Real-Time Programming,* April 1980, Liebnitz, Austria.

[15] Alford, M., and I. Burns, "R-Nets: A Graph Model for Real-Time Software Requirements," *Symposium on Computer Software Engineering,* New York: Polytechnic Press, 1976, pp. 97–100.

[16] Lee, J., and N. Xue, "Analyzing User Requirements by Use Cases: A Goal-Driven Approach," *IEEE Software, 16,* 4 (July/August 1999), pp. 92–101.

[17] Gottesdiener, E., *Requirements by Collaboration,* Reading, Massachusetts: Addison-Wesley, 2000.

[18] Paulk, M., et al., "Capability Maturity Model 1.1," *IEEE Software, 10,* 4 (July 1993), pp. 18–27.

[19] Kulpa, M., and K. Johnson, *Understanding the CMMI,* New York: Auerbach, 2003

[20] Bollinger, T., and C. McGowan, "A Critical Look at Software Capability Evaluations," *IEEE Software, 8,* 4 (July 1991), pp. 25–41.

[21] McConnell, S., "Capability Maturity Model for Software (SW-CMM)," in "The Best Influences on Software Engineering," *IEEE Software, 17,* 1 (January/February 2000), pp. 14–15.

[22] Cockburn, A., *Agile Software Development,* Reading, Massachusetts: Addison-Wesley, 2001

[23] Beck, K., *Extreme Programming Explained,* Reading, Massachusetts: Addison-Wesley, 1999.

[24] Anton, A., "Successful Software Projects Need Requirements Planning," *IEEE Software, 20,* 3 (May/June 2003), pp. 44, 46–47.

[25] Reifer, D., "XP and the CMM," *IEEE Software, 20,* 3 (May/June 2003), pp. 14–15

[26] *American Heritage Dictionary of the English Language,* 4th Edition, Houghton Mifflin. 1990.

[27] Davis, A., *201 Principles of Software Development,* New York: McGraw-Hill, 1995.

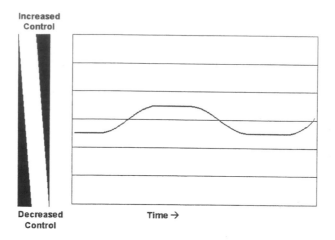

Figure 4.5. A More Moderate Cycle of Software Processes.

SEEDS FOR DEBATE

1. You may consider yourself to be an adherent of one or more of the approaches to software development that I characterize as being either fundamentalist or libertarian, and you resent me pigeon-holing you or your approach as one of those two extremes. That's okay! Put forth an argument for why your approach is perfect for your environment.

2. Perhaps you believe that the graph of Figure 4.4 is too extreme. Perhaps you feel it is more accurately portrayed in Figure 4.5.[2] Perhaps you feel that although the extremists are the most vocal, they are not the majority, and that the majority of development efforts make incremental changes for the better, without blowing in the wind caused by extremists. If so, present a case that includes statistics showing what percentage of development efforts really do follow the extreme positions I describe herein, and libertarianism

3. Take the position that the fundamentalist and libertarian views I portray in this essay are just the same as the fads I described in the software lemmings essay starting on page 3. Argue your position with actual examples.

4. Take the position that the fundamentalist and libertarian views I portray in this essay are different than the fads I described in the software lemmings essay on p. 3. Argue your position with actual examples.

---

[2]Of course, without a scale on the vertical axis, the two graphs are identical. My point is that perhaps you feel the swings are far more moderate than I.

Art or Engineering, One More Time*

Debates about whether software development is an engineering discipline or an art have persisted for many years. Should software development be considered engineering? The complexity of software systems and the criticality of applications in which software is embedded argue that it should—proven principles, techniques, and tools must be adhered to. Or should it be considered art? That the creation of software requires great innovation and "great" (resilient, supportable, understandable, reliable) programs, often exhibiting simplicity, beauty, and elegance argues in favor of this interpretation.

COMPARE DEFINITIONS

Regularly, we see articles mapping out how we can become more like engineers (see Mary Shaw's "Prospects for an Engineering Discipline of Software" article in the Nov. 1990 issue [of *IEEE Software*]). Regularly we see articles arguing why it is so important to preserve the art in software development (see Maarten Boasson's "The Artistry of Software Architecture" in the Nov. 1995 issue [of *IEEE Software*]). The following definitions (from *Webster's Third New International Dictionary*, 1986) give us a place to start:

> *Engineering is the disciplined application of demonstrably valid principles, techniques, and tools for creating useful products.*

> *Art is "the conscious use of skill, taste, and creative imagination in the practical definition or production of beauty."*

BOTH, OR NEITHER

Our discipline is perhaps more like custom home construction than either electrical engineering or oil on canvas. When we examine the mature (relative to software development) field of custom home development, we see many attributes with obvious software counterparts. As the boxed text on pages 28–29 shows, it is remarkable

*Originally published in *IEEE Software, 13*, 6 (November 1996), pp. 4–5.

Great Software Debates. By Alan M. Davis
ISBN 0-471-649880 © 2004 Institute of Electrical and Electronics Engineers.

how similar the activities are. Even more remarkable, the skill mixes required at each step are quite similar. In home design there are no arguments about whether it is engineering or art. Instead, it is recognized that different skills are required at different times: problem analysis people at the beginning, artists (architects and designers) next, specification-following laborers next, and finally quality-demanding inspectors.

Software development is the same. It doesn't need to be engineering, or science, or art. We do need to recognize that different skills are required for each activity that comprises software development. As our discipline matures, we should become more user-oriented during requirements, more creative during design, and more attentive to detail during coding.

COMPARING TWO DISCIPLINES

Custom Home

1. At the early stages, analysts must be visionaries, with a keen understanding of the homeowners' needs, strong communication skills, and an appreciation for what homes can and cannot do.

2. Such visionaries generally gather and document the gleaned information in words, without regard to what the home might look like. However, on occasion, models or photographs of existing homes may help the customer better appreciate the implications of their decisions or realize additional needs. The process is often iterative. The resulting document sets out the home's requirements: number of bedrooms, whether sleeping areas should be isolated from recreational areas, the need for heat/cold retention, an understanding of the climatic attributes of the home's expected locale.

3. Next, architects create external elevations and floor plans showing room layouts. The resulting blueprints are considered the home's high-level design. This step requires great creativity and an eye for elegance and beauty, as well as knowledge of building codes and the structural properties of construction materials. This step may be repeated until a satisfactory solution is found.

4. Once the room layouts and external views are approved and baselined (that is, agreed to), more detailed designs are created: framing, facade, doorways, electrical, plumbing. Unexpected problems may force previous steps to be modified. This step requires intimate knowledge of building codes.

5. A building code inspector (an independent third party) inspects and approves the designs.

6. The home is constructed. Scaffolds may be erected and removed. The people who do this step are hired for their accuracy, ability to follow specifications, knowledge of codes, and willingness and ability to do hard work. Artistic quality is not a requirement, and may even be considered a detriment.

7. Again, an independent third party inspects and approves the building before customers take ownership of it.

SEEDS FOR DEBATE

1. In the January–February 1998 issue of *IEEE Software*, Steve McConnell puts forth an excellent argument that we should ignore the question "*Is* software development engineering?" and instead ask the question "*Should* software development be engineering?" Read his essay titled "The Art, Science, and Engineering of Software Development," and see what you think. If you agree with him, take the opposite position, and put forth an argument for why he is wrong. If you disagree with him, put forth an argument for why he may be right. (Yes, I am asking you to argue for a position opposite of what you believe!)

2. Read the following four terrific articles:

Software

1. At the early stages, analysts must be visionaries, with a keen understanding of customers needs, strong communication skills, and an appreciation for what software can and cannot do.

2. Such visionaries generally gather and document the gleaned information into words, without regard to what the software might look like. However, on occasion, software prototypes may help the customer better appreciate the implications of their decisions or realize additional needs. The process is often iterative. The resulting document sets out the software's requirements: what features, how many users, security needs, adaptability needs, response times, an understanding of the attributes of the software's expected external environment.

3. Next, software designers create a software architecture showing the subcomponents and how they interrelate temporally and physically. Called high-level design, this step requires great creativity and an eye for elegance and beauty, as well as knowledge of software standards and capabilities. This step may be repeated until a satisfactory solution is found.

4. Once the architecture is approved and baselined, more detailed designs are created: algorithms, data structures, interfaces, protocols, flows. Unexpected problems may force previous steps to be modified. This step requires intimate knowledge of data structures, algorithms, system performance, and development standards.

5. A quality assurance person (an independent third party) inspects and approves the designs.

6. The software is constructed. Scaffolds may be erected and removed. The people who do this step are hired for their accuracy, ability to follow specifications, knowledge of coding conventions, and willingness and ability to do hard work. Artistic quality is not a requirement, and may even be considered a detriment.

7. An independent third party inspects and approves the software before customers take ownership of it.

---

a. Shaw, M., "Prospects for an Engineering Discipline of Software." *IEEE Software, 7,* 6 (November 1990), pp. 15–24.

b. Boasson, M., "The Artistry of Software Architecture," *IEEE Software, 12,* 6 (November 1995), pp. 13, 15–16.

c. Bollinger, T., "The Interplay of Art and Science in Software," *IEEE Computer, 30,* 10 (October 1997), pp. 125–128.

d. Pfleeger, S., "What Software Engineering Can Learn from Soccer," *IEEE Software, 19,* 6 (November–December 2002), pp. 64–65.

Which of these take the position that software development is primarily an art? Which take the position that it is primarily an engineering discipline. Compare and contrast their positions with the one I put forth in the current essay.

3. Describe all the ways that home construction and software development are dissimilar.

Why Build Software?*

If I can stop one heart from breaking,
I shall not live in vain.
If I can ease one life the aching,
or cool one pain,
or help one fainting robin
unto his nest again,
I shall not live in vain.

—Emily Dickenson

Why do we build software anyway? In reading the literature, I sometimes get the impression that building software is an end in itself. We build software to see how good we can get a product quality measure, or how high we can push our process maturity level.

For those of you who haven't figured it out yet, we really build software to solve real problems. If we successfully solve the intended problem and thus satisfy the customers' needs, we have done a good job—regardless of the measured quality of our product or process. If we fail to solve the intended problem and fail to satisfy the customers' needs, we have failed. It is that simple.

MEANINGFUL MEASURES

I'd like to propose some new measures that tell us if we've done a good job. They are tied to our real purpose, not to some secondary aspect of the software development phenomenon. The new (and essential) measures:

1. Complaints per user per month
2. Profit made
3. Contribution to society/humanity

I contend that it is always valuable to measure complaints, as opposed to enhancement requests. After all, enhancement requests indicate the good health of the

*Originally published in *IEEE Software, 14*, 1 (January/February 1997), pp. 4, 6.

product (see M. Lehman, "Software Engineering, the Software Process, and Their Support," *Software Engineering Journal,* Sept. 1991, pp. 243–258). Lots of complaints indicate poor customer satisfaction. Few complaints indicate good customer satisfaction. This applies to any aspect of the software industry you find yourself working in. If you build custom software for a few select users or shrink-wrap software for thousands of diverse users, customer complaints are bad. Normalizing by number of users and by time period equalizes all parties; no complaints is great, as long as you do have users.

PROFIT IS IMPORTANT

Mass production of software is extremely inexpensive, so obviously the more copies you sell of a software product, the larger the base over which to amortize the fixed development cost, and thus the more profit you make. Although this is Accounting 101, it does say something profound for software development companies. The more copies sold the more profit; the more profit, the more you can afford to invest in other development efforts anti thus solve more customer needs. As Dave Card points out so well ("Measurement for Project Management," *First Upper Midwest Conference on Practical Software Quality Techniques,* Univ. of St. Thomas Software Engineering Program, Minneapolis, Minn., Oct 1996), market share is also important. The larger the share of a large market, the more copies you sell and the more profit you make. The larger the share of a small market, the more significant your unique contribution is and the more margin can be built into each product.

THE HUMAN TOUCH

The third and equally important measure is the most difficult to quantify: contribution to humanity and/or society. If omitted, you might conclude that I believe that making money with few complaints is not only necessary but also sufficient. I do not. Corporations exist for many reasons (providing employment, providing good return for investors, and so on), but one very important reason is to make a difference somehow. I believe that every human has a responsibility to somehow make this world a better place as a result of his or her existence. Companies need the same charter. I don't know how to measure it, but, please, don't lose sight of it as a goal. A company's product may save lives, prevent disasters, protect a nation, aid a community, preserve integrity, increase enjoyment when recreating, or make somebody's life easier. However you measure it, a company's and a product's contribution to helping people is important.

IN SUMMARY

In summary, if the software you are building contributes to humanity, generates few complaints, and makes a profit, your software is good. All other measures are secondary to the real goal. All other measures have but a second-order relationship to quality. On the other hand, there are many other reasons to measure things other than to assess after the fact whether your software is "good." For example, we need measurement to help assess the health of a development project, the status of a product under development, and the like. For these goals, there are obviously many other measures that make sense and are critical. Just don't lose sight of the real goal: satisfying customer needs.

SEEDS FOR DEBATE

1. Take the position that two of the three measures* I propose in this essay are really very good. Describe how you could subvert the use of these measures. That is, argue for what you can do to make your project score high marks for these metrics, yet really fails miserably.

2. Look at the metrics that your company uses to quantify the "goodness" of your software products. Correlate each with one of the three metrics I proposed in this essay. If any of your metrics have no relation to my three metrics, argue for why they are necessary anyway. Then take the opposite viewpoint: argue for why they are extraneous or erroneous.

3. A company I was consulting for a few years ago wanted me to endorse its use of the measure "number of requirements agreed upon per hour" as a means to measure the quality of their requirements process. Can you relate this to any of the three metrics I proposed herein? How or why not?

---

*"Contribution to society/humanity" is almost impossible to quantify.

It Feels Like Déjà Vu All Over Again*

We still, by and large, lack the necessary methods to increase our ability to design and implement high-quality systems. We do not have, nor are we able to teach to those entering the field, methods to significantly increase programming productivity. We need to make short-term progress in a variety of areas because of ever-increasing demands made on our industry.

These words were written by then editor-in-chief Bruce Shriver in January 1984 for this magazine's first issue. Why is it that words that described our industry so well then are still so appropriate 12 years later?

PROGRESS?

Our industry is making incredible progress toward the construction of reliable, complex systems. The problems we are solving today are enormously more complex. And yet our systems reliability is certainly not getting any worse. The news reports we hear regularly about software-assisted disasters should be expected; after all, software has permeated every aspect of our lives. As software engineers, we fail to credit the overall health of the forest (the industry's generally excellent soundness) because we obsess about the diseases afflicting specific trees (the mini-disasters that transpire on every software project).

STAGNATION?

Our industry is stagnating. No matter how many lessons we're exposed to, we absorb little. Not only are projects poorly managed, we make the same mistakes over and over again. We underestimate our project schedules and costs by the same degrees repeatedly. With each new project, we turn to the latest industry panacea, hoping naively that it—unlike the dozens we've tried before—will really work. We

---

*Originally published in *IEEE Software, 13,* 4 (July 1996), p. 4.

Great Software Debates. By Alan M. Davis
ISBN 0-471-649880 © 2004 Institute of Electrical and Electronics Engineers.

think that tools without technique will save the day. And on and on. When will we learn?

SYNTHESIS

The truth of our industry lies somewhere between the extremes of progress and stagnation. We do tend to make the same mistakes repeatedly. On the other hand, we are able to solve increasingly complex problems. And their software-dependent solutions *do* work and *do* integrate seamlessly into our societal tapestry.

Having a large dose of both views is probably healthy. After all, if we believe only the progress view we might become complacent or careless, and create more disasters than we otherwise would. On the other hand, if we believe only the stagnation view, then we become obsessive or depressed.

Many of my recent editorials have taken one extreme view or the other about our industry. All were intended to serve as a moderating force for those readers polarized to the other extreme. I'm heartened by the many letters written to me concerning these editorials. It tells me that you are interested in some of the tough issues in our industry today. It tells me that you care. Your concern indicates that I'm justified in feeling optimistic about the future of software development.

SEEDS FOR DEBATE

1. Do you believe that Bruce Shriver's comment is still as true today as it was in 1984? If so, create a list of six arguments (along with examples) for why it is so. If not, create a list of six arguments (along with examples) for why it is no longer the case.

2. The above essay argues for moderation between the two extreme beliefs. Perhaps I am totally wrong. Maybe things are much better in the industry than I am portraying them. Perhaps things are much worse. Construct two logical (not emotional) arguments each of which supports the two extremes.

Eras of Software Engineering Technology Transfer*

In the beginning, software was developed and put to work. If it solved the problem at hand, the project was considered a success. If it failed to solve or exacerbated the problem, the project was deemed a failure. Life was simple.

Occasionally, somebody thought of a new way to write software, say, by creating a library of mathematical subroutines. The success of such breakthroughs was judged on whether or not people used the subroutines. If lots of people used the routines, they were successful, and they would pass the test of time. If few people used the routines, they were unsuccessful, and time would destroy them.

RATIONAL ERA

This was the rational era, when new ideas that were good ideas were widely used because their goodness was obvious. Any Fortran programmer of the 1960s would quickly see that it was more efficient and reliable to call a built-in sine function than to write one from scratch. Of course, if the sine function returned a wrong answer, the programmer quickly learned not to call it the next time.

These were the good ol' days. Even today, most of the day-to-day decisions we make follow this protocol: If it makes sense, do it! If you bake cakes regularly, you don't mix ingredients with a spoon—you buy a mixer. You don't need a cost-benefit analysis. If you believe you need a mixer, and you believe you can afford it, and you believe it will do the job better (in some way), you just buy it. If you are so unsure about the need for a mixer that you require a statistical analysis, you probably don't need it!

EMPIRICAL ERA

In the late 1980s, a new philosophy of software-engineering technology transfer arose. People began to preach that before adopting any "new" method or tool, you

*Originally published in *IEEE Software, 13,* 2 (March 1996), pp. 4, 6–7.

Great Software Debates. By Alan M. Davis
ISBN 0-471-649880 © 2004 Institute of Electrical and Electronics Engineers.

must first measure its effect. We are all now brainwashed into believing that before you introduce method X into your process, you must first determine a statistical baseline for your current performance, start using X, and then do another statistical analysis to compare the "before" and "after." Only then can you determine if adding X was a good or bad decision.

This approach has two flaws:

• *Significance of results.* If the positive effect of buying a mixer is not absolutely obvious, then you probably should not waste your money buying it. Furthermore, statistical evidence shouldn't convince you otherwise. The same holds for new software methods or tools: If their positive effect is not absolutely obvious, forget them! Statistics shouldn't convince you otherwise.

• *Poor control of variables.* Every experiment should limit the freedom of most variables (at least the significant ones). Assuming that Barry Boehm and Tom De-Marco are correct, by far the most significant factor influencing productivity and quality is the skill (and experience) of the developers (see "Nontechnological issues in Software Engineering" in *Why Does Software Cost So Much?*, Dorset House, 1995). How can we possibly expect to measure the effect of changing a method when it (and everything else) is so greatly influenced by the most important variable of all—the skill of the developers who use it? In essence, most of our empirical studies are flawed because we cannot control (or even measure) the inherent productivity or quality of individuals or teams.

BACK-TO-BASICS ERA

I predict that software engineering will soon move toward a synthesis of rationalism and empiricism. (Obviously, I have already revealed myself as a rationalist!) This era should be guided by four tenets:

Tenet 1.   If a new method or tool has an *obvious* positive effect on quality and/or productivity, adopt it. If you must run an experiment to determine the degree of usefulness, then the benefit is not obvious. Don't adopt it (and don't experiment with it). Remember, if the benefit is obvious and the data proves otherwise, you would ignore the data anyway.

Tenet 2.   If the effect of a new method or tool on quality and/or productivity is questionable, then the benefit is probably minor. Don't bother with it. In fact, if the effect is minor, you won't be able to measure it anyway!

Tenet 3.   Let researchers do the research. It makes no sense for 100 companies to independently evaluate whether object orientation (or anything else) will work. Let trained empiricists (like Vic Basili) run the experiments.

Tenet 4.   Don't blame a lack of personally acquired data for your failure to use a new technology. Inspections, which are hardly new, feel right (just like the mixer), have little risk involved, and have been subjected to dozens of experiments. All of them indicate quality and productivity gains. Just do it!

SEEDS FOR DEBATE

1. I admit the position that this essay takes is highly controversial. Let's say that I am totally wrong. Let's say that without empirical methods we have nothing; we are just wandering around aimlessly. Construct an argument for why this is the case.

2. Natalia Juristo and Ana Moreno wrote a book on the value of experimentation and empiricism in software. It is so good that it almost convinced me to change my ways. If my essay convinced you that I am right, you must read their *Basics of Software Engineering Experimentation* (2001, Kluwer). Then you will have proper balance and knowledge so you can reach your own conclusions. Now put together your case for one position or the other.

3. Examine the latest popular techniques (or select some from the software lemmings essay starting on page 3). Which of them have been validated through multiple experiments? Which of them are being used just because they are "cool?" And which of them are being used because they just seem like they make sense?

Fifteen Principles of
Software Engineering*

This is an excerpt from my book, 201 Principles of Software Engineering, published [in 1995] by McGraw-Hill. Here I can only highlight the 15 most important principles that underlie software engineering, then list the next 15 in the table on page 46.

Other engineering disciplines have principles based on the laws of physics, biology, chemistry, or mathematics. Principles are rules to live by; they represent the collected wisdom of many dozens of people who have learned through experience. A discipline's principles evolve as the discipline grows: Existing principles are modified; new ones added; old ones discarded. Practice, and experience gained through practice, are the basis for the evolution of principles.

Because the product of software engineering is not physical, physical laws do not form a suitable foundation. Instead, software engineering has had to evolve its principles based solely on observations of thousands of projects. If we were to examine software engineering's principles from 1964 ("always use short variable names;" "do whatever it takes to make your program smaller"), they would look downright silly. Today's principles will look equally silly in 30 years. Nevertheless, I think it's important to describe what our principles are today. The following are probably the 15 most important.

1. MAKE QUALITY NUMBER 1

A customer will not tolerate a poor-quality product, regardless of how you define "quality." Quality must be quantified and mechanisms put into place to motivate and reward its achievement. It may seem politically correct to deliver a product on time, even though its quality is poor, but this is correct only in the short term; it is suicide in the middle and long term. There is no tradeoff to be made here. The first requirement must be quality.

However, there is no one definition of software quality. To developers, it might

*Originally published in *IEEE Software, 11,* 6 (November 1994), pp. 94–96, 101.

Great Software Debates. By Alan M. Davis
ISBN 0-471-649880 © 2004 Institute of Electrical and Electronics Engineers.

be elegant design or elegant code. To users, it might be good response time or high capacity. For cost-conscious managers, it might be low development cost. For some customers, it might be satisfying all their perceived *and* not-yet-perceived needs. The dilemma is that these definitions may not be compatible.

2. HIGH-QUALITY SOFTWARE IS POSSIBLE

Although our industry is saturated with examples of software systems that perform poorly, are full of bugs, or otherwise fail to satisfy user needs, there are counterexamples. Large software systems *can* be built with very high quality, but they carry a steep price tag—on the order of $1,000 per line of code. One example is IBM's onboard flight software for the space shuffle: three million lines of code with less than one error per 10,000 lines.

Techniques that have been demonstrated to increase quality considerably include involving the customer, prototyping (to verify requirements before full-scale development), simplifying design, conducting inspections, and hiring the best people.

3. GIVE PRODUCTS TO CUSTOMERS EARLY

No matter how hard you try to learn users' needs during the requirements phase, the most effective way to ascertain *real* needs is to give users a product and let them play with it. The conventional waterfall model delivers the first product after 99 percent of the development resources have been expended. Thus, the majority of customer feedback on need occurs after resources are expended. Contrast this with an approach that has you deliver a quick-and-dirty prototype early in development, gather feedback, write a requirements specification, and then proceed with full-scale development. In this scenario, only five to 20 percent of development resources have been expended when customers first see the product.

4. DETERMINE THE PROBLEM BEFORE WRITING THE REQUIREMENTS

When faced with what they believe is a problem, most engineers rush to offer a solution. If the engineer's perception of the problem is accurate, the solution *may* work. However, problems are often elusive. In *Are Your Lights On?* (Dorset House, 1990), Donald Gause and Gerald Weinberg describe a "problem" in a high-rise office building. The occupants complain of long waits for an elevator. Is this really the problem? And whose problem is it? From the occupants' perspective, the problem might be that the wait is a waste of time. From the building owner's perspective, the problem might be that long waits will reduce occupancy (and thus rental income). The obvious solution is to increase the speed of the elevators. But you could also add elevators, stagger working hours, reserve some elevators for express service, increase the rent, or refine the "homing algorithm" so elevators go to high-demand floors when they are idle. The range of costs, risks, and time associated with these solutions is enormous. Yet any one *could* work, depending on the situation. Before you try to solve a problem, be sure to explore all the alternatives and don't be blinded by the "obvious" solution.

5. EVALUATE DESIGN ALTERNATIVES

After the requirements are agreed upon, you *must* examine a variety of architectures and algorithms. You certainly do not want to use an "architecture" simply because it was used in the requirements specification. After all, that "architecture" was selected to optimize the understandability of the system's external behavior. The architecture you want is the one that optimizes conformance with the requirements.

For example, architectures are generally selected to optimize constructability, throughput, response time, modifiability, portability, interoperability, safety, and availability, while also satisfying the functional requirements. The best way to do this is to enumerate a variety of software architectures, analyze (or simulate) each with respect to the goals, and select the best alternative. Some design methods result in specific architectures, so one way to generate a variety of architectures is to use a variety of methods.

6. USE AN APPROPRIATE PROCESS MODEL

There are dozens of process models: waterfall, throwaway prototyping, incremental, spiral, operational prototyping, and so on. There is no such thing as a process model that works for every project. Each project must select a process that makes the most sense for that project, on the basis of corporate culture, willingness to take risks, application area, volatility of requirements, and the extent to which requirements are well-understood.

Study your project's characteristics and select a process model that makes the most sense. When building a prototype, for example, choose a process that minimizes protocol, facilitates rapid development and does not worry about checks and balances. Choose the opposite when building a life-critical product.

7. USE DIFFERENT LANGUAGES FOR DIFFERENT PHASES

Our industry's eternal thirst for simple solutions to complex problems has driven many to declare that the best development method is one that uses the same notation throughout the life cycle. This is not the practice in any other engineering discipline. Electrical engineers use different notations for different design activities: Block diagrams, circuit diagrams, logic diagrams, timing diagrams, state-transition tables, check plots, stick diagrams, and so on. Why should software engineers use, say, Ada for requirements, design, and code unless Ada was optimal for all these phases? Why should they use object orientation for all phases unless it was optimal for all phases? Select a set of techniques and languages that is best for the phase you are working in. The transitions between phases are difficult, but using the same language doesn't help. On the other hand, if a language is optimal for certain aspects of two phases, by all means use it.

8. MINIMIZE INTELLECTUAL DISTANCE

Edsger Dijkstra defined *intellectual distance* as the distance between the real-world problem and the computerized solution to the problem. Richard Fairley has argued that the smaller the intellectual distance, the easier it is to maintain the software. To minimize intellectual distance, the software's structure should be as close as possible to the real-world structure. This is the primary motivation for approaches such as object-oriented design and Jackson System Development. But you can minimize intellectual distance using *any* design approach. Of course, the real-world structure can vary, as Jawed Siddiqi points out ("Challenging Universal Truths of Requirements Engineering," *IEEE Software,* Mar. 1994, pp. 18–19). Different humans perceive different structures when they examine the same real world and thus construct quite different "realities."

9. PUT TECHNIQUE BEFORE TOOLS

An undisciplined carpenter with a power tool becomes a dangerous undisciplined carpenter. An undisciplined software engineer with a tool becomes a dangerous undisciplined software engineer. Before you use a tool, you should understand and be able to follow an appropriate software technique. Of course, you also need to know how to use the tool, but that is secondary to having discipline.

10. GET IT RIGHT BEFORE YOU MAKE IT FASTER

It is far easier to make a working program run faster than to make a fast program work. Don't worry about optimization during initial coding (but don't use a ridiculously inefficient algorithm or data structure, either). Every software project has tough schedule pressures. Given this situation, any time a component is produced on (or ahead of) time and it works reliably, there is cause for celebration. Try to be the reason for celebration rather than desperation. If your program works, everyone on your team will appreciate it.

II. INSPECT CODE

Inspecting the detailed design and code, first proposed by Michael Fagan (*IBM Systems Journal,* July 1976), is a much better way to find errors than testing. Inspection can find as many as 82 percent of all errors, consumes about 15 percent of development resources, and reduces net development costs by 25 to 30 percent. Your schedule should account for time to inspect (and correct) every component. You might think your project cannot tolerate such a "luxury." However, data shows that inspections can reduce time-to-test by 50 to 90 percent (Tom Gilb and Dorothy Graham, *Software Inspections,* Addison-Wesley, 1993). If that's not incentive, I don't know what is.

12. GOOD MANAGEMENT IS MORE IMPORTANT THAN GOOD TECHNOLOGY

The best technology will not compensate for poor management, and a good manager can produce great results even with meager resources. Successful software start-ups are not successful because they have great process or great tools (or great products for that matter!). Most are successful because of great management and great marketing.

Good management motivates people to do their best, but there are no universal "right" styles of management. Management style must be adapted to the situation. It is not uncommon for a successful leader to be an autocrat in one situation and a consensus-based leader in another. Some styles are innate; others can be learned.

13. PEOPLE ARE THE KEY TO SUCCESS

Highly skilled people with appropriate experience, talent, and training are key. The right people with insufficient tools, languages, and process will succeed. The wrong people with appropriate tools, languages and process will probably fail (as will the right people with insufficient training or experience). When interviewing prospective employees, remember that there is no substitute for quality. Don't compare two people by saying, "Person x is better than person y, but person y is good enough and less expensive." You can't have all superstars, but unless you truly have an overabundance, hire them when you find them!

14. FOLLOW WITH CARE

Just because everybody is doing something does not make it right for you. It *may* be right, but you must carefully assess its applicability to your environment. Object orientation, measurement, reuse, process improvement, CASE, prototyping—all these might increase quality, decrease cost, and increase user satisfaction.

However, only those organizations that can take advantage of them will reap the rewards. The potential of such techniques is often oversold, and benefits are by no means guaranteed or universal. You can't afford to ignore a "new" technology. But don't believe the inevitable hype associated with it. Read carefully. Be realistic with

Fifteen More Software Principles

---

16. **Understand The Customers' Priorities.** It is possible the customer would tolerate 90 percent of functionality delivered late if they could just have 10 percent of it on time. Find out!

17. **The More They See, The More They Need.** The more functionality (or performance) you provide a user, the more functionality (or performance) the user wants.

18. **Plan to Throw One Away.** One of the most important critical success factors is whether or not a product is entirely new. Such brand-new applications, architectures, interfaces, or algorithms rarely work the first time.

19. **Design for Change.** The architectures, components, and specification techniques you use must accommodate major and incessant change.

20. **Design Without Documentation is *Not* Design.** I have often heard software engineers say "I have finished the design. All that's left is its documentation." Can you imagine a building architect saying "I have completed the design of your new home. All that's left is to draw a picture of it"?

21. **Use Tools, but be Realistic.** Software tools make their users more efficient. By all means, use them. Just as a word processor is essential to a writer, a CASE tool is essential to a software engineer.

22. **Avoid Tricks.** Many programmers love to create programs with tricks—constructs that perform a function correctly, but in an obscure way. Show the world how smart you are by avoiding tricky code.

23. **Encapsulate.** Information-hiding is a simple, proven concept that results in software that is easier to test and much easier to maintain.

24. **Use Coupling and Cohesion.** Coupling and cohesion are the best ways to measure software's inherent maintainability and adaptability. Learn them. Use them to guide your design decisions (Larry Constantine and Edward Yourdon, *Structured Design,* Prentice-Hall, 1979).

25. **Use McCabe Complexity Measure.** Although there are many metrics available to report inherent complexity of software, none is as intuitive and easy-to-use as Tom McCabe's ("A Complexity Measure," *IEEE Trans. Software Eng.,* Dec. 1976, pp. 308–320).

26. **Don't Test Your Own Software.** Software developers should never be the primary testers of their own software.

27. **Analyze Causes for Errors.** It is far more cost-effective to reduce the effect of an error by preventing it than it is to find and fix it. One way to do this is to analyze the causes of errors as they are detected.

28. **Realize that Software's Entropy Increases.** Any software system that undergoes continuous change will grow in complexity and will become more and more disorganized.

29. **People and Time are Not Interchangable.** Measuring a project solely by person-months makes little sense. If a project can be completed in one year by six people, does that mean that 72 people could complete it in one month? Of course not!

30. **Expect Excellence.** Your employees will do much better if you have high expectations for them.

respect to payoffs and risks. And run experiments before you make a major commitment.

15. TAKE RESPONSIBILITY

When a bridge collapses we ask, "what did the engineers do wrong?" When software fails we rarely ask this. When we do, the response is, "I was just following the 15 steps of this method," or "My manager made me do it," or "The schedule left insufficient time to do it right." The fact is that in any engineering discipline the best methods can be used to produce awful designs, and the most antiquated methods to produce elegant designs.

There are no excuses. If you develop a system, it is your responsibility to do it right. Take that responsibility. Do it right, or don't do it at all.

SEEDS FOR DEBATE

1. The thirty principles listed here were extracted from my 1995 book titled *201 Principles of Software Development* (McGraw-Hill). I am now revising that book, and am surprised by how many of the so-called principles have actually changed. If these were truly principles, they should have remained true forever. Do you think that any of the thirty listed here have changed? Why or why not?

2. Construct an argument for why each of the thirty principles is neither a principle nor even valid.

Thoughts on Software Estimation

The average software project completes its job between 10% and 75% later than was originally predicted [1]. The challenge in software schedule estimation is to convert some estimate of the "size" of a software product, along with some project characteristics. into an accurate prediction of when the software will be delivered. Pfleeger, et at. [2] have written an excellent article on how metrics and measurement should be used, but are often abused. Jørgensen [3] has done a great job surveying the many studies that concerned the accuracy of estimation efforts. In the current essay, I will explore some common issues relating to the practicalities of this particular measurement challenge, and will offer some recommended solutions.

Few aspects of software development and management are subject to as much "game playing" as estimating software development costs and schedules. Our industry is extremely poor at delivering products on time. The reasons are some combination of poor estimates [4] and requirements creep as high as 2% per month [1]. This paper explores some of the problems we face in the 21st century concerning estimation, and recommends what we can do to change our abysmal record of achievement to date.

THE PROBLEMS

Some of the problems we face are:

- Some think there is a "magic" measure of size and/or complexity
- Developers play many games when providing estimates
- Many projects are told their expected delivery date
- Neither project managers nor team members believe the date
- Estimation tools are based on actuals, not estimates
- Estimation tools report a most probable outcome
- After a sound estimate is made, the "market"* demands the estimate be compressed

The following sections describe each of these.

*Typically, blamed on "management."

Great Software Debates. By Alan M. Davis
ISBN 0-471-649880 © 2004 Institute of Electrical and Electronics Engineers.

Magic Measures

All estimation approaches transform some independent variables concerning the project to be undertaken into an estimate of schedule. Fundamental to these independent variables is a measure of size. The earliest approaches used lines of code as the measure of size [5]. The problems with using this as a primary measure are: lines of code measure the size of the solution, not the size of the problem; how do you estimate lines of code; solving the same sized problem with less lines of code is generally considered better than solving it with more lines of code; which lines of code do you count; and so on [6]. Albrecht and Gaffney [7] suggested using function points as an alternative. Function points have the benefit of measuring the size of the problem rather than the solution, but it too suffers from some major problems: function points are difficult to estimate; just because there is an algorithm for counting function points, does not mean it is an accurate assessment of the size or complexity of the problem; use ordinal measures that do not exhibit straightforward mathematical properties; much subjectivity, and so on [8]. More recently, Jones [1] expanded the concept of function points to include feature points, but it fails to alleviate the aforementioned problems. In more recent years, estimation methods have been developed for object-oriented development [9].

Let me make an argument for why lines of code are a better measure. If my task were to construct a bridge over a river, I could design two different bridges. One could be relatively conventional, and include lots of steel and rivets, and would take 5 years to construct. The other could use an extremely innovative design that would take 2 years to design on paper, but just 1 year to construct. If the goal of estimation is solely to determine how long it will take to complete, then we must base the estimate on the size of the solution, not the problem. If my task is to construct a new software system, I could build it with 1 million lines of code, or with just 100,000 lines of code. The million-line program *will* take much longer to construct than the smaller version, even though they are both addressing the same "size" problem.

Let me make an argument for why function or feature points are a better measure. Let us assume that I have built 100 bridges over a wide range of span lengths. I should be able to correlate the length of the span with the amount of time required to construct the bridge. So when a new river awaits my bridge-building efforts, I can easily predict the time required by comparing the new river width with the past records. Similarly, if I have constructed 100 software systems and recorded the size and complexity of the requirements vs. the time required, it seems intuitive that there would be a strong enough correlation to enable me to estimate my next effort accurately.

Game Playing

When an individual is asked, "How long will it take to build this software," myriad games are played. For example, here are but a few:

- I will compute my honest estimate and then double it because
  - I know that my boss is going to halve it. Well, of course if you consistently double your estimate, yes, the boss will consistently halve it! You have trained him/her to do so!
- I will compute my honest estimate and then halve it because
  - I know that my boss is going to double it. Well, of course if you consistently halve your estimate, yes, the boss will consistently double it! You have trained him/her to do so!
- I will compute my honest estimate and then decrease it significantly because
  - If I give my boss an honest estimate, he'll tell me that he'll find somebody else to replace me who can do the work with a more reasonable schedule.
  - I really want to do this job.
  - I know I am one of the world's best software developers. I can do anything in just a few days, especially with enough caffeine.
  - I work better when I am under pressure.
  - I want my boss to like me.
- I will compute my honest estimate and then increase it significantly because
  - I really do not want to do this job.
  - My boss is stupid, and why should I work any harder than I have to?
  - I will look good when I complete the job in less time than planned.

Dates "Given"

In most companies, the product delivery date is selected by marketing (or directly by the customer when the customer is internal), and given to the development organization. Many developers consider themselves victims in such cases, but this is not the case. It is marketing's job to determine the optimal time to deliver a product. It is based on such factors as market window, competition, seasonal purchasing trends, specific feedback ascertained from potential customers, and so on.

When you move to a new city and want to rent an apartment, you have a specific date at which you want to move in. If you find a "perfect" apartment that is not available until 6 months after you move to town, you simply find another apartment. The customers, in this case you, decide when they want the product. It is the apartment owners' choice then to offer an alternative apartment (perhaps a "less than perfect" one), or to admit that they cannot satisfy your needs. And now the customers can decide if they want the less than perfect alternative apartment or find a source elsewhere.

Role of Belief

Few companies appreciate the important role that belief plays in the satisfaction of a delivery date. If the developers do not believe a date is reasonable, it will *not* be met! After all, if the developers estimated 6 months, and management insisted on 4

	The Schedule is Reasonable	The Schedule is Unreasonable
Development Believes Schedule	A	B
Development Doesn't Believe Schedule	C	D

Figure 10.1. The Role of Belief in Meeting a Schedule.

months, the developers are motivated to complete it in 6 months, not 4. After all, by completing in 6 months, they prove that they were right in the first place, and it sort of teaches the boss a lesson to not compress the schedule in the future. If they actually complete it in 4 months, the developers are proven wrong, and even worse, would be encouraging the boss to compress the schedule next time as well.

Let's look at the four possible situations that can occur on a development project. In Situation A of Figure 10.1, the schedule will likely be met; after all, it is a good schedule and the developers believe it is good. In Situation B, the schedule will likely be met as well; after all, although it is a tight schedule, the developers believe it is good and will therefore strive to make it happen. Situation B presents a big, hairy, audacious goal (BHAG*) [10] to the team members. The presence of BHAGs, and the belief that the BHAG *must* be met, is as critical to the success of teams as it is for corporations [10]. In Situation C, the schedule will likely be missed; although it is a good schedule, the developers do not believe it and will likely not be particularly committed to its success [10]. In Situation D, the schedule will likely be missed as well; after all, the schedule is unreasonable and the developers know it. Thus, Situations A and B are likely to be successful, and C and D are likely to be unsuccessful. From this we can see that the primary driver of schedule success is belief, not reasonableness.

Tools Based on Actuals

Barry Boehm [11], Larry Putnam [5], Capers Jones [12], etc., have spent years collecting data from past projects in order to improve the accuracy of their respective predictive estimation models, COCOMO, SLIM, and KnowledgePLAN®. In its most elemental form, a past project (from an estimation perspective), looks like Figure 10.2.

The data extracted from these past projects come from the right column. That is, these models (and the tools based on them) use the actual values and measures for past projects in order to predict what schedules future projects will need. However, this ignores the fact that on these past projects conditions changed during the development effort, and most importantly, requirements creep occurred making the pro-

---

*Pronounced "Bee-Hag."

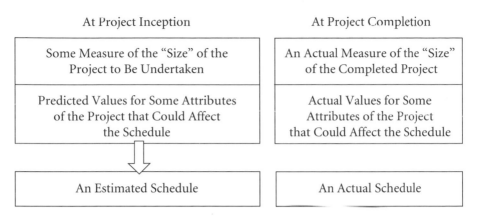

At Project Inception	At Project Completion
Some Measure of the "Size" of the Project to Be Undertaken	An Actual Measure of the "Size" of the Completed Project
Predicted Values for Some Attributes of the Project that Could Affect the Schedule	Actual Values for Some Attributes of the Project that Could Affect the Schedule
An Estimated Schedule	An Actual Schedule

Figure 10.2. Relationship of Measures at Beginning and End of a Project.

ject at completion look very different than the project did at inception. Fast forward now to your next proposed project. This project is likely to undergo the same degree of requirements creep that your past projects did. Furthermore, you are likely to make the same mistakes in predicting project attributes that you have in the past. Therefore, the data concerning past projects should be the items in the top two boxes of the *left* column together with the *actual* schedule! Then, the models are mapping *predictions* (as opposed to actuals) of project size and project attributes to actual schedule. And this is exactly what you have on your new project; you know your predictions for these values, not the actuals.

Most Probable?

If I told you that I was going to flip a coin 170 times and asked you to make your best guess concerning how many times it would be heads, what would you guess? 85, right? And the fact is you would be selecting the most likely outcome. See Figure 10.3. However, if I now actually did the 170 tosses, would you be surprised if it resulted to exactly 85 heads? Absolutely! That is because although 85 is the *best* guess, its probability of being right is extremely small, only about 6%. However, if we interpret your guess of 85 heads to mean you "win" if there are 85 heads or less, then your probability of winning soars from 6% to 50%.

Most software schedule estimation models provide you with the most probable estimate given a set of factors. Let's say for example that you estimate your software product to be x lines of code (or feature points if you prefer), and your project has characteristics $c1$, $c2$, $c3$, and $c4$. The model provides you with some schedule estimate, say 5 months. Like the 85 heads in the previous examples, 5 months is the most likely outcome as shown in Figure 10.4, but unfortunately the probability of the project actually completing in exactly 5 months is slim. The good news is that in the case of software development estimation, being late is always bad,

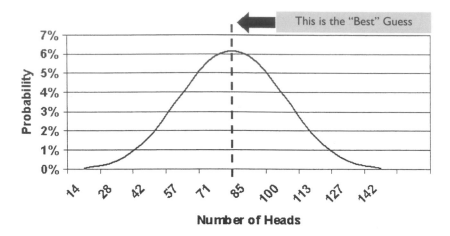

Figure 10.3. Probability of *x* Heads After 170 Coin Tosses.

and being early is generally acceptable. Thus, you have a 50/50 chance of being at 5 months or earlier. Do you want to stake your career on 50/50 odds? Of course not.

Now I must admit that software development is not just a pure probabilistic series of events. Many, many actions by management during development can actually affect the outcome, which is not the case with the coin toss.

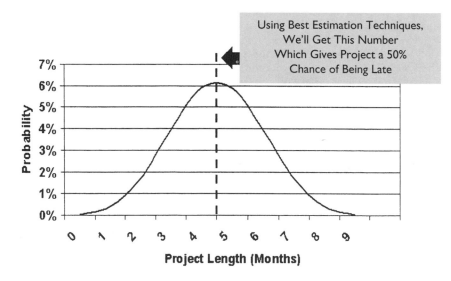

Figure 10.4. Probability of Completing a Project in 5 Months.

Compression Pressure

Regardless of how an initial schedule estimate is created, pressure will exist to compress that schedule. The pressure may come directly from customers (I *need* it earlier), from middle management (my bonus increases if we get it out earlier), marketing (we must beat the competition), or from executive management (we promised the board of directors that we would increase our revenues by 20% by the third quarter). Typically, the plea is made like this, "Can't you shave *just* 20% off the schedule?" That sounds fairly innocent, and often development teams comply. However, look at what that innocent "*just* 20%" does! It could lower the probability of success from 50% to 25%, as shown in Figure 10.5.

SOLUTIONS

Some Solutions to "Magic Measures"

The real problem is not whether you estimate using lines of code, function points, feature points, or anything else that suits your fancy. Honestly, as soon as Jones [1] provided us with tables that convert among these variables (based on a set of project characteristics such as implementation language), it became clear that the choice really didn't matter. The problem is that we naïvely believe that there should be some magical universal way to estimate the size of software, and thus accurately predict the schedule. There isn't. Every organization must make its own choice of inde-

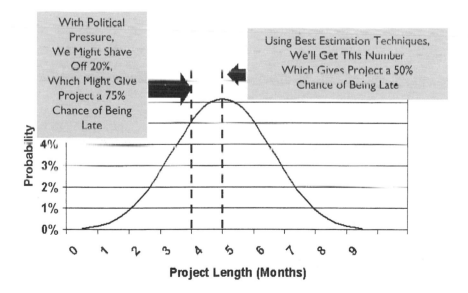

Figure 10.5. Political Pressure Makes Situation Much Worse.

pendent variables to use. And it is highly likely that what works well in one organization may produce dismal results in another.

Some Solutions to "Game Playing"

At Omni-Vista, Inc., Ann Zweig (then Vice President of Development) and I (then CEO) asked developers for their estimates of how long it would take them to do various tasks. As managers, we vowed to *never* alter an estimate that was given to us by a person responsible for doing the work. Our belief was that as soon as we did that, we would lose the trust of the employees, and rampant game playing would result. Also, we did not ask them to avoid playing games. Instead, we asked them to simply tell us what games they were playing. So, for example, a developer might say to us, "10 weeks, 'cause I don't want to do it." We would record the estimate of 10 weeks, and record the game being played. Over time, as developers saw that we never second-guessed their estimates, all game playing ceased.

Any other management response to game playing incites additional game playing. For example, confronting developers builds distrust. Changing the estimate builds distrust. And so on. Some readers may argue that this will not work in large companies. A large company is composed of a collection of small organizations and teams. The culture of a large company can change one project at a time.

Some Solutions to "Dates Given"

As explained above, it is the right (and in fact the *responsibility*) for marketing, management, and customers to specify the date by which a product is expected. It is also their responsibility to specify what requirements are desired. So how does a development organization respond when the deadline and the requirements are incompatible? The answers are (a) manage by cumulative probabilities of successful outcomes, rather than absolutes, and (b) let schedule drive requirements, not the reverse.

The probability graphs shown earlier in this essay show the probability of each outcome. What we really need is a graph like Figure 10.6 that shows the *cumulative* probability of outcomes. When the marketing department says we need these *x* requirements and we need them delivered in three months, all that is needed is to display the graph shown in Figure 10.7. All parties will now see that the situation is untenable; moving ahead with the plan almost guarantees failure. The only solutions are to extend the schedule or remove some requirements.

As mentioned above, many companies dictate both requirements and schedules to the development organization. When that happens, Figures 10.6 and 10.7 are the solution. In other companies, the requirements are defined, and development is asked how long it will take. When they report a date, they are told it is unacceptably late. The solution is to allow schedules to drive requirements. Say we decide that we are going to release successively larger increments of a product every 5 months. Now we distribute the requirements among the next 2 or 3 builds in such a way that the probabilities of success on each delivery are acceptable.

The data used to create Figure 10.6 is the same data used to create any estimation

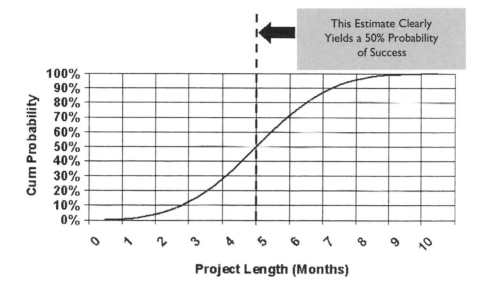

Figure 10.6. Cumulative Probability Graph.

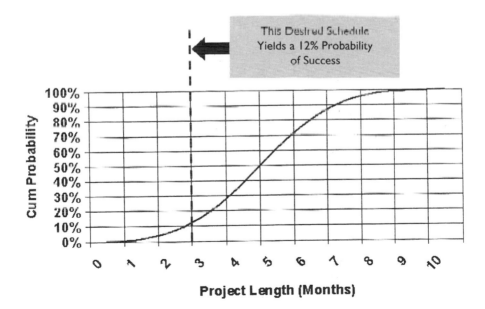

Figure 10.7. Low Likelihood of Success.

model, i.e., information about the original estimates of size and characteristics for a set of projects. The only difference is the presentation.

Some Solutions to the "Role of Belief"

Since belief in a schedule is such a strong driver in meeting that schedule, it behooves us to do everything we can do to ensure that the development team believes the estimate. This includes many of the items described within this essay, including,

- Let the development team make the estimates.
- As a manager, *never* change the development team's estimates.
- Use cumulative probability graphs so that the developers (and everybody else) can see the success likelihood.
- Allow developers to sit in on triage [13] meetings so they can witness the compromise process.

Some Solutions to "Tools Based on Actuals"

As mentioned before, most estimation models use a project's actual completion characteristics and measures of size as their data. I propose that we all start using the project's original estimates of characteristics and measures of size instead.

Some Solutions to "Most Probable?"

Instead of planning projects based on the most probable outcome, plan them using cumulative probability graphs like Figure 10.6. First establish a lower limit on a success probability that the entire team would find acceptable, say 75%. Now all that's left to do is to make sure that every product release contains baselined requirements and a schedule that can be met with at least a 75% cumulative probability of success.

At Omni-Vista, we did not use our own historic project data. Instead we used the COCOMO project database and formulae. Although we started using COCOMO data because we did not have our own data, the decision ended up helping us predict our success. Here is how it happened. Our first project manager had very little practical software experience but wanted dearly to be successful. As a result, she decided to be conservative in her project planning. At the first triage session, she demanded that the cumulative probability graphs (using COCOMO data) show at least a 95% likelihood of success before she would agree to a requirements baseline and schedule. The vice president of marketing was furious because it seemed to him that the project manager was making no sacrifices, and he, the marketing guy, was forced to exclude requirements in order to arrive at a "compromise." That project ended up being delivered on time, but with a great many extra bonus requirements. That convinced the project manager that she could tolerate a lower likelihood of success, and still succeed. So, at the triage session for the next product release, the project manager accepted a 75% likelihood of success. The vice president of marketing was thrilled. That second release was able to include most of the vice president's highly desired requirements. Once again, the project completed on schedule, and this time it included many (but not as many as earlier) extra requirements. This process continued for two more iterations. By then, the project manager had learned that if she accepted a set of requirements that gave her team a 45% probability of success based on COCOMO historic data, she knew she would be able to lead her team to an on-time completion. We never added our own project data. If we had done so, the project manager would have naturally tried to get agreement at a much higher level than 45%, and meanwhile, the vice president of marketing saw her as a real team player!

Some Solutions to "Compression Pressure"

Marketing and development organizations typically express little respect for each other. Each side accuses the other side of dishonesty, making up numbers, and poor reliability (i.e., they change their minds too often). And yet when it comes to schedule estimation, members of both disciplines practice the same degree hocus-pocus. For example, when marketing says, "we must have this product by March 2005," is that really a fact? Absolutely not! It is a best guess based on a large body of experience, a sampling of data, and some probably shaky business intelligence about competitors. Not only that, but any of those variables could change drastically at any moment. When development says, "we cannot produce this product before June 2005," is that really a fact? Absolutely not! It is a best guess based on a large body of experience, a sampling of data, a great many assumptions about what the product is supposed to do. Not only that, but any of these variables could change drastically at any moment. So the first thing to do to solve the compression problem is for all parties to recognize what is really happening.

Note also that when marketing asks for a product three months earlier than development can produce it, marketing is in some way "covering its rear." After all, if the product is delivered according to development's schedule, and the product fails in the marketplace, marketing can easily blame development. "If development had only produced the product by the date we wanted it, we would have had no problem making our revenue numbers." And the reverse is also the case. If marketing gets its way, and development succumbs to a ridiculously tight schedule, the product will likely be delivered with poor quality. But development has "covered its rear." "If you had allowed us to produce the product according to our originally scheduled delivery date, the product would have been of much better quality." Although these scenarios are replayed continually in software companies, we are not in business to "cover our rears." We are in business for some combination of satisfying customer needs, providing a return to the shareholders, and employing people in a pleasant work environment.

So, then what is the answer to the dilemma of delivering a product early with poor quality, late with sufficient quality, or early with less functionality? First, however, let me eliminate the consideration of delivering with poor quality. I think that delivering poor quality software products will just continue to erode our industry's poor reputation (not to mention your company's!). Beyond quality, the answer is balance. You need to find 2 or 3 balanced alternatives, and then decide which is best. The best won't be perfect; it is just the best of the alternatives. Here are some likely alternatives where 25 requirements have been selected, and we expect that March 2005 is the optimal time to deliver from the market perspective:

- Deliver the product in March 2005 with only 20 of the requirements satisfied—with a 90% likelihood of meeting the date.
- Deliver the product in January 2005 (early!) with only 15 of the requirements satisfied—with a 90% likelihood of meeting the date.
- Deliver the product in June 2005 with all 25 requirements satisfied—with a 90% likelihood of meeting the date.
- Delivery the product in March 2005 with all 25 of the requirements satisfied—with a 20% likelihood of meeting the date.
- Don't build the product.

Like I said, none of these is perfect. But this is real life. "Covering your rear" and letting the company fail is just not a responsible alternative.

SUMMARY AND PREDICTIONS

I do not have a good feeling about how today's software companies arrive at a delivery date. The fact that we are so consistently late supports my feeling. I wish I could be optimistic concerning our future, but at the time I write this essay, I am not. It took the tragedy of September 11 to make the United States and the World aware of the need to make our airlines safer for the flying public. It may take an equally grave disaster to get us to change our schedule prediction techniques. For example, one organization insists on a product delivery date, and the development organization insists that it is impossible to do so. The buying organization threatens with "produce it by this date or I will find another source." The development organization capitulates. The product is delivered "on time" but with poor quality. The software is implicated in the deaths of many people, and in the subsequent high-profile court case, the scheduling disagreement surfaces.

REFERENCES

[1] Jones, C., *Applied Software Measurement*, 2nd edition, New York: McGraw-Hill, 1997.
[2] Pfleeger, S., et al., "Status Report on Software Measurement," *IEEE Software*, 14, 2 (March/April 1997), pp. 33–43.
[3] Jørgensen, M., "A Review of Studies on Expert Estimation of Software Development Effort," *Journal of Systems and Software*, 70, 1–2 (February 2004), pp. 37–60.

[4] DeMarco, T., "Why Does Software Cost So Much," *IEEE Software, 10,* 2 (March 1993), pp. 89–90.

[5] Putnam, L., "A General Empirical Solution to the Macro Software Sizing and Estimation Problem," *IEEE Transactions on Software Engineering,* 4, 4 (July 1978), pp. 345–361.

[6] Furey, S., "Why We Should Use Function Points," *IEEE Software,* 14, 2 (March/April 1997), pp. 28, 30.

[7] Albrecht, A., and J. Gaffney, "Software Function, Source Lines of Code and Development Effort Prediction," *IEEE Transactions of Software Engineering,* 9, 6 (June 1983), pp. 639–648.

[8] Kitchenham, B., "The Problem with Function Points," *IEEE Software,* 14, 2 (March/April 1997), pp. 29, 31.

[9] Laranjeira, L., "Software Size Estimation of Object-Oriented Systems," *IEEE Transactions on Software Engineering,* 16, 5 (May 1990), pp. 510–522.

[10] Collins, J., and J. Porras, *Built To Last,* New York: HarperCollins, 1994.

[11] Boehm, B., et al., *Software Cost Estimation with COCOMO* II, Upper Saddle River, New Jersey: Prentice Hall, 2000.

[12] Jones, C., *Estimating Software Costs,* New York: McGraw-Hill, 1998.

[13] Davis, A., "Requirements Triage," *IEEE Computer,* 36, 3 (March 2003), pp. 42–49.

SEEDS FOR DEBATE

1. I argued in this essay that the only meaningful historic "size" data to use when estimating software development efforts are those that were created at the inceptions of past projects. Construct an argument for why estimation tool vendors are correct in using *actual* size data ascertained at project completion.

2. One of this book's reviewers commented that my recommendation for management to never alter a software developer's estimate of work would never work in a large company. Construct an argument for why the recommendation would work in all sized companies. Construct an argument for why it would work only in small companies. Construct an argument for why it would never work.

3. One could argue that marketing is by definition "right" when they say they need *this* system by *this* date. After all, making these kinds of calls is their job. Put forth an argument why this is the case, and describe how you think the software developers should respond to such a decree.

4. One could argue that development is by definition "right" when they say they need *this* much time to build *this* system. After all, making these estimates is their job, and they have (presumably) built such systems before. Put forth an argument why this is the case, and describe how you think marketing should respond to such a decree.

5. In the essay, I construct an argument that belief in a schedule (by the team members) is a bigger driver of success than the inherent reasonableness of the

schedule. I do so using Collins and Porras' argument that successful companies often have BHAGs that drive them toward excellence. To really justify the argument, however, an experiment may be in order. Such an experiment would need multiple teams, all with the same challenging deadline. But some would need to believe that the deadline was achievable, while others would need to believe it was unachievable. Conduct such an experiment.

6. If you are a strong proponent of function points or feature points, construct a *solid* case in favor of lines-of-code as the best measure of size of a software development effort. Leave out all those arguments against lines-of-code, just as you do when you are arguing for function or feature points.

7. If you are a strong proponent of lines-of-code as a measure of program/problem size, construct a *solid* case in favor of function or feature points as the best measure of size of a software development effort. Leave out all those arguments against fp's, just as you do when you are arguing for lines-of-code.

8. On page 60, I list five alternative routes for you to take when the market demands requirements in a timeframe that you cannot deliver. Can you think of any other alternatives? What does your organization do?

MANAGEMENT

I have spent most of my career as a manager in various high-tech companies. It is from this experience that I present to you this collection of nine essays concerning (a) my personal experiences, and (b) the state of the software industry's management practices.

Trial by Fire: Saga of a Rookie Manager tells the story of my first few months as a manager, a job I was given with no training, no background, and unfortunately no skills (at the time, at least).

Can You Survive Your Management Mistakes describes a death march [1] project I participated in back when I was a very inexperienced and quite naïve manager. In retrospect, it also turns out to be one of the most "fun" pieces in this book. I can laugh at it only now. The subsequent essay, *Should He Stay or Should He Go? Advice for a Beleaguered Manager,* tells the rest of the same story.

If you are trained as a software engineer, you likely have little understanding of how a company works. *The Software Company Machine* is a short and simple description of how a software company actually works—all in words that an engineer can understand.

From 1998 through 2002, Ann Zweig and I took time off from our respective careers to operate a software startup called Omni-Vista, Inc. Omni-Vista made a big splash in the software industry and then died a quiet death. *The Rise and Fall of a Software Startup* tells the cradle to grave story of this fascinating little company with great prospects.

Omni-Vista had been my third startup, and my first "failure." The next essay, *Anatomy of a Software Start-Up,* tells the story of my first. Written by the founder and president of the company, BTG, Inc., Ed Bersoff, this is a fascinating up-and-down story of a startup that made it.

Information for Decision Makers elaborates on management's role in the software lemming problem.

The last two essays, *Some Tips for the Would-Be Entrepreneur,* and *Some More Tips for the Would-Be Entrepreneur,* were written for the Colorado Springs Gazette, the local newspaper, for local high technology startups. These short articles provide advice to new or prospective entrepreneurs.

REFERENCES

1. Yourdon, E., *Death March*, Englewood Cliffs, New Jersey: Prentice-Hall, 1997.

Trial By Firing: Saga of a Rookie Manager*

I have managed small and large software organizations for twelve years. I have managed groups as large as 140 professionals. Although I have been in many stressful circumstances, one of my most emotional episodes occurred when I first became a manager in 1978. This is the story of my first management experience. I hope you can learn from my mistakes.

—*Al Davis*

I joined the industrial world for the first time in 1977. As a member of the technical staff I was expected to work individually doing innovative software engineering. My employer, a large telecommunications research laboratory, expected me to do research, publish the results, and generally "carry the flag" at public forums.

One year after I joined the company, my department manager resigned. Upper management decided, in its infinite wisdom, to fill the vacant position with the "best technical person" in the department. (A mistake made by so many companies. They assume great technical contributors are great leaders as well.) The director, Richard (not his real name, of course), entered my office. He told me Thomas had resigned, and the company believed I was the right person to fill his shoes.

OFFER I COULDN'T REFUSE

I told Richard I was a computer specialist and had neither training nor interest in management. Richard explained the "facts" to me:

- I would be letting down the company if I did not accept.
- My career would be greatly enhanced if I had management credentials.
- I could make a lot more money in management.
- Richard would personally guide me through the job.

*Originally published in *IEEE Software*, 9, 4 (July 1992), pp. 72, 85.

Great Software Debates. By Alan M. Davis
ISBN 0-471-649880 © 2004 Institute of Electrical and Electronics Engineers.

How could I refuse? I accepted the job. I would be a "one-of-the-guys" manager. I would not let being a manager interfere with the trust and friendship I had developed with my colleagues (now my employees). I was in for a rude awakening.

Richard coached me through a wide variety of challenges during those first few months. Although I was actually enjoying the job, it was obvious that some members of the department had decided to change their relationship with me. They expressed growing suspicion of my motives and growing resentment that I had been promoted instead of them. Whether this attitude resulted from their own perceptions or my altered behavior, I will never know.

FIRING LINE

In addition to many little problems, I had two large ones. First, there was George. A member of the technical staff, George regularly arrived at 10 or so in the morning and often left by three or four in the afternoon. When he was at work, he acted belligerently, refusing to attend review meetings. His work was late and of poor quality.

Then there was the recruitment problem. The department was trying to grow rapidly. We were interviewing two to three candidates a week and making numerous offers, but everyone was turning us down. I could not figure out what was wrong.

One day, Richard called me into his office. He said he had become aware of both problems from anonymous sources. (I had discussed my woes with a few peers and with the people in personnel, but I had not yet approached Richard.) He asked me what I thought we should do. I had no idea. He had ideas. Richard wanted me to fire George immediately. Also, he had heard a rumor that another member of my technical staff, Bob, was bad-mouthing me and the department to prospective employees—that's why everyone was turning us down. Richard asked me to verify this information.

At this stage in my management career, I knew very little about management. I did not know about coaching. I did not know about my obligation to do everything in my power to understand my employees and to help them overcome any barriers that prevented them from excelling. Without such knowledge, I was a pawn of my boss. He told me to fire George, so I prepared to fire George.

Richard spent the next two days with me, role-playing the firing. He taught me to say the words, "You are fired," in a way that left no room for misunderstanding. He taught me to tell the employee to leave at once and come back, supervised, on the weekend to pick up all personal belongings. (I guess this was to prevent him from "polluting" other employees.) He taught me to always fire an employee on the ground floor of the building. (I guess this was just in case the employee decided to jump out—or throw me out—the window.)

I planned to fire George at 4:00 p.m. At 3:00 p.m., he walked into my office and resigned. I still do not know if he had seen the writing on the wall, if there had been a leak, if he had planned all along to quit and his performance was suffering because his heart was no longer in the job, or if it was just a coincidence. In any case, I felt fairly proud that problem number one had been solved.

LONELY AT THE TOP

With Bob, I decided to take a direct approach. I called him into my office, having not yet learned that communication is easier when meeting with employees in their offices. I asked him, "Do you know why none of our prospective new hires has accepted our offers?"

He responded without hesitation: "Of course! Why would anybody possibly want to work here? This place is awful." I asked him if he knew how the candidates learned of this. Once again he responded quickly, "Oh, I tell them. You don't want me to lie to them, do you?" I tried to explain to him that the state of the department and my managerial competence were matters of opinion, but my words fell on deaf ears. He made it clear that he felt it was his responsibility to tell everybody. For the next couple of days, news of my meeting with Bob spread. Many of the other employees dropped by to tell me how appalled they were by Bob's actions. They all told me I needed to fire Bob or the department would never grow.

I went to Richard and explained the situation. His answer was predictable. To Richard, surgery was always the preferred cure. Once again, he role-played with me for two days. I learned my lines. I memorized my responses to all possible comments Bob might make. Humanity, tenderness, caring, and thoughtfulness were not considered. We rehearsed a hard-hearted, brainless severing of the relationship.

I planned to fire Bob at 4:00 p.m. (on the first floor!). At 3:00 p.m., I stared at my door, expecting him to enter and resign. Silence. For one very long hour, I stared at the door, the floor, the walls. The only visitor was another employee, who dropped in to tell me that Bob was in the hallway bragging about how he was going to make me fail as a manager. That added to my resolve.

Four o'clock came. I called Bob into the office and played my role exactly as rehearsed. I told him he was fired. I told him to leave the premises at once. It did not feel real. I was but an actor in a play. I felt a mile of insulation surrounding me, insulating me from Bob and this dreadful task.

But Bob didn't leave at once. Instead, he went to the department's other employees and told them he had been fired. Within the hour, a parade of employees began that was to continue for the next few days. They all said something like, "How dare you fire Bob?" I did not sleep for many weeks. I kept seeing Bob, his wife, his kids. I tortured myself with guilt about what I had done to this family.

I learned two very important lessons that day:

- Firing somebody is very painful.
- No matter how many people are "behind you" when you make a painful decision, you are all alone once you implement it.

EPILOGUE

Looking back, I realize how little I knew about management then. I now know that your most important resource as a manager is people. You have a responsibility to know them, understand them, respect them, and coach and train them so each of them can reach their full potential. You have a responsibility to work around problems, to predict and prevent them, to be proactive, and to "carry the water" (sometimes literally by fetching refreshments when your employees are working long hours). In short, good managers serve their employees, not the reverse.

Quality management requires you to maintain a fine balance between "representing your people" to your company and "representing your company" to your people. Just like every aspect of management style, you must vary your actions and words for each situation, deciding carefully based on the emotions, politics, and facts of the situation. Always listen to others' opinions before taking action. Above all, be as objective as possible, honest, and ethical. Be what you expect others to be—nothing less.

SEEDS FOR DEBATE

1. What can companies do to ensure that technical personnel with no interest in management careers are "rewarded" and "appreciated" as much as they would be if they selected a managerial career path?
2. If you were in Richard's shoes and you needed to replace Thomas, what would *you* say to me to convince me to take the job?
3. Do you think that a manager can do well being "one of the guys?"
4. Would you have fired George? What would you have done instead?
5. In this essay, I wrote, "good managers serve their employees, not the reverse." Put together an argument for why this is true? What benefits accrue? Now put together an argument for why you believe this would never work. What benefits accrue when employees serve the manager?

Can You Survive Your Management Mistakes?*

Every manager has a memorable project or two that seems to attract disaster. Things that seemed destined to go right inevitably go wrong. Why? Many times, it's the executive decisions—a mix of personality quirks, experience, sixth sense, whatever—that determine the outcome. There are a few management laws, but most of us learn by doing, and often doing means making mistakes or observing the mistakes of others. Consider this scenario, and test your skill. How would you get out of this situation?

I was the director of a group of 30 to 40 software engineering researchers in a large telecommunications company. One of our many goals was to experiment with language-independent compiler technology to translate CHILL, a language that had the potential of becoming the new international standard for our business.

I started looking for someone to manage this important effort and became impressed by George (not his real name), a computer science professor who wanted to enter industry. George had a PhD from a major university, had published many papers on compilers, and had a great personality. What else could I possibly want? I hired him. *Mistake #1: A great technical person does not necessarily make a great manager.* He proceeded to staff the project with very capable, fine people. About three months into the project, one of the company's divisions called me and said they needed a CHILL compiler as soon as possible for a critical product development. Could we deliver? I said yes. *Mistake #2: A research laboratory should not be on the critical path of an important product development.*

George and I discussed a schedule and agreed on a specific date for delivery, about nine months away. We contacted the division that needed the compiler and told them the date. They said, "That's too late. We need it three months earlier than that." Because we were afraid of losing this "opportunity," George and I agreed to a six-month, rather than a nine-month, schedule. *Mistake #3: Just because the customer says the product is needed earlier than you can deliver it is not good enough reason to promise it earlier.*

*Originally published in *IEEE Software, 11*, 5 (September 1994), pp. 109–110.

George had decided that the best way to judge progress on this development was to have the compiler try to compile itself. When the compiler successfully translated 25 percent of itself, clearly the compiler was 25 percent finished testing, and so on. I agreed to use it. *Mistake #4: Do not use unproven measures for testing project completion.*

After five months of development, we were one month from delivery and George reported that we were right on schedule. In the last four weeks, we had moved from 50 percent to 75 percent of the compiler successfully translating itself. I called the customer and told him all was fine. *Mistake #5: Do not tell the customer that you are on schedule unless you know you are on schedule.* The customer was happy.

Three days before the scheduled delivery, 99 percent of the compiler was successfully translated. Everything looked great. George was busy preparing the delivery package. In the late afternoon on the delivery date, the customer called me to ask, "What do you mean the compiler will be a month late?" *Mistake #6: Don't fail to establish sufficient rapport with your employees, so they tell you the bad news before they tell the customer.* I went to George's office to find out what had happened. He explained the team's jubilation when the compiler had successfully translated itself entirely. He also explained how quickly the jubilation ended when they discovered that the compiler could not translate many much simpler test cases. They were nowhere near ready to deliver.

Although George estimated one more month to completion, I started getting suspicious. After discussions with my boss, we convinced the customer to wait three months—we were back to our originally scheduled delivery date. The customer was not happy, but agreed. At this point, George asked me if he and a number of his employees could take a short vacation to recoup their energies in preparation for the coming long haul. I thought this was an unreasonable request from the viewpoint of our image. What would the customer think if he heard we were all on vacation while he was waiting nervously for our now late product? But I said yes. *Mistake #7: When you believe you are right don't be afraid to be the bad guy.*

With some trepidation, I went to my boss for advice. *Mistake #8: Don't ask your boss for advice if you know he has no common sense.* My boss's response was, extreme. He issued a proclamation to me, to George, and to all workers on the project: Effective immediately, all of us were to be in the office a minimum of 10 hours per day, six days per week with no vacation, no travel, and no sick leave, period! The team continued to work hard for a few weeks.

After a few weeks, my boss came to me for a progress report. I reported that everybody was working as he wanted, that they were tired, but doing the best job they could. My boss's response was, "Effective next week, I'm transferring six people from another project to the CHILL project to bolster the ranks." I knew this would be a bad move. As Frederick Brooks discovered years ago, adding more people to a project at the wrong time only delays product delivery. But I was tired. I argued, but did not have enough strength to refuse. *Mistake #9: If you know you're right, don't let your boss bully you into making the wrong decision.*

The team continued to work the long hours for another six weeks. We were one month from the new scheduled delivery. The customer called me. He explained that his own development schedule had undergone a major revision for reasons unrelated to the CHILL compiler. As a result, we could relax our schedule even further if we wanted. He asked if I could fly out to his office the next day to exchange status and discuss a new, more reasonable schedule. I explained that my boss had given me a direct order not to leave the office for any reason. The customer explained that if we could meet face to face, there would no longer be a need to work so hard.

What should I do? Should I disobey my boss and visit the customer to resolve the problem? Or should I obey my boss, ignore the customer, and stay and work?

I tried to call my boss, but he was out of town and inaccessible. So I made reservations and flew to the customer the next day.

[I] received an overwhelming response from the readers [to the above question]. See the next essay for some highlights.

SEEDS FOR DEBATE

1. If you wanted to hire a project manager for a compiler project, what qualities would you look for in the candidates? Argue for why your choices are better than the ones I used.

2. What would you do if you were given the choice: (a) agree to build the CHILL compiler in six months (when you knew it would take longer), or (b) you would not have a job?

3. How often would you have expected George to report project status to you? And would information would you want from him? Would earned value* have helped?

4. What would you have done if you were my boss and I asked you if the team could go on vacation?

5. Before you read the next essay, think about the dilemma described in the last few paragraphs. If you were in my shoes, would you stay at the office, or fly to the customer?

---

*See Q. Fleming, and J. Koppelman, *Earned Value Project Management*, Newtown Square, Pennsylvania: Project Management Institute, 2000.

Should He Stay or Should He Go?
Advice for a Beleaguered Manager*

This is what happened to [me] in the previous [essay]. As you may recall, my boss had given me strict orders not to leave the office for any reason. But the customer said he wanted to talk to me in his office halfway across the country. I tried to call my boss, but he was out of town and inaccessible. So I made reservations and flew to the customer the next day.

We received an overwhelming response from the readers. . . . Here are some highlights:

- From Ed Evers of Herndon, Virginia. "This . . . is a good opportunity to practice the 'it is better to ask forgiveness than permission' paradigm, especially when the person isn't around from whom the permission must be asked. I would make plans to do the face-to-face. . . I would then make the visit, learn the new requirements, . . . [and] draft a plan, . . . which I would review with my boss when he did return. I would not reduce the work activity until my boss had returned and he agreed with the revised plan."

- From Noah Davids, Marlboro, Massachusetts: ". . . while I read many of IEEE Software's articles with interest I cannot say that most of them are [as] enjoyable. . . . Ignore the boss and travel to the customer to resolve the problem. Then present the boss with a *fait accompli* and loudly and widely give the boss credit for giving you the environment that allowed you to resolve the problem."

- Santosh K. Misra of Cleveland, Ohio, suggests: ". . . visit your customer IMMEDIATELY and discuss the updated schedule. . . . If your boss does not like your travel violating his direct instruction, what is he going to do . . . fire you? I think not. You may actually receive his whole-hearted approval."

- Mafedh Mili of Montreal, Quebec, made similar suggestions, but added that I should have covered my bases better: "Clearly . . . [you are] too worried about [your] image, and most of the mistakes . . . have to do with . . . trying to cultivate . . . image. . . . For the good of the project, and the morale of the project team and the client, . . . fly to meet the customer . . . and keep the client hap-

*Originally published in *IEEE Software*, 9, 5 (September 1992), pp. 100–101.

py. . . . I [also] would make honest efforts to contact my boss (and let it be known/recorded that I tried)."

- Lorraine Duvall, Syracuse, New York, also advised me to make multiple attempts to contact the boss.
- Thomas Knoedler, Springfield, Illinois, offers a variation on this theme: "Going to the customer . . . is fine if the staff doesn't mind being fired on the spot. However, the boss . . . said nothing about . . . paying for the customer to fly to the manager's office for the face-to-face meeting. . . My overall answer is [to] attend to the needs of the customer and ignore the boss . . . somehow."

This is a nice suggestion. Unfortunately, the customer was a very busy vice president and I was a lowly center director who clearly had more time on his hands now that the schedule had slipped.

- John Whited went beyond ignoring the boss, and suggested I go around him: "Talk to your boss's boss or other person acting on his behalf while he's gone. See if you can get approved via that means."
- Yuval Lirou was a bit harder on me: "You forget that you must meet the customer, since ignoring the customer defies the reason for your job. Your next mistake is that you assume your boss is an ignorant tyrant. Visiting the customer would not mean necessarily ignoring the boss; his grounding direction was issued in different circumstances. There is [however] no point worrying about how you look to your customer. . . . You already look bad . . . since you just demonstrated your impotence by not delivering a promised product on time. You cannot look any worse no matter what you do. I suggest you look for an easier job . . . not . . . managerial."

Only three readers suggested I not visit the customer.

- Garurank Saxena of Arlingon Heights, Illinois, had some great advice: "If we can make the schedule within . . . one month, I would stick to [it] and finish. . . . If not, I would complete the project to the next milestone, . . . write a detailed status report, [and] continue or terminate the project. There is [no] . . . need for a meeting [with the customer]."
- And from Jay Schutawie, Austin, Texas: "Your boss seems to have no faith in you so I wouldn't push it by disobeying his/her order. Ask the customer to wait until your boss returns. The customer should have plenty of time to wait another week. Until then, work at the same level. You've been working this way for eight weeks, [so] you can do it another one or two."
- Sarah Kooshian also suggested I stay on the course: "It is difficult to tell who had responsibility for managing the customer . . . so I am suggesting you play it conservatively . . . enough things have gone wrong under current management of this project that slower reaction to the news of being able to slip the schedule would be prudent."

The best overall advice, in my opinion, came from

- Nancy Mead, Pittsburgh, Pennsylvania: "Disobey the boss, visit the customer, reorganize to beat the new schedule by a month . . . and inform the boss when he gets back. Don't ask him what to do—tell him what you have done. In the meantime, get some real project-control and project-management mechanisms in place so you know where you stand. The worst case is that you won't be able to negotiate a new schedule and you'll get fired. That would be a blessing in disguise."

WHAT I DID

I reasoned that the customer and I would be able to work out a deal that would make the ridiculous work restrictions placed by my boss obsolete, so I made the trip.

While at the customer's site, I received a call from my boss. He had returned from his vacation and come to my office for a status report. I wasn't there. He wanted me to get on the next flight back. He would be waiting for me in my office. I tried to explain why I had left. All he kept saying on the phone was, "I told you to not leave your office for any reason. You disobeyed me." *Mistake #10: Don't Think That Logic Has Any Role in Some Management Decisions.*

When I got back to the office late that afternoon, my boss was waiting for me in my office. All he said was, "Pack up your things. Leave today. You are no longer working here." I was fired! *Mistake #11: Don't Think That You are Invulnerable Just Because You are Doing the "Right" Thing for the Company.*

I was fired on a Thursday. Friday morning, I called my boss's boss to ask him if there was anything I could do to get my job back. He was shocked! He did not even know I had been fired. He immediately reversed the decision and rehired me. The CHILL compiler was completed on the new schedule. Three months later, the research laboratory was reorganized. My boss was "put out to pasture."

Many thanks to all of you who wrote in.

EPILOGUE

A few years after I wrote this story, I started working again with "George." It turns out that George has actually learned a lot about management in the ensuing years; he even knows how to keep a project on schedule. He is now a very successful small business executive in Florida.

SEEDS FOR DEBATE

1. What lessons do you suspect that George learned from all of this?
2. One of the messages of this essay is that it is better to do the right thing (and

be able to sleep well at night) than have a job (and sleep poorly because you are worried about having done the wrong thing). Is this always the case? Can you construct a situation where having a job is more important than your ethical stand?

The Software Company Machine*

Software company employees live in silos. Software developers learn how to develop software but learn little or nothing about marketing, sales, or finance. Marketing personnel learn how to market software but not how to develop it or manage the finances. And the financial personnel learn little or nothing about software development or marketing.

If our industry enjoyed a reputation of regularly satisfying our customers, I would have no concern for the current situation. However, we have a dismal reputation. Every survey of our success record (whether performed in the early 1970s or the late 1990s) reports the same: Most software development efforts result in shelfware—software its intended users never use. Perhaps one reason for this is that we all live in our own silos.

Unfortunately, our silos are not accidents. After all, software developers receive their education in universities where they are taught to specialize in narrow technical areas. A student has no reasonable expectation of meeting—let alone learning from—a faculty member with interest or knowledge in software development, marketing, and finance. When leaving academia to join the world of industry, few interdisciplinary role models exist—the employees being products of the same educational system. Identical phenomena apply to finance or marketing graduates.

Consequently, software development companies do not function as systems. Instead, they function as a set of totally asynchronous and rarely communicating divisions that succeed by accident, not by design.

A WELL-TUNED SOFTWARE MACHINE

A software development company (in fact, any company) might achieve more success if it thinks of itself as a finely crafted and well-tuned machine. As Figure 14.1 shows, a software development company is a machine comprising three engines: the financial engine provides resources to power the other two engines. Its criteria for success are well understood and well documented. It must provide a "return" to

*Originally published in *IEEE Software, 17,* 2 (March/April 2000), pp. 14–15.

Great Software Debates. By Alan M. Davis
ISBN 0-471-649880 © 2004 Institute of Electrical and Electronics Engineers.

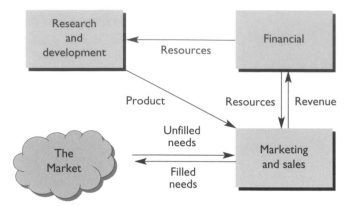

Figure 14.1. A software development company requires three engines—research and development, financial, and marketing and sales—which must exchange various resources to satisfy the company's market.

those parties who provide the resources (whether the parties include lenders or shareholders). Thus, you can't let this engine run out of resources—it may never possess negative cash.

The marketing and sales engine must transform unsatisfied (customer or user) needs into satisfied needs. It takes fuel (resources) from the financial engine to create interest in the company's products, draw potential customers, and then sell the products. Its criteria for success are also well understood and well documented. This engine acts as the primary source of new cash, so it must return to the financial engine (considerably) more than it takes in.

The research and development must create products (and services) that help satisfy customers' unsatisfied needs. It takes fuel (resources) from the financial engine and delivers products to the marketing and sales engine, which sells the products to customers.

From this perspective, it is remarkable that developers often consider marketing the enemy ("What do they know about our customers anyway?") and marketing personnel often consider development the enemy ("They can never produce a product on time, within budget, that also satisfies customers' needs"). Each party considers the other party incompetent, yet the reality is not their respective incompetence, but their total lack of knowledge about the other disciplines.

HOW TO KEEP THE ENGINES RUNNING

Each engine can thrive only when all three engines thrive. Imagine how long the system would survive if any of the engines failed. For example, if the financial engine runs out of cash or the marketing or development engines try to consume more cash than is available, the other two engines will lack the necessary resources to maintain their own inner workings. Negative cash flow on the cash-flow statement clearly indicates serious problems. Additionally, if the financial engine can't provide adequate returns to the shareholders or lenders, they desert and valuations plummet, consuming the reserves and providing little cushion for future hard times. Similarly, if the marketing engine consumes more resources than it returns to the company, the resulting lack of profitability can break the lenders and shareholders' confidence, resulting in valuation decreases. If the development engine falls significantly behind schedule or creates a product that does not fill unsatisfied needs, the marketing engine won't be able to satisfy customer demands and thus will consume more resources than it can return, leading to decreased valuation.

Properly maintaining the engines requires a plan that shows how resources move across the engine boundaries as a function of time. We can easily create this plan with a set of cooperating worksheets in a spreadsheet. Each worksheet adheres to its engine's rules. Meanwhile, each worksheet "sends" key resources to the other two worksheets.

The financial worksheets are typical financial reports: an income statement (which reports on the machine's efficiency, showing how many resources the company produces and how many it consumes), a cash-flow statement (showing the company's monetary status), and a balance sheet (charting the company's health). The marketing and sales worksheets capture where the company spends its money (to generate leads, close deals, and so forth) and the revenue it generates. The development worksheets are the most straightforward; they mostly keep track of the costs. If development or marketing consumes cash too quickly, the cash-flow statement sounds an alert. If development builds the wrong product or marketing is inefficient, the income statement sounds an alert.

Software development companies will thrive more when managers of individual engines understand how the entire machine behaves. We need to escape from our silos and learn how the other engines work. We need not all become experts for all three machines, but we must develop an appreciation for the other disciplines if we have any hope of thriving.

SEEDS FOR DEBATE

1. For each of the three engines shown in Figure 14.1, (a) describe what happens when it runs out of fuel, (b) describe what happens to the other two engines when this engine runs out of fuel, and (c) find an example of a company that failed because this engine failed to perform its job.

2. This entire essay reveals a left-brained bias. Take a right-brained approach to understanding the company as an organism, not a machine. Argue for why that is a more realistic and helpful model.

The Rise and Fall of a Software Startup

A. DAVIS AND A. ZWEIG

Between 1998 and 2002, the authors founded and subsequently managed Omni-Vista, Inc., a software startup based in Colorado Springs, Colorado. This is the story of how the events surrounding this company unfolded. We start with a quick glimpse of the final days of the company, then do a rewind back to the beginning of the story and the backgrounds of the two authors. The remainder of this essay contains seven stories that run in parallel, each detailing the events with respect to a different aspect of the company. The objective is to help you, the reader, better understand the intricacies of managing a software startup, and hopefully enable you to lead a startup and make fewer mistakes than we made.

THE END

In May 2002, Omni-Vista had its last shareholder meeting. Only one issue was to be discussed and voted upon: the recommendation by the officers and directors of the company to dissolve the company. Just three individuals attended: the authors and the corporate counsel. The proxies were counted. The decision was to close the company.

In June 2002, we notified all shareholders and interested parties about the availability of all our assets, both physical and intangible. We received bids for almost all our assets, and they were all distributed. We held a garage sale to sell off the remaining pieces of furniture and office supplies. We closed the doors.

In the end, Omni-Vista was able to pay off all its creditors. And the remaining cash was distributed to the shareholders on a pro rata basis, returning approximately 15 cents on the dollar.

THE BEGINNING

On September 22, 1997, Al Davis was leading a discussion at Storage Tek in Colorado. Present in the room were around 25 employees including a few senior pro-

Great Software Debates. By Alan M. Davis
ISBN 0-471-649880 © 2004 Institute of Electrical and Electronics Engineers.

ject managers. Al had just finished talking about the importance of verifying that a requirements baseline is consistent with the available schedule and resources, when one of the project managers in the room asked whether commercially available estimation tools could be used to verify such consistency. Al explained that many such tools used feature- or function-points to create an estimate and that these tools could tell you what a good schedule and a good budget would be for any given set of requirements. The project manager said, "but how would I know what would happen to my schedule if I had to remove a requirement?" Al drew a picture on the whiteboard something like that shown in Figure 15.1. He had no idea what either of the axes meant. He simply wanted to indicate that when you have a desired schedule (the vertical bar), you'd like it to reside close to some optimal point (the low point in the center of the smooth graph). If you are right on the low point, the project's requirements and the desired schedule are perfectly compatible with some historic database of projects, and the further away from the center point the vertical bar appears, the less compatible the requirements are with desired schedule. Al stewed on this idea for about a month after returning to his office.

In October 1997, Al started drawing a set of graphs similar to Figure 15.1 that showed various kinds of optimality that should be considered when agreeing to a set of requirements. Thus, in addition to the original "how close are we to an optimal schedule," there was "how close are we to an optimal set of resources," and "how close are we to describing a system that would produce an optimal return on investment." At around the same time, he was growing increasingly dissatisfied with the engineering school in which he was a professor. So, he walked into the office of one of his graduate students, Ann Zweig, to tell her that he was going to start a company. The intent was to get some feedback from Ann concerning whether she thought it was a good idea—from a business viability and a personal perspective. To Al's surprise, Ann's response was simply, "Okay, I want to join the company."

Al and Ann knew they had some great product ideas, but lacked marketing and financial know-how. Al quickly turned to a respected colleague, Rob Geller, an ex-

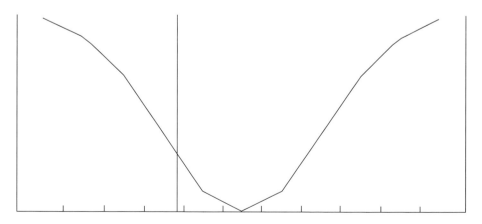

Figure 15.1. The Initial Concept.

pert in financing strategies for early-stage, fast-growth companies. Rob and Al had been co-investors and co-board members at Requisite, Inc. Rob also liked the ideas. Little by little, they brought in more trusted expertise and six of us decided to become co-founders of Omni-Vista, Inc. The six were Al, Ann, and Rob, as well as Bob Keeley, a former venture capitalist and then professor of finance (now retired), Jay Billups, an Air Force captain (now a major) and another of Al's graduate students with an incredibly good understanding of user interfaces, and Kemp Bohlen, a former Hewlett-Packard executive with intimate knowledge of a typical customer for our nascent product.

BACKGROUND OF THE FOUNDERS

Before co-founding Omni-Vista, Al Davis had spent a good deal of time in both academe and industry, in both small and large companies. After receiving a PhD in Computer Science from the University of Illinois at Urbana-Champaign in 1975, he became an assistant professor at the University of Tennessee. He took his first "real" job as a member of technical staff at GTE Laboratories in 1977. After a few years and a few promotions, he became the Director of the Software Technology Center, responsible for automated tools and techniques for the GTE Corporation. In 1983, he transferred within GTE to become a Director of R&D at GTE Communication Systems. This was his first exposure to developing software products for a large commercial market. A year later, he left GTE to join Ed Bersoff at BTG, Inc., a startup where he served as Vice President for one of the divisions for 6 years. This was his first exposure to building custom solutions for individual customers. It was also his first time interacting face-to-face with actual paying customers. It was under Ed's tutelage that Al learned the importance of acquiring and continuing to please customers. After BTG, Al spent nine more years in academe (at George Mason University and the University of Colorado at Colorado Springs) before the story of Omni-Vista began. However during these nine years, Al became a founding member of the board of directors of another software startup in Boulder, Colorado, Requisite, Inc., which subsequently was acquired by Rational Software, which in turn was acquired by IBM. He was also a non-managing general partner in Catalyst Ventures, a venture capital company in Colorado Springs. So, in summary, he spent around 8 years in small companies, 7 years in large companies, and 11 years in academe. It was this broad and diverse background that enabled him to take on the challenge of Omni-Vista's leadership and to gain the support of the investment community.

Ann Zweig's experience was even broader than Al's, although it spanned fewer years. After earning her undergraduate degree in biology from the University of Kansas in 1984, she became a research field biologist. After 12 years of doing this, she and her husband both decided to switch careers. He studied for and earned an MBA in finance, while she studied for and earned a master's degree in computer science in 1997, both at the University of Colorado at Colorado Springs. It was during the pursuit of her masters degree that she took courses from Al Davis, and was subsequently hired as his graduate research assistant to work in requirements engineering and requirements management. It was Ann's leadership skills, natural caring for other human beings, and abundance of common sense that caused Al to invite her to participate with him in the founding of Omni-Vista, Inc.

PRODUCT DIRECTION

Omni-Vista was envisioned from the start to be a product company. We filed early on for three patents to protect the intellectual property (IP). The general idea was to build a series of applications, each destined for a specific vertical market, but all sporting a common architecture and look-and-feel. We would go to market with just one vertical application, and be successful in that market. Then, based on that experience and the capital acquired, we could move on to other verticals. Meanwhile, we could also license the underlying architecture to other companies who could customize it for domains within their expertise. And we always had in the back of our minds the possibility that a large company (like Microsoft or IBM, for example) would be interested in buying our underlying technology outright as an extension to their existing products.

The underlying technology consisted of a set of layers built around a spreadsheet, in our case, Microsoft Excel. The first layer enabled bi-directional propagation of changes to spreadsheet cells. Unlike native Excel, which could not resolve circular references, this layer allowed changes to cell x to propagate to cell y, and changes to cell y to propagate back to cell x. Our patent search turned up nothing similar to this concept, and we ended up filing for a patent, but it was denied many years later by the US Patent and Trademark Office because another patent had been filed earlier for the identical concept. The next layer was the customizable layer that enabled us and others to construct vertical applications. And the outermost layer was a user interface that displayed a set of user-selectable graphs simultaneously on the display. The graphs were linked to the spreadsheet. User edits were made directly to the graphs by dragging and dropping. Any change to any graph was automatically propagated to all other graphs being displayed. The bi-directional propagation in the spreadsheet allowed us to allow users to change graph g on the screen, and have the change propagated to graph h, and allow users to change graph h on the screen, and have the change propagated to graph g.

We embedded the IP into our first product, called Omni-Vista SP (or OVSP; "SP" for "software planning"). OVSP was to be used by software companies to select the "right" set of features to include in their next release. It enabled users to find a balance among such variables as features, time-to-market, revenue, profit, market size, pricing, R&D cost, and breakeven point. Each was represented as a graph. The user could change any of these graphs, and the other graphs would display the implications. We selected this application primarily because it was (a) the first market we had conceived of based on the IP, and (b) for an industry that we understood.

We learned fairly quickly that the market was not ready for OVSP. We found few companies that even estimated the size of their markets, let alone made a conscious decision to include or exclude any particular feature. Almost every company we visited followed the same procedure for release planning: (1) select the features we need, (2) select the date we need it by, and (3) too bad if the development organization says they cannot deliver it by then. From previous consulting, Al knew this was the typical scenario, but he underestimated the effort required to get them to change their practices. He thought they would welcome a solution. Instead, Omni-Vista discovered that development organizations did not want a solution; they were content because they could blame marketing (for demanding an outrageous schedule) when their product delivery was late. And marketing organizations did not want a solution; they were content because they could blame development (for being late) when a product failed in the market. As long as you have a scapegoat, why fix the problem? Developing and marketing organizations seem to thrive on this 'blaming mentality.'"

Another problem we had with OVSP was the need to capture the commitment of both marketing and development. The alternative (which we also tried) was to sell to general management because they were the ones with the most to gain by finding product solutions that met the needs of both development and marketing, and most importantly, the customer. Unfortunately, we found most general managers simply passed us on to either their marketing or their development organizations, with a statement like, "well, if development [marketing] won't use your product, I have no interest in it."

After OVSP failed to capture the attention of the market, we turned our attention to a simpler scaled-down version of the concept, called OnYourMark Pro. This product presented just three views to the user: (a) a list of annotated prospective features, (b) a graph showing the probability of making the desired schedule, and (c) a graph showing the probability of making the desired budget. These last two graphs looked basically like Figure 15.2, a natural and more easy to understand presentation than Figure 15.1. This figure shows that there is an 88% probability that the selected features can be delivered on time by the desired delivery date of November 1, 2005.

OnYourMark Pro was much easier to sell than OVSP, but it still failed to make the revenue numbers that we had proposed to the investment community.

Throughout the years during which we sold OVSP and OnYourMark Pro, we also provided consulting and training services, delivered almost exclusively by Al. Much of this business was just a continuation of the business (with the same customers) that Al had run as The Davis Company before co-founding Omni-Vista. And from the very beginning we had been more successful at selling these services than our products.

Finally, late in the life of the company, we were forced to reduce our development staff dramatically. We rewrote the business plan so that the company turned to the services business as its sole revenue generator. We retrained our sales force to focus on selling services instead of products. We felt that the services could sustain us through the economic downturn that started in 2000, but the poor economy also

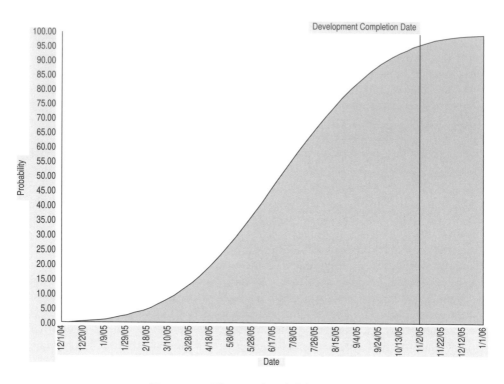

Figure 15.2. The Actual Probability Graph.

reduced demand for our services.

STAFFING

The initial employees were Al Davis (with no salary for the first eight months) as CEO and Chairman, Ann Zweig as Manager of Product Development, and Jay Billups as (part time) software engineer. We quickly hired our first non-insider Quinn Capen, another software engineer. Within a year, we grew to 11 people by adding: a vice president for marketing and sales, one salesperson, one marketing communications person, and four more developers. All employees voluntarily accepted stock options in lieu of competitive salaries.

At its peak, Omni-Vista employed thirteen people: Al as chairman and CEO. Ann as president and chief operating officer, a vice president of marketing and sales, 4 sales and marketing personnel, 5 software developers, and an administrative assistant.

As the cash situation deteriorated late in the company's life, Ann and Al created sets of what-if models using Excel. In some cases, we determined that the best course of action was to reduce salaries. Ann and Al always took a salary reduction prior to asking the employees to take a smaller reduction themselves. This insured that we remained a team, and we never received complaints about the cuts in salary. We also made the amounts of our salary public knowledge, so all the employees knew that we were not making excessive amounts. In a few instances, we determined that the only way to survive was to somehow reduce the cost of personnel. In some cases, we determined that the best course was to reduce the labor force, and that we did reluctantly. These cases tended to be somewhat teary-eyed; we had all grown to be a family. Almost all of those laid off expressed the desire to work for this management team again. To this day, we stay in close touch with these folks. In fact, we assisted most of them in getting good jobs elsewhere after they lost their jobs with us.

During the worst cash crunch of all, we found we could not make payroll (in our opinion, the worst crime a company can commit!). Ann and Al solved the problem by writing personal checks to every employee. Once again, we did what we believed we had to do to keep the team together.

During the final year of the company's existence, when we had moved to our services-only based plan, all employees were on commission-only. Basically, if you were a salesperson and sold something, you received a commission. And if you delivered a revenue-generating service to a customer, you were paid a percent of the revenues. Otherwise, you were not paid. These were lean times. All employees continued to hang around for the ride.

MARKETING AND SALES

Omni-Vista had an interesting history concerning its marketing and sales department. When we were around halfway through developing our first product, we hired our first vice president of marketing and sales. He seemed to have all the right qualifications, having been through a few successful and not so successful startups. Neither Ann nor Al had had much experience with hiring such a person, so we called upon two board members to assist in the interviewing and assessment. Everybody agreed that he was the best of the 3-4 finalists we had interviewed, and seemed to have the right skills and attitude. Within a few months, it became clear that he was not going to work out. He came to the company with a sales and marketing "silver bullet." He believed that the only way to elicit requirements from customers is to videotape them using and commenting on the use of a prototype. And he believed that the only way to sell software was via low-paid telesales people with little or no background in the software industry. As a result, we kept overhead down, but sold very few seats; the potential customers were quick to ascertain that they were talking to somebody who did not understand their business or their problems. Meanwhile, the VP never understood what our product did; he thought it was a competitor of Microsoft Project. Within about six months, we reached a mutual decision that he should leave Omni-Vista.

What followed was a period of a few months where Al and Ann took over sales, while our marketing communications person continued to create marketing materials, do mass-mailings, and create new leads. Revenues increased, not because Ann and Al were good salespeople, but because we knew the customers' environment intimately. We felt their pain and could speak their language.

As Ann and Al spent more time in sales, less attention was being spent on corporate functions such as watching the cash, finding new investors, developing strategic partnerships, and so on. Finally, we agreed we needed to hire another vice president of sales and marketing.

This time, we retained a consultant to do the job. But like the vice president, he had a philosophy of one-size fits all situations. His approach was to analyze the market to death. He made his job to understand everything he could about the potential customer. He conducted focus groups, interviewed customers who used competing tools, dredged up the customers' worst pains, and made several SWOT* charts—a typical marketing analysis tool that did actually shed some light for us onto the customer. In short, he did everything except sell the product. He did not last long, and finally after a series of interviews by Ann, Al, and board members, we made our decision to hire another full-time vice president of sales and marketing.

This VP believed that the only way to sell software effectively was to hire very expensive (high base salary and high commission) seasoned sales professionals using "solution selling." The idea was that they would make contacts at the highest levels in the companies, convince them that our products solved their problems, and sell large site licenses. She brought with her three individuals, two of whom had worked for her in previous jobs. These folks were "typical" salespeople. For around a year, we overheard all kinds of "lines," and even witnessed one salesman sending a dozen roses to the female president of a prospective customer! (That did not go over well with us, and went over even worse with the recipient. And no, the prospect did not buy our product.) Our expenses skyrocketed, and our sales plummeted. Al and Ann were not happy, and our frustration with how the sales process was progressing was apparently clear to the VP. After nine months, the VP finally resigned, and her staff followed her out the door.

Once again, Al and Ann took over the sales function, and revenues went back on the increase, slowly but surely. As our successes grew, so did our confidence, and we finally had to admit that we actually were not that bad at selling. It was clear that selling the Omni-Vista products took someone who really understood the customers and their pains.

Toward the end of Omni-Vista, when we changed our business course away from product and toward services, we once again hired a VP of sales and marketing. This VP was a close friend of both Al's and Ann's. His strength was that he (like Ann and Al) understood the customers' environment and needs intimately. With a couple of commission-only salespeople under his tutelage, he was able to effectively sell our consulting and training services. Our expenses once again came under control, and revenues continued to increase. We were even profitable during our last few months in existence!

*Strengths, weaknesses, opportunities and threats

THE BOARDS

We tried to populate our board of directors with individuals who had the following qualities:

- Had an expertise lacking in the core officer team.
- Were seasoned professionals.
- Were strongly opinionated.
- Were never afraid to express their opinions.
- Had a history of mutual respect with the Omni-Vista insiders.

The initial board consisted of:

- Ed Bersoff. Founder and president of BTG, Inc. Founded BTG in 1983, and brought it public in 1992. A master at all aspects of running a corporation. Understands politics. Understands the sales process. Knows finance and accounting. Has close ties to capital. A close friend and colleague of Al's for 15+ years.
- Kemp Bohlen, co-founder of Omni-Vista, formerly head of financial operations for HP, masterminded the split of financial functions for HP when it split into HP and Agilent. Spends much time listening and thinking, but expresses his views vehemently when he is stirred to comment. An eight-year friend of Al's.
- Rob Geller, co-founder of Omni-Vista; president of Growth Strategies, Inc., of Boulder, Colorado. Frequent board member on startups. Expert in financing strategies that ensure fairness in equity distribution to all parties. Great communicator. Never afraid to voice his opinion. Always on top of issues, regardless of subject. Rob and Al co-invested in Requisite, and were both board members of that company.
- Bob Keeley, co-founder of Omni-Vista, former venture capitalist, former CEO, former professor at Stanford, now professor of finance at the University of Colorado at Colorado Springs. An eight-year colleague and friend of Al's. Former MBA teacher of Ann's husband. Relatively quiet, but very outspoken and articulate when appropriate.
- Al Davis

We later added Roger Oberg to the board. He was a veteran marketing and sales executive with a series of successful software startups. He had been vice president of sales and marketing with Requisite, Inc., at the time of the acquisition by Rational, and was a vice president at Rational at the time of his appointment to the board. When Omni-Vista modified its marketing message from "product planning" to "requirements management light," we were in direct competition with Rational, and we had to agree to part ways. But Roger remained an active investor in Omni-Vista right to the end.

Meanwhile, we also maintained an active board of advisors. The goal of this board was to provide product direction for Omni-Vista. And we filled it with folks as distinguished as the board of directors:

- Dick Fairley is one of the world's experts at risk management and software cost estimation. Currently a professor at the Oregon Graduate Institute.
- Al Steiner was formerly a general manager and executive at Hewlett-Packard. A great out-of-the-box thinker, he ensured that the board of advisors did not get too carried away with technical ideas and lose sight of the real company mission. His background made him an excellent candidate for the board of directors as well.
- Ed Yourdon is one of the most famous and qualified software consultants and authors in the industry. Al Davis was instrumental in bringing Ed onto the board of directors of Requisite. Well respected. Could easily use him as a consultant to our customers. Formerly CEO of Yourdon, Inc., he sold his consulting and publishing company before mergers and acquisitions became popular.

FINANCING

To help establish a corporate culture of fairness, a plan was put into place to divide the stock into three equal pools. One third would be earmarked for the founders, one third would be earmarked for investors, and one third would be reserved for employees as incentives. Rob and Al created spreadsheets that showed how 3 successively higher priced rounds of financing over a period of 2 years would:

- Generate sufficient capital of around $2.5M to sustain the company until its revenues were sufficient for self-funded growth.
- Distribute approximately one third of the pool of shares to the investors.
- Provide high rates of return for investors in all three rounds, with decreasing rates of return and risk for each successive round—assuming that we met our business goals.

Since most of those involved had had previous positive experience with angel investors*, we decided to limit our fund-raising plans to angels. We liked the open, honest, and peer-to-peer type of communication that often can be established with individual investors who are risking their own capital.

The founders purchased the "founder's shares" in February 1998. With help from a terrific lawyer in Colorado Springs, Ben Sparks, we put together the first set of disclosures and other paperwork. We created a powerful business plan, which in retrospect was probably too long: around 100 pages. But we had a lot to say about the exciting path we were on. The plan was to sell 400,000 shares at $1.00 per share

*Basically individual investors with a minimum net worth

by mid July 1998. Al and Rob invested first. As it turned out, 18 individuals, including several of the employees, ended up investing a total of $250K. That was enough to get us started and we revised the plan to include making significant product progress by the end of the year and accelerate round two to January 1999.

For the second round, we hoped to sell 375,000 shares at $2.00 per share, for a net of $750,000 more. Al invested first. Eight of the original round one investors were joined by 10 new investors, to create an additional $500K. Once again, we fell short of the goal, but had enough cash to get us through to the next milestone if we were very careful spending money. Notice how different angel-financed companies behave relative to their venture capitalist-financed counterparts. As a general rule, VC's like the companies to spend money at a high rate. The result is that the company can (at least in theory) hit their markets more quickly, and with good early revenue numbers; the VC's are happy to invest even more if the company starts running out of cash. Meanwhile, angels like to see their money spent carefully and in a calculated manner. The result might be a delay in hitting the market, but fewer resources squandered in the process.

Omni-Vista was close to meeting its milestones with respect to creating product, but was falling short of its revenues numbers. The lack of early marketing expertise was taking its toll.

On the other hand, revenues were steady and growing, and as cash started to dwindle, we prepared for a third round of investments. This time we wanted to generate an additional $1M with equities priced at $2.25 per share. By September 1999, ten of the previous investors and two new investors had infused an additional $1M into the company. This was used to staff up the sales and marketing engine of the company for a major product release to the market.

In early 2000, we were once again running low on cash, but revenues were still growing (although not as rapidly as planned). We decided to offer the same equities we offered last time, again at $2.25 per share. By April, we had managed to scrape up only $80,000 in new investment money. Investor confidence was waning as the result of our less-than-stellar revenue results and the crash of the public markets.

The shares we sold in these four rounds represented preferred stock. As opposed to common shares (e.g., those sold to the founders, and those used as incentives for the employees), these shares gave the investors an advantage in the case of a poor ending. In particular, when a company undergoes a "liquidity event," e.g., an initial public offering, a sale to another company, a bankruptcy, or a closure, proceeds must be distributed among various parties. First to be paid are creditors. Next are the preferred shareholders, who receive an amount equal to their original investment, and finally the remaining cash if any is distributed among all shareholders (the common and preferred shareholders combined). Thus, the preferred shareholders receive a small "kicker," well-deserved in our opinion, because they are investing in a company in which they have no direct control. In addition, if the proceeds are relatively low, the preferred shareholders may get back all or some of their original investment, while holders of common shares may get nothing. A company could try to sell common shares to angel investors, but the probability is high that savvy angels would decline to invest.

At the May 2000 meeting of the board of directors, it became clear that we were in significant financial distress. Cash was burning at a high rate, and the last round had generated almost nothing. The Board made a tough decision to:

- redirect the company toward services rather than product, in order to ride out the slow economy,
- reduce staff (and thus burn rate),
- approach a few selected external investors* for a little more sustaining cash, in order to validate the services model,
- and the Board members would make one more financial infusion in the company.

At that meeting, pledges amounting to roughly $130,000 were made by Board members and officers, and over the next few weeks, we received around $60,000 more from other parties excited about our new direction.

By summer of 2001, it was clear that the economic downturn had taken its toll. Few of our customers were buying anything but the most essential items. Our cost of sales was skyrocketing; our cash was just about depleted; our R&D staff had been decimated; the officers were taking no wages. It seemed the end had arrived.

The dream had been to create a company that could by acquired by another at a great price. The dream was not to be. Ann and Al tried to find any alternative to closing down the company, in the vain hope of providing the investors with some return. But we were not being paid salaries, and as common shareholders, we knew we would receive nothing if we remained with the company.

We knew that the likelihood of a turnaround was miniscule, but we still wanted to try. We crafted a proposal to the entire family of investors telling them that the company was at its end. We proposed to transform the company into a life-style company, which could keep a few individuals employed as the Requirements Management Institute, with no plans for dramatic growth. Meanwhile, it would hold onto its intellectual property and perhaps sell it to another company sometime over the next few years. This would enable us to provide *some* return for the investors. But there was absolutely no reason for us as individuals to stay with the company under the current terms. We proposed to the shareholders to convert all shares to common shares on a one-to-one basis. This would dissolve the preferred shareholders' additional rights, but would at least enable them to get something out of the company. This proposal was embraced by most, but not all, of the Board members, and represented a clear demarcation point for the company: no longer were we one big family dedicated to a common cause.

All the shareholders who decided to vote voted to accept the proposal. With all the shares now converted to common, and the share price devalued to just five cents per share, we were able to sell $50,000 more shares, mostly to current shareholders.

---

*As a courtesy to current investors, we also wrote to them all offering them the opportunity to invest at the same new terms.

The effect of this was to further dilute the other investor's stakes, but they were also afforded the opportunity to buy more shares at this new low price and most declined to do so.

In the final dissolution of the company, all shareholders received a small return for their original investments.

ACQUISITIONS AND PARTNERSHIPS

In November 1999, we approached a supplier of a high-end requirements management tool. It seemed to us that they should be losing some sales because they were not offering a low-end requirements tool as some of their competitors were offering. OnYourMark Pro could be positioned as such a tool, and could be used as a door-opener for some of their potential customers. After using it for some time, they may be convinced to upgrade to the more powerful requirements management tool. By late 2000, this company had gotten to the point of performing a serious due-diligence on every aspect of Omni-Vista's business. As we got closer to the likelihood of them acquiring Omni-Vista, they started running into cash problems of their own. In the middle of our negotiations with them, they were acquired by a much larger company. And that company had no interest in a low-end requirements tool.

In December 1999, we approached a key player in the project management tool space to see if they were interested in a close partnership. It seemed to all of us to be a natural fit. Omni-Vista's product planning tools would ensure that features were compatible with schedules and budgets, and then would feed that information into the project management tool. As the project progressed, and problems arose, actuals could be fed back from the project management tool into Omni-Vista tools to see what made sense next, e.g., to extend schedules or delete requirements, or add resources, or whatever. The two companies met many times and developed a good working relationship. In the end however, the other company did not see enough advantages to them. If we had more revenues and customers, they probably would have acquired us, and used our customer database to extend sales of their existing products. But without the ability to quantify the short-term revenue advantages to their company, they could not do the deal. Talks ceased in April 2000.

In August 2000, we were approached by a website-development division of a large corporation. This division specialized in providing custom websites to other very large corporate clients. To be more competitive, they wanted to be able to present a business case to their prospective clients. The business case would use our OVSP product to show them how they would achieve a positive and quick return on investment from a new website. We wined and dined each other for a couple of months, and then they had a massive layoff. All of our contacts there were terminated. Discussions ceased. Six months later, the division was closed, and a year later the parent company folded.

In September–October 2000, we approached a Fortune 100 company about buying our company. They had recently started a venture capital arm that had the mission to invest in promising high-technology companies that could eventually be folded into the larger parent company. We spent many hours with these folks, telling them about our products and capabilities. They had decided that they wanted to have internal capability in the area of requirements; one of their desired core competencies. After careful analysis of our products, they finally hired us as consultants to them to help them evaluate our competitors' products. Although it was clear at this point that they were not going to help Omni-Vista in the long-term, at least they were a source of short-term revenue for us.

In December 2000, we contacted the presidents of two other Fortune 100 companies to see if they had interest in acquiring Omni-Vista. In January, they responded with a flat "NO!"

From December 2000 through March 2001, we met extensively with a vendor of software tools concerning the acquisition of Omni-Vista. They wanted desperately to have a tool in the requirements space. Things looked real good, but they were in the middle of huge internal crisis; their board of directors was deeply divided on some issue and was considering firing the president and/or tearing the company into two pieces. Our contacts were associated with major players on one side of this argument. When the issue was finally resolved, the company kicked out the president and changed its direction considerably. Our contacts lost their jobs as well. And neither of the resulting entities was in a healthy enough position to consider an acquisition.

In February 2001, we approached a successful government contractor whose primary expertise was project- and program-management. The goal was to sell them our intellectual property so they could augment their services to the government with up-front ROI analyses. After 4 months of negotiation, we learned that the president really liked the way his company worked currently. He liked the life-style it afforded, and could not see any reason to change the company's business much. We ended up with a strong partnership agreement however. This resulted in some effective cross-marketing, and numerous referrals of customers in both directions.

FACILITIES

Many start-ups start in the basement of a home or a garage. Omni-Vista was no exception: its first office was in the basement of Al Davis' home. We occupied this space for over a year, and managed to squeeze nine people into two small rooms. Bursting at the seams, and with an irate neighbor threatening to call the police for violating the subdivision's covenants, we were forced to find new digs.

We found an office building whose owner was willing to allow us to occupy 1,800 square feet of unfinished space for a period of time for no rent prior to moving into finished space within the same building. This seemed ideal. It preserved our cash short term, and allowed us to move into nicer space after we became more financially solid. We ended up staying in this unfinished space for nine months, although neither the landlord nor we thought it would be that long. But the real problem was that this unfinished space had no bathrooms. We knew we could not live without them. We found a gym next door that had bathrooms; only problem: we needed to be members to use the bathroom facilities. Ann had a great idea: the company could offer to pay half the club membership fees for any of our employees who wished to join. We cut a deal with the gym; if most of our employees joined, they would allow all of our employees to use the bathrooms.

In October 1999, we finally moved into our new grand 3,000 square feet of offices. It included a server room, bathrooms (great news!), a reception room, a large classroom that could double as a boardroom, a break room with kitchenette, a storage room (for future expansion), and around 10 offices. The space was not luxurious, but it was certainly very nice. We had to sign a five-year lease, and Al was required to be a personal guarantor for the full five years of rent! Ouch.

After a year in the nice office space, with our cash dwindling, and our need to reduce staff, it was clear that we needed to get out of the lease. But where would we move to? And what about Al's personal guarantee for the rent for all five years? Ann and Al discussed this at length and decided we needed to simply present the dilemma to the landlord and see if we could reach some mutually agreeable termination terms. Al stewed for a couple of days before finally getting up enough nerve to approach the landlord. He woke the next morning with the plan to call the landlord and discuss this sensitive matter. Al expected the worst. He rehearsed his words from 6 am to 8 am that morning. At 8 am the phone rang. The landlord was calling Al! The landlord explained that he had something very awkward to discuss with Al and would like to meet with him right away. Later that day, the landlord explained to Al that he had another tenant in the building who needed more space, and he would like to "buy out" our lease. Would we be willing to vacate the space within thirty days? We agreed. The landlord made our departure quite pleasant, and released Al's personal guarantee. Sometimes, things do go right!

From there, we moved into much smaller, and less pleasant office space in downtown Colorado Springs. Here we had a 6-month lease (once again, with a personal guarantee from Al, but for just 6, rather than 60, months rent!), and the ability afterwards to extend it month-by-month. We were considerably downsized at this point, and we crammed ourselves into the crowded space. We stayed in this space for about a year, and finally used it for our farewell "garage sale."

SUMMARY

In summary, here are some of the lessons learned:

- *Sell a simple product before you sell a feature-rich one.* The reasons seem obvious: (a) you'll produce the product a lot faster, and thus hit the market earlier, (b) you'll receive early customer feedback about whether you are on the right track, (c) you'll get early customer feedback about what more complex features they really want, (d) cost-of-sales are far less, (e) average-time-to-close a sale is decreased considerably, and (f) you can use the revenues generated from the simple product to fund development of the more complex one.

Ironically, Al had been teaching this philosophy for at least 15 years just prior to the creation of Omni-Vista; and still he became so enamored by the full product that the lesson was lost on him.

- *Don't move into fancy offices if you have nobody to impress.* We thought we had earned the nice offices after living in basements and unfinished space for so long. But who were we trying to impress? Customers never visited us at our offices.

- *Don't be a personal guarantor for leases.* Easier said than done. We found ourselves in a situation where we had to live on the street or sign a lease with a personal guarantee, so we signed. Similarly, our choice was to live with no computers, or sign a personal guarantee for leasing them. Every entrepreneur has to make this decision. Al will likely try to never do this again, but sometimes desire and reality do not coalesce.

- *Marketing needs to be involved on Day One.* This is another adage that Al had been teaching for many years. But in this case, he said "But I know the customers far better than any marketing person because I have been consulting for them for 20+ years." Wrong!

- *Maintain strong external boards.* This gives you a constant source of wisdom and experience to tap from. When running the day-to-day operations of a company, it is sometimes difficult to see the forest from the trees. These folks ensure that you stay on course.

- *Keep your investors informed.* This is one rule we followed throughout the company's life. By telling the investors everything, they were able to make wiser investment decisions, even if that was not always favorable to us. At least we could sleep well at night.

- *The principals should invest in every round.* The advantages of this are: (a) when talking to prospective investors, they will ask "and how much have you raised so far?" and you will have something greater than zero to say, and (b) when you put your own money into a potentially risky situation, others are more likely to trust you (and rightly so!).

- *Keep your employees informed.* This is also one at which we did well. Throughout the company's history, the employees knew everything: cash flow, projections, milestones, revenues, balance sheet, and so on. The result was no surprises and an extremely loyal set of employees. And when we delivered any kind of bad news, the employees saw all the events heading up to it, including what we were doing to prevent it. Even when it was layoff time, nobody was surprised. To this day, Al and Ann stay in close contact with most of the former Omni-Vista employees.

- *Eliminate symbols of hierarchy.* At Omni-Vista, every employee had the identical desk, and the same amount of space. When in space without janitorial service, the officers emptied the trash. When documents needed to be bound, or envelopes needed to be stuffed and stamped, everybody pitched in.

SEEDS FOR DEBATE

1. Omni-Vista had built an underlying infrastructure platform capable of supporting many different software products. The first such product was chosen for a specific vertical market, software development companies. As stated on page 84, we selected it because it was (a) the first market we had conceived of based on the intellectual property, and (b) for an industry that we understood. Are those valid reasons? Develop a list of other reasons for selecting a specific vertical segment, and argue for why Omni-Vista should have used these other reasons.

2. One of the ironies of the fall of Omni-Vista is that the company's primary value to other companies was its ability to help them select the right features for the right products in their markets. Yet, Omni-Vista's own products were not as successful in the market as expected. Create a list of things that can make or break a product in the marketplace that were not analyzed by either OnYourMark Pro or OVSP. Could these oversights have been the cause of Omni-Vista's demise?

3. If you were hiring a vice president of marketing and/or sales for Omni-Vista's products, what qualities would you look for? Would these same qualities have been applicable when Omni-Vista became a services company?

4. Did the team of Al, Ann, plus the two boards cover the full breadth of skills required to run the company successfully? If not, what was missing, and why would that talent be critical?

5. Do you think Omni-Vista would have been more successful if it had been financed using a means others than angels, e.g., venture capital financed, debt-financed, customer-financed or F^3 (friends and family financed)?

6. Many startup advisors recommend a relatively succinct business plan, instead of the 100-page tome created by Omni-Vista. At the time of financing, none of the potential investors commented on the size. Do you think Omni-Vista would have been more successful at financing if it had a shorter business plan?

7. The above story talks about seven of the dozen or so attempts to merge with or be acquired by other companies. Why do you suspect none of these were successful? Would the outcome have been different had we made different choices concerning (a) product mix, (b) equity structure, (c) marketing approach, or (d) who would negotiate the M&A with the companies?

Anatomy of a Software Startup*

E. BERSOFF

This essay is an edited transcript of a speech by Ed Bersoff for the University of Colorado at Colorado Springs in November 1993. Bersoff, president and founder of BTG, shared some of the trials and tribulations of the 12 years he spent building BTG.

—Al Davis

I want to talk to you today about starting and building a business. I've always been very uncomfortable with the word *entrepreneur*—never considered myself one—but I'll wear the label for the time being. I want to talk a little about what an entrepreneur is, and what sets entrepreneurs apart from normal people.

First let me tell you about BTG. We're just about 12 years old, largely employee-owned. We are a computer-engineering, software-development, and value-added reselling company. In 12 years, we have done about a total of $300 million in business. Our total assets are around $30 million.

KNOW WHERE YOU'RE GOING

The key to what we've done in the last 12 years is that we set goals. If there's one thing I'm going to leave you with, it's the importance of planting a stake in the ground about what it is you are as a company. Think of that as a visual image. As the Cheshire Cat said to Alice, "If you don't know where you're going, any road will get you there."

It's important that your goals are known not only to you, but to everybody else. It's hard to mobilize your team if the team doesn't know where it's going. It can be a great personal risk to divulge the plan, because if you don't achieve your goals, it gets to be embarrassing.

*Originally published in *IEEE Software*, 11, 1 (January 1994), pp. 92–94, 100.

Great Software Debates. By Alan M. Davis
ISBN 0-471-649880 © 2004 Institute of Electrical and Electronics Engineers.

99

But I believe goals are somewhat self-fulfilling. You'll achieve as much as you set out to achieve, hopefully. But generally no more. So if you don't set goals that everybody understands, you're not going to achieve much of anything.

I also believe that if you think you've achieved success, you're done for. I remember when I figured that when our company grew to 20 people we'd be a good, solid company. When we got to 20 people, it seemed that 50 was a good number. And of course, we're at about 400 now and it's still scary. It's always scary.

If you haven't read it since you were 20 years old, I recommend that you read Robert Persig's *Zen and the Art of Motorcycle Maintenance* (Morrow, 1974). It explains that in business, as in art, you can describe and dissect what success is. And you can kind of list the ingredients to success. But knowing the ingredients doesn't necessarily mean you'll have success. It takes more than just doing those things. It takes putting them all together in a holistic way.

Finally, if you want to go into business solely to make money or to become the master of your own destiny, then don't bother. Because that focus is not going to lead you anywhere. You have to go into business to do business. The process is what counts. With that as a backdrop, I present the anatomy of a startup company.

EMOTIONAL DECISION

Before I started BTG, I was with another startup company, except I didn't start it. I was the sixth employee and I ultimately became president, but I still had a boss—the CEO. About a year and a half after I became president, something happened that was so horrendous that I decided to quit. When you're a company president, the only respectable thing to do when you quit is to say you're going to start your own company. So that's what I said. Even though I talk about planning and setting goals, the process of getting started was very emotional.

Then comes the first level of commitment. Putting your toe in the water. Because if you say you're going to start a company, then you actually have to start a company. So I registered the company name, BTG, and got some space. I rented 500 square feet in the basement of the office building of my previous company. They had already moved, so I went back there because the landlord knew me and didn't ask for a security deposit.

I put $1,000 into a bank account, and that was the capitalization. Until very recently, that was the only money I ever put in the company. Then I rented a desk for three months. And I remember thinking I needed a Xerox machine. When the Xerox salesman came, there was no furniture—I could tell he wasn't too excited about renting me a Xerox machine. But while he was there, the furniture and the telephone arrived, so he called to arrange delivery, and I heard him say, "Well yeah, he's got a desk now and he's got a phone." So I guess I was respectable at that point.

I went to the accountant we used in my previous company and went to the same bank and consultants and so on. Then I found out that my previous employer had called them and said if they worked for us, they'd lose his account. The bank and the accountant bailed. Others didn't. You find out who your friends are pretty quickly.

The next thing we did was to decide what it is we were. We had a company name but we didn't have a mission. So we made a little brochure and company announcement, and we decided—I decided, there wasn't much of a we—I decided that we were going to be a systems company. We were going to build software-based systems. You don't get much of an opportunity to do that when you're by yourself, but that was what we said we were going to do.

ROLODEX ROULETTE

By this time I was getting some interest from some companies I had done business with. A company called System Development Corporation—SDC—now part of Unisys, called and said "We'd like you to work with us on this contract we have." And so I went over there and they said "we'd like you to be a consultant."

Here's a key turning point in my life. I knew I didn't want to be a consultant—I wanted to build a company. So I gulped and said, "I can't do that, but tell you what. Why don't you give me a $250,000 contract for the next six months and I'll bring a couple people over and we'll do work for you, because I think we can help you on this contract. But I won't take a consulting contract, and by the way, I'm not going to work on it full time, either. I'll work on it half-time, because I need some time to go out and sell."

I left wondering what kind of fool I was, but eventually they took the deal. Then we went after a couple of competitive contracts, and we actually won a $9,000 competitive contract, which was the biggest thrill. But the $250,000 was going to run out in six months and time was going by. We sat around and said, what are we going to do?

What I did was I took out my Rolodex and I started in the front and I just started calling people. As luck would have it, a friend of mine named Bill Atwood worked for RCA. He wasn't under the Rs, thank goodness. I called him and he said, "You know, I was just thinking about you. We have this job with the FAA and we need some help, and the kind of stuff you know is the kind of stuff we need."

So about a week later we had a contract with RCA. I should point out that we are still working for the FAA. So that one phone call to Bill Atwood represents 12 years worth of business. So don't give up hope. If you have a Rolodex, start making calls. It might turn into something.

IT'S A STRETCH

Well now I knew the kind of business we were going to do, but I wanted to quantify it. So I said the objective of BTG is to be a $50 million company in 10 years. And I drew a curve from zero, where we were, to 50. There was a point, after seven years, where we would be at $25 million.

It was very aggressive, obviously. We were about growth, we were about systems, we were about building. And I gotta tell you that there were people I interviewed who didn't believe. And they didn't join the company.

But our relationship with SDC was very positive, and we negotiated a considerably larger add-on contract. We couldn't fit in the basement anymore, so we went to a building a few blocks away and took 5,516 of square space. I remember the number—it's one of those things you don't forget. This was getting serious now. We occupy today about 120,000 square feet throughout various offices. But the 5,516 square feet was a tough move.

Anyway, we moved in. Then we were presented with an opportunity with the National Security Agency. They had a requirement for something that we knew a lot about, but in addition to people, we needed facilities: A VAX and what they call a SCIF, a secure facility. It would cost $250,000 to do both.

To put this in perspective, our first year's revenue—which we hadn't finished yet, we were still in the middle of our first year—was $700,000. Our profit was $26,000. So that's a stretch trying to get a quarter of a million dollars from somebody.

I went to our bank right across the street. And they chuckled and talked about ratios and stuff like that and said, "Look, if you can come up with half the money, then we'd think seriously about giving you the other half on a term loan." Well, where was I going to get $125,000? After talking with some other people, my idea was to see if the people in the company—we had about 15 employees by now—were willing to invest in the company.

This was my second big decision. I got some very good advice. The idea is to separate control of the company and ownership of the company—equity and control don't necessarily mean the same thing. What I did was create a second class of stock, B shares. And I asked the employees for—I had to learn a lot of new words—convertible, subordinated debentures. It was a loan, but at a fixed price, determined in advance, for conversion in the future. They could convert their loan to shares in the company, but they'd be nonvoting B shares. The equity would be distributed equally among the A and B shares, but they would only get the B shares. Using this mechanism, I collected $116,000 from the employees and one outside board member.

Sometimes things happen that are awesome. One of the employees, who is still with us, had lost a relative in an automobile accident the year before. The estate had just been settled. He invested $15,000. And you gotta know how that feels, when somebody gives you money like that and says they're going to invest in your company. So it gives you a sense of responsibility that doesn't quit.

I think about that all the time. This fellow was with my previous company. He was a phys ed major. We hired him out of school to run the Xerox machine. And he's a vice president now, running a huge segment of BTG's business. So don't ever shut anything out. People have capacities that you just can't believe.

With our money in hand, we went off to the bank and they gave us the rest.

As it turned out, the NSA canceled the procurement soon after we were done building our SCIF. But we went to another customer and said "Look at the capacity we have," and sure enough we got a contract with this other customer. And that started the ball rolling.

So the commitment to the facilities gave us the energy to go off to use what we had. A lot of people wait for something to be put on the table before they go and make the commitment. And that may work, but sometimes it's more important to make the commitment first.

GROWING PAINS

The first year we did $700,000. The next years we were kind of feeding off that momentum; we did $1.3 million the second year, and $2.8 million the third year. We were now a real business, effectively doubling for the first three years.

Then the government asked us if we would do something that was technically very risky, something none of the big companies felt was achievable. When you have no alternatives you do things that people say are unachievable, so of course we said yes. And we built a system that was pretty successful. We showed it to some Navy people and they liked it.

To make a long story short, the system was adopted by the Navy and put on several hundred ships. Now it didn't happen all at once, obviously, but we were now growing yet again at a 100-percent rate, only now the numbers were bigger. And so it was a little more difficult.

We had a lot of very good, creative engineering types. But as we got more and more business, as we became more and more successful, the question came up about the quality of our work. Some said we didn't have any rigor in our systems; we were kind of throwing stuff out the door.

For the first time, we faced the customer satisfaction issue. What we struggled with was, what does quality really mean? There's the technical excellence of the product, and then there's the utility of whatever the product is to the user. Are you willing to live with a system that could save your life, but every once in a while it crashes, or do you want to make sure it doesn't crash before you give it to the person? Now I'm really talking about life and death situations. Our systems were used on aircraft carriers to make decisions about targeting, and so on. But sometimes they didn't work as well as they should.

The question that drove some of our engineers up a wall was, was it really appropriate for us to have our name on it and have it go out like that? As Admiral Gorshkov of the Russian fleet said, "Better is the enemy of good enough." We didn't like to quote Russian admirals in those days, but that was the issue. We made the commitment to deliver a product that was useful and include maintenance as part of what we had to deliver. But deliver it sooner rather than later.

This was the late '80s. The banks were always there for us. Great time to build a company. These are things that you don't see today, necessarily. And we started getting an invincible feeling about ourselves that we could do anything and would. We were feeling pretty good about getting rich at that point. We got an offer to sell the company, and we negotiated a sale.

That was another interesting milestone, because here was an entrepreneur deciding to sell his business, announcing to the employees that it was sold, and just waiting for the check. I remember it was Labor Day weekend. I went to the headquarters of the company out in Torrance, California, and my new boss was telling me how we had to raise our overhead rates and, you know, all the things we were doing wrong. And I hadn't had a boss for five years, so that felt funny. But I was counting the money, so it didn't feel that bad.

Remember what happened October '87? The market went to hell, and the value of the buying company—they were traded on the market, I wasn't—fell about 50 percent overnight. So they wanted to renegotiate, but I said just because you lost 50 percent in value, doesn't mean I did. They didn't buy that argument at all. So the deal fell through. When that happened, we had to regroup and start over.

We decided that what we needed now that we were a more than $20-million company was some discipline and rigor. So I hired a vice president out of the Navy. He had been one of our customers, and he was terrific . . . mostly. He knew everything and everyone, and we started getting new business through him. But he thought he was still in the Navy, and he was horrible to the employees. If you look at the turnover curve over the life of our company, you see this spike. That's when he was with us. So I had another realization. No matter how good somebody is in one area, if they're a jerk, get rid of them. Putting up with jerks is not what being in business is all about.

I put in a hierarchical organization and we wrote a five-year plan. The problem was nobody read it. In fact, instead of rigor we had rigor mortis. We flattened out because we put in too much control; we didn't let people do what they were naturally able to do. We had to do something to grow again.

So we went out and bought companies. Again, this is the late '80s, when banks were giving me all the money I wanted. Don't worry about profit, we're just going to grow.

But what about profit? People start to ask when you're a $26 million company, where's your profits? And what about liquidity? I now had people who had owned part of the company for seven, eight, nine years. The folks who started with me when they were 27 or whatever are now in their 30s and they want to buy a house; some of them want to send their kids to college. All they had was worthless paper. So liquidity started to become an issue.

About that same time, our debt/equity ratios were getting pretty high, and our banks were getting nervous. I was in Denver on my way home from some meeting, and I called the office. I was told that to meet payroll we had to go over our line of credit by $20,000. And the bank said no.

You start thinking of the "B" word. You're liquid, you've got more collateral than you need for your line of credit, you've never missed a payment, and yet you're thinking about bankruptcy. Very, very scary flight from Denver back to Washington. The next day a large check came in and the payroll was met. The bank had failed us. Needless to say, we're not with that bank anymore.

So all of this is raining down upon us in our tenth year, and the question is, do we pull our horns in and just stick it out or do we redefine the plan? We decided that sitting back and letting things happen was not us.

A NEW PLAN

What we did over a fairly extended period of time—a year or so—was to reorient ourselves and effect some organizational change. We eliminated a layer of management, which was kind of when it became vogue, but I don't think we read that somewhere; we just figured that out. We focused on quality, on making sure we did things right the first time. Living within our budgets. And making money. We finally focused on profits.

I don't think I ever thought seriously about the company making a lot of money until it became clear that the banks wouldn't lend us any money unless we made some.

We started planning a different way. We still have the five-year plan. In addition, we have a three-year plan, which kind of takes the next level of detail. Then each of our groups has an annual operating plan. So the plan isn't all in one big document.

About this time we acquired another company. As a result, I went below 50-percent ownership. Now control doesn't come from the fact that I have the votes; control comes from convincing people that I ought to have control. It's a little different.

Our next step is to take on a bit more debt, because debt today is very inexpensive and available, and make another acquisition or two. And then most likely find a mechanism for full liquidity. There's only a couple that you can think of, one of which of course is going public and using the public money to retire the debt. That's what will probably happen over the next three to five years. Our stated goal is to be a $500 million company at 20 years. I won't say it will be easy, but it's much more probable we'll make this goal than it was that we would go from zero to 50 in 10 years.

WHAT SETS US APART

So let me leave you with what I said I would when I started, which is what sets entrepreneurs apart. The first thing is to plant your stake in the ground. Figure out where you're going and tell everybody about it. The second is never give up. If there's anything that I think sets entrepreneurs apart from everybody else, it's the ability to get up after you get knocked down. Third, take care of yourself. The government's not there to help you, the bank's not there to help you, nobody's there to help you. You're there to help you, so take care of yourself. Fourth, life's too short to deal with jerks. Don't compromise your plan, your principles, your people, or your purpose. Fifth, balance the needs of your customers, your employees, your investors, and the community. And the bottom line: Try to have fun while you're doing it.

EPILOGUE

Ed brought BTG public in 1995. It was subsequently acquired in 2002 by another publicly traded company, Titan Systems, Inc. Ed Bersoff is no longer involved as a hands-on manager, but he does remain on Titan's board of directors. As of early 2004, Lockheed Martin was negotiating the acquisition of Titan.

SEEDS FOR DEBATE

1. Present a case for why "becoming rich" or "being the master of your own destiny" as a primary goal will likely cause your company to fail. Now take the reverse position, and argue for why those two goals are keys to success.

2. You have now read about two companies: Omni-Vista (essay starting on page 81) and BTG (essay starting on page 99). The two companies have similarities (e.g., both involved Ed Bersoff and Al Davis; both built software) and many differences (e.g., angel-funded vs. customer-financed, mass-marketed software vs. custom software). By all accounts, one must consider BTG a huge success. Although Omni-Vista did succeed in many things, it ultimately closed and returned little to the investors. Create a more thorough list of similarities and differences. Highlight those differences that were critical to why one succeeded and the other did not.

3. In the section on "Emotional Decision," Ed Bersoff talks about what he needed to do to get BTG started back in 1982. Many years have passed now. Describe what needs to be done to start a company now that was not true in 1982. And describe what needed to be done to start a company in 1982 that is no longer true.

4. During the six or seven years I was at BTG, the company kept leasing more and more office space. In my opinion at the time, every one of these expansions was too large and too early, and thus too risky (I do not believe I ever expressed that concern to Ed; but I know he'll be reading this book, and so he'll know now). When history proved that he was right with every expansion, I thought I had learned a valuable lesson, i.e., when you are planning to grow, you need to have convenient office space ready. How do you think my BTG experience effected my decision to expand Omni-Vista's office space (see facilities description starting on page 94)?

5. I consider the last paragraph of Ed Bersoff's essay to be one of the most important in this entire book. Read it a few times. Can you argue with any of the points he raises?

Information for Decision Makers*

I have spent a lot of time trying to understand why so many software managers and engineers follow the crowds toward popular fads (see Essay 1) rather than thinking about what is really needed. I have decided that the problem is caused by

- a software industry that has a reputation of being irresponsible (many projects are late and over budget and do not satisfy needs); and
- lack of real information about which technology is really useful.

The first difficulty causes managers and engineers to work harder at protecting themselves from inevitable blame than at doing a good job. Thus, a software manager who embraces the latest fad and fails can skirt blame by saying, "But everybody's doing it!" The manager who takes a path less traveled and fails presents an easy target.

As Warren Bennis wrote (*Why Leaders Can't Lead*, Jossey-Bass, 1997):

An unconscious conspiracy in contemporary society prevents leaders ... from taking charge and making changes. Within any organization, an entrenched bureaucracy with a commitment to the status quo [or the latest fad] undermines the unwary leader.

The second difficulty means managers have inadequate information on which to base an intelligent decision. Thus, managers have little choice but to follow the latest fad. After all, what other criteria do they have, other than "everybody's doing it?"

SEEDS FOR DEBATE

1. List ten reasons why managers are safer to go with the fad than to do what they think is right.

2. List ten reasons why managers should do what they think is right, rather than going with the latest fad.

*Originally published in *IEEE Software*, 12, 2 (March 1995), p. 4.

Great Software Debates. By Alan M. Davis
ISBN 0-471-649880 © 2004 Institute of Electrical and Electronics Engineers.

Some Tips for the Would-Be Entrepreneur*

I have been involved in the entrepreneurial world since 1983 and have been giving advice to entrepreneurs and entrepreneur wannabes in Colorado Springs since 1992. Much of what I now know I learned from incredibly talented individuals.

Here is a summary of some of those lessons:

- Surround yourself with excellence—I learned this from Dean Leffingwell, president and founder of Requisite Inc., a 1995 start-up acquired by Rational Software in 1997 [and since acquired by IBM in 2002].

    When I founded Omni-Vista in 1998, I surrounded myself with people I could trust, who had deep experience, who knew a lot about things I didn't know and were not afraid to speak their mind. I didn't always sound smart, but I sure learned a lot. When you're spending other people's money, and when you feel responsible for maintaining your employees' jobs, there is little room for ego. Every morsel of help you can get is worth it, even if you feel stupid when asking for it.

- Don't hog ownership [I learned this from Rob Geller, president of Growth Strategies, Inc., of Boulder, Colorado].

    Many entrepreneurs demand 51 percent ownership of the company. One motivation for this is fear of losing control. The problem here is that true control is earned via mutual respect and influence; it is not something you can buy. Another motivation is the desire to become richer than the sum of all the other players when or if a liquidity event occurs. I have worked in companies in which I had a stake and for companies in which I didn't. I can assure you I worked a lot harder for those companies in which I chased the larger carrot.

    This applies to you as well as your employees and colleagues. Share ownership with them, and they will work twice as hard. This aligns your colleagues' goals with yours. You want to establish an environment in which their success is your success, and vice versa. It is better to own 20 percent of a lot than 100 percent of nothing.

---

*Originally published as "To Succeed, Have the Strength to Know Your Weaknesses" in *Colorado Springs Gazette* (August 30. 1999). p. B5. Reprinted with permission.

Great Software Debates. By Alan M. Davis
ISBN 0-471-649880 © 2004 Institute of Electrical and Electronics Engineers.

- Know your own weaknesses.

  Few individuals are talented in every area of business. An entrepreneurial company needs expertise in finance, accounting, law, product planning, technology, marketing, people management and sales. You must understand which of these you are good at and where you need help. Then, make sure you have access to the right help. The talent you recruit can come in the form of cofounders, [board members], employees or consultants, but you must know where this talent is going to come from. If you are a technologist, don't think you can fake marketing. If you are a marketing expert, don't think you can fake technology.

- Do it yourself before asking others to do it [I learned this from Bob Keeley].

  Although I practice this principle, I am not entirely convinced everybody should do this. I can say with great assurance that managing the books for Omni-Vista for the past 18 months has been critical to helping me understand how the company really operates. I now see how every dollar is spent and how every dollar is earned. Until March 1999, I was comfortable allowing others to run the marketing side of the company. Without the availability of such talent between March and July 1999, I personally led the marketing efforts with help from a band of talented consultants. During those four months, I really learned how hard and complex marketing is. Now I have been a software developer, an accountant and a marketing manager, and I'm in a far better position to fully understand the activities performed by each of the departments within Omni-Vista.

EPILOGUE

This article was written during the time of Omni-Vista. See more lessons learned from my Omni-Vista experience on pages 81–97, written after the demise of the company.

SEEDS FOR DEBATE

1. Present arguments for why each of the four "lessons" described in this essay are wrong. If you cannot create such an argument for one or more, then at least cite some specific cases where they would be wrong.

Some More Tips for the Would-Be Entrepreneur*

Since 1983, I have been involved in the entrepreneurial world and have been giving advice to local entrepreneurs since 1992. [In the previous essay,] I began presenting a summary of lessons I've learned from experience and from several talented individuals. Here is a continuation of that list:

- Have an exit strategy.

    Whether you are self financed, customer-financed, angel-financed, boot-strapped, or venture capital-financed, you must have a plan for how the company will produce a return for its investors. In the case of angel or venture capital, your investors will demand this and they'll expect to hear your exit strategy early in your discussions.

    Typical exit strategies are acquisition or initial public stock offering (also called "going public"). Many people have been through these processes. Make sure you have talked with some of these folks, so you are fully informed about the pros and cons of each alternative. Of course, if you are self-financed, customer-financed, or bootstrapped, your exit strategy might not be to exit at all, but instead [your goal may be] to create a company that maintains a number of employees in an acceptable lifestyle via lucrative salaries. There is nothing wrong with such a company, but all parties should understand the big plan.

- Plan for the long term [I learned this from Ed Bersoff].

    Even if you plan to be acquired within three to five years, make business decisions as if the company will be around for a long time. Decisions that [do nothing other than] make the company look good to acquirers in the short-term are [often] unethical. If you do the right thing for the long-term growth of the company, you will be far more attractive to a responsible prospective acquisition partner. Remember in most cases "looking for a company to acquire you" is similar to "looking for a spouse." If you have to look, you will likely not find a partner.

*Originally published as "All Businesses Need Exit Strategies" in *Colorado Springs Gazette,* (September 6, 1999). p. 85. Reprinted with permission.

- Have a fully integrated financial plan [I learned this from Rob Geller].

    One of your first priorities when deciding whether to start a new business is to make sure everything holds together financially. I do this with a complex series of worksheets that I put together in one large Excel spreadsheet. Three of these worksheets contain the standard financial reports: Income Statement. Balance Sheet and Cash Flow Statement. Another set of worksheets models the marketing, sales and revenue aspects of each primary market segment of the business. [See additional discussion of these worksheets on page 79.]

- Have a fully integrated product or service plan.

    Understand the relationships between features to be included in your product or service, costs associated with providing them, development risks, time-to-market, price, market size, market penetration, revenues, profits, break-even point.

- Practice integrity above all—a standard drilled into me by Ed Bersoff, president and founder of BTG Inc., a successful 1982 start-up company [see article starting on page 99].

    I have learned [that] doing business without integrity is not business at all. Honesty and openness are essential ingredients for dealing with everybody in business: customers, users, employees, colleagues and investors. There is no other alternative.

EPILOGUE

This article was written during the time of Omni-Vista. See more lessons learned from my Omni-Vista experience on pages 81–97, written after the demise of the company.

SEEDS FOR DEBATE

1. Present arguments for why each of the five "lessons" described in this essay are wrong. If you cannot create such an argument for one or more, then at least cite some specific cases where they could be wrong.

2. This essay states, "'looking for a company to acquire you' is similar to 'looking for a spouse.' If you have to look, you will likely not find a partner." Contrast this with the discussion of acquisitions on pages 93 and 94. Was there good justification for looking for an acquisition partner in the case of Omni-Vista'?

REQUIREMENTS

I have spent a majority of my technical career experiencing and investigating requirements. Although most people in the industry think of a requirement as something that is documented in a requirements specification, I take a much broader view. Requirements activities span the range of activities from trying to understand/analyze the world of the customers and users to the detailed documentation of individual descriptions of desired external behavior of a system that could improve that world in some way. I have always been fascinated by requirements because the field requires a large dose of both left- and right-brained talent.

Although I have written hundreds of technical articles on the subject of requirements, I was careful to select the most controversial and the most practical for this collection.

The first essay, *The Harmony in Requirements*, addresses the point I just made, i.e., how an effective requirements practitioner needs both a left and a right brain. They must *feel* the customers pains and be able to *communicate* with those customers, while also being able to write precisely and concisely.

The second essay, *System Phenotypes*, helps readers understand what requirements are by drawing an analogy between requirements and that which geneticists call a phenotype.

Ann Zweig and I wrote *The Missing Piece of Software Development* as a guest editorial for Bob Glass when we first founded Omni-Vista, Inc. (see article on page 81) At the time, and still today, we feel that the software industry is making a big mistake by not taking requirements triage seriously. Triage is the process of analytically deciding what features to include in a product before commencing its development. We're not saying it is easy to do. But not doing it guarantees that our industry will continue its awful record of poor customer satisfaction.

When object-oriented programming and design emerged as popular paradigms, I embraced them because they appealed to my common sense, and seemed to me to offer considerable advantages with respect to development and maintenance cost over more traditional approaches. But when object-oriented analysis (OOA) surfaced, I was utterly confused. I could not see how OOA could possibly work. Then a few of the object pundits started giving speeches on how object-orientation makes it easy to transition from requirements to design. This really bothered me because it seemed like such misdirected advice. So, I wrote the next essay entitled *Object-Oriented Analysis to Object-Oriented Design: An Easy Transition?* to capture some of my thoughts and hopefully persuade a few object-oriented lemmings to look before leaping into the tar pit.

Achieving Quality in Software Requirements is not particularly controversial, but it is an excellent (and brief) summary of the types of activities one needs to perform, and the kinds of quality you want to aim for, while involved with requirements.

I suspect that I have contributed to the belief so prevalent in the industry today that requirements gathering, selecting, and documenting is incredibly complicated. Certainly my textbook of 1993, *Software Requirements: Objects, Functions and States,* has helped people believe that you have to be a computer scientist or mathematician to do a good job of requirements. But I do not believe that. The next piece, *Requirements Management Made Easy,* shows the danger in getting too carried away with the requirements process. This essay suggests moderation, and explains how little you really have to do.

Elicitation: How Do the Experts Do It? is definitely the most research-y of the articles contained in this entire book. I didn't include this paper by Ann Hickey and me to overwhelm you with experimental method. I included it because the paper tells you just how others perform requirements activities in real life.

The last essay, *Requirements Are But a Snapshot in Time,* emphasizes the fact that you will *never* be able to record the requirements for a system and then just go and build it. It tells the story about how requirements undergo constant, significant, and eternal changes. Your only choice is to accept this fact, not to avoid the changes.

The Harmony in Rechoirments*

I remember well that day in 1977 when my boss plopped a thick document on my desk and asked me to critique it. I stared at the title: Software Requirements Specification for the GTD-120 PABX. I tried in vain to parse the three adjacent nouns, "software requirements specification." Did it mean software for requirements specification? Or specification of software requirements? Or requirements specification of software? And even if I could determine which of the three it meant, their semantics still puzzled me—I had never before seen "requirements" or "specification" used with regard to software, let alone used together. As I started reading, I quickly saw that the document detailed the intended external behavior of the software for a small telephone switch called the GTD-120, and then I knew what the title meant.

Twenty years have passed since I first started thinking about requirements specification. I spent most of that time trapped in the belief that requirements specification, requirements management, requirements analysis, and requirements engineering were all about documentation. Their purpose was to document something, that is, a desired system's external behavior.

NOW I KNOW BETTER

I find it remarkable how long my views were tainted by that first exposure to a document in 1977, but I now know better. The field of requirements (and it no longer matters to me what word you like to append to "requirements" to make it sound more esoteric) has to do with understanding, not documentation. Sure, we need to document the desired external behavior of a solution system, but that is the easiest part of the process. The hard part, and the true essence of requirements, is trying to understand your customer's needs. This is true whether you are building custom or mass-marketed software (or systems)—or, for that matter, if you don't intend to build software (or systems) at all.

Requirements involves more than knowing how to analyze using the latest method such as structured whatever or object-oriented whatever, or knowing how to specify systems using finite-state machines or Petri nets, or knowing how to pro-

*Originally published in *IEEE Software, 15*, 2 (March/April 1998), pp. 6, 8.

gram in a specification language such as Z. A person involved in requirements needs human skills, communication skills, understanding skills, feeling skills, listening skills—so that he can function in his setting as harmoniously as a seasoned choir member (with all due respect to Tom DeMarco, *Why Does Software Cost So Much?*, Dorset House, 1995).

These qualities typify individuals with highly developed right-side brains; yet most engineers and managers tend to be left-brained. In *The Management of the Absurd* (Touchstone Books, 1996), Richard Farson reports the results of a survey of employees asked to name and describe their favorite bosses. None said their favorite boss was the one who brought projects in on schedule, or was great at planning, or was great at tracking progress, or possessed strong financial skills. Lo and behold, their favorite bosses were those who sat down on a busy day and found the time to help them with their career planning, or expressed sincere interest in the employee as a fellow human being, or admitted that they too were scared to do something, and so on. These are precisely the same special moments we all remember about our parents, our favorite teachers, our best friends. I find it interesting that out of the thousands of people we meet in our lifetimes, the ones we remember most are those who exhibit kindness, understanding, spontaneity, caring, and humanity, not the most profound thinkers or those with the most analytical or precise minds.

IF YOU'RE GOOD, YOU'RE GOOD

Over the years, I have often claimed that good programmers are good programmers regardless of the language—if you're a good C programmer, you're also a good Ada programmer and a good assembler programmer because the real skills that make a programmer good are independent of language. If you meet a programmer who claims he is good in only one language, he probably isn't.

Farson makes the same claim for managers: The real skills that make a good manager are much like those that make a good lover, friend, teacher, parent—you don't learn them from courses or books. I'd like to add requirements analyst to Farson's list.

If you sincerely care about the customer, just be yourself and you will be more than halfway to your goal. As with management, tactical skills such as interviewing, brainstorm facilitation, information organization, and formal specification can improve your effectiveness. But these are relatively useless if you don't have the most basic people skills: listening, open-mindedness, feeling, compassion, caring.

SEEDS FOR DEBATE

1. This one is for you left-brained readers: Assemble an argument for why this essay is absolutely wrong. Explain why right-braininess will just interfere with the real job, i.e., to get and record the facts. If those customers can't express

their requirements well, then that's their loss; they'll just have to use the product I build!

2. This one if for you right-brained readers: Try and predict how your left-brained colleagues are going to respond to the Seeds for Debate #1 above. For each argument that they can come up with, assemble a counter-argument.

3. Debate both sides of the statement "The skills that make a good requirements analyst are much like those that make a good lover, friend, teacher, parent."

System Phenotypes*

Over the years of working in the requirements world, I have been repeatedly shocked by people's inability to comprehend the fact that requirements describe the external view of a system. Perhaps this is because many years ago, somebody provided the term "requirement" with the ridiculous definition of "a requirement specifies what a system is to do without specifying how it does it." Perhaps we have produced an entire generation of people who think that there really is a way to differentiate between a "what" and a "how." I certainly cannot. My how is your what. My what is your how.

In genetics, scientists have long ago realized that the external view of an organism may hide internal characteristics of that organism. Geneticists use the term "phenotype" to represent all those externally observable characteristics of an organism. And they use the term "genotype" to represent all characteristics of the organism hidden within its genetic code. Thus, when we say that a fruit fly has red eyes, nobody is confused about what we are talking about. We are stating that the phenotype of the fruit fly includes red eyes. When we say that a fruit fly carries a recessive gene for black eyes, we are talking about its genotype. Notice that we can place the fruit fly under a microscope with successively higher power lenses. As we do so, we are simply examining finer and finer details of the fly's phenotype.

REQUIREMENTS AS PHENOTYPES

Stating requirements is no different than defining the phenotype of the system that we desire. As in the case of the microscope and the fly, requirements can be stated at many levels of detail from the most abstract,**

> The system shall allow hotel residents to make long-distance phone calls.

to the more detailed,

> When the user lifts the receiver, the system shall generate a dial tone.

> When the system is generating a dial tone and the user dials a "9," the system shall generate a distinctive dial tone.

*Originally published in *IEEE Software, 20,* 4 (July/August 2003).
**Some people use the term "features" for such abstract phenotypes/requirements.

Great Software Debates. By Alan M. Davis
ISBN 0-471-649880 © 2004 Institute of Electrical and Electronics Engineers.

to even more detailed,

When the system generates a dial tone, it shall be a tone of x MHz, plus or minus y MHz.

Whenever I present examples like these, I receive complaints that this example is too vague or that example is too detailed. The degree of detail has little to do with whether or not the example is a valid requirement, just as the degree of specificity has nothing to do with whether something is a valid description of an organism's phenotype. The correct level of detail for a requirement is all about the degree of risk tolerance and degree to which the customer demands a characteristic. If a customer would be happy with any interpretation of a vaguely specified requirement, then the lack of detail in the requirement is acceptable. And if some interpretation of that requirement would render the system unacceptable by the customers, then it needs more detail. It is as simple as that.

This worries many customers, developers, and consultants. Product customers regularly call me to ask, "Isn't this requirement too vague?" and I answer, "Is it?" For if they think it is too vague, then it is. Development personnel often call me to ask, "Isn't this requirement that my client gave to me too detailed? Doesn't is suppress our creativity?" to which I respond, "Would you rather have your creativity suppressed or have a dissatisfied customer?"

So, a *requirement* is an externally observable characteristic of a desired system. In other words, a requirement describes the phenotype of a system. It will be up to the system designers to craft the optimal genotype (i.e., the architecture, design, code) in order to realize the phenotype. Some may argue that an overly detailed phenotype unduly restricts the genotype designers. In reality *every* requirement limits the choices available to the design team. As soon as the requirement,

The system shall allow residents to move up and down floors through a vertical shaft in the building.

is recorded, we eliminate a telephone system from consideration. As soon as the requirement,

The system shall display the error message "The zip code entered is incorrect. It must be exactly 5 digits, or 5 digits followed by a dash followed by 4 digits."

is recorded, we eliminate all solutions that do not generate that exact error message.

IMPLICATIONS ON REQUIREMENTS ACTIVITIES

Once we understand that the essential nature of a requirement is that it describes externally observable characteristics (at any level of detail), the activities conducted as part of requirements engineering become better defined. For example, elicitation is the activity of determining the problems being experienced or the opportunities afforded the customers and users, as well as ascertaining what external system behaviors could address these problems or surface the opportunities. Triage (see article in March 2003 issue of *Computer* titled "The Art of Requirements Triage") is the activity of determining which problems, which opportunities, and which external behaviors can be addressed in light of insufficient resources. And requirements specification is the activity of documenting the desired external behaviors of the system to be constructed or procured. Notice how often the word *external* appears in these three descriptions.

IMPLICATIONS ON REQUIREMENTS ELICITATION

During elicitation, the focus must remain on problems and opportunities (which are *external* to the system) and *external* behaviors of the solution system. Note that the oft-quoted advice of some expert analysts to keep the discussion on the problems and opportunities and to avoid discussing the solution simply cannot work. It is natural for humans to discuss their problems and opportunities in terms of solutions. Stating "I am hungry" is not much different than stating "I wish I had food." Stating "I feel vulnerable" is not much different than stating "I wish the system would tell me which incoming missiles are the most threatening." Since one of the most important goals of requirements activities is to define a system that makes customers happy, we should spend more time listening to customers than trying to limit their vocabulary. If customers can visualize (and describe) aspects of the solution system that would make them happy, that is good news. Our role as analysts is to understand the customer; it is not to preserve the designers' ideal of creating a system that they think is somehow optimal

During elicitation, analysts often utilize modeling notations in order to add structure and understanding to the problem or its solution. This is of course beneficial. However, notations should be selected from among those that are relatively easy for the customer to understand. Furthermore, analysts should draw using the modeling notation but should speak exclusively in terms customers understand. Let's say, for example, that the application lends itself to modeling using a statechart (see D. Harel and M. Politi, *Modeling Reactive Systems with Statecharts*, McGraw-Hill, 1998). There is no reason for the analyst to ever use the term "statechart." Instead, the analyst could say "As I understand it, when the user selects the 'seating plan' menu item, you want the system to display a seating plan?" Or, "What I think I hear you saying is that if the user does nothing for 2 minutes, you want the system to return them back to the original log-on screen?" While the analyst is saying the above, he/she is drawing Figure 21.1 on the whiteboard or computer screen.

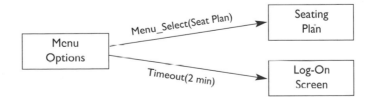

Figure 21.1. Statechart Used During Elicitation.

Notice there is no need to *teach* the customer about a statechart. The customer happens to be learning about statecharts *in situ,* and that is a nice side effect, but the spoken dialog is all in terms of the problem, the opportunity, and the desired external behaviors of the solution system. Contrast this with the incompetent analyst who draw the above diagram while saying, "Once in the state named Menu Options, two transitions are possible. The first transition is triggered by the user selecting Seat Plan from among the menu options. In this case, the system transitions to the state Seating Plan. The second transition occurs as the result of a two-minute timeout. If that timeout occurs, the system transitions to the state Log-On Screen." In the first case, the customer is completely "on board" and may even have learned something. In the second case, the customer is totally alienated.

All candidate requirements must be stated in terms of externally observable phenomena. For example, if a designer wants to make an algorithm faster, that requirement should be stated as, "The system performance shall be improved so that response time (or throughput or capacity) decreases (or increases) from x to y."

At the end of elicitation, we have created a list of problems and opportunities as we understand them, and a list of possible abstract phenotypes we desire the system to possess in order to address those problems and opportunities.

IMPLICATIONS ON REQUIREMENTS TRIAGE

Similarly during triage, the focus must remain on problems, opportunities, and phenotypes. Everything that is discussed should be in terms of the requirements gathered during elicitation, plus available resources (e.g., people, money, equipment) and desired delivery dates.

Modeling notations are rarely used during triage, but trade-offs between the benefits of multiple, competing (for the same resources) requirements are the norm. As long as everything is discussed in terms of benefits to the stakeholders (i.e., observable from a perspective external to the system), comparisons are possible. The questions become something like, "Would I rather have the system (a) be 20% faster and be delivered on time, or (b) perform some specific new feature and be delivered on time, or (c) be 20% faster, perform that specific new feature, cost $250K more, and be delivered two months late?"

At the end of triage, we have subsetted the list of problems and opportunities to isolate those that we *will* address, and subsetted the list of abstract phenotypes to isolate those the system *will* possess, given available resources.

IMPLICATIONS ON REQUIREMENTS SPECIFICATION

During requirements specification, the focus must be exclusively on external behaviors. As mentioned before, as a consultant, I am regularly called upon to resolve conflicts between customers and developers about the level of detail included in a requirements specification. The correct answer is that the level of detail simply is not a major issue. Requirements should be stated at a level of detail sufficient to insure that a system is built that satisfies the customers. As seen in Figure 21.2, there is no well-defined line between abstract and detailed, but a very distinct line exists between externally observable and internally-observable. In genetics, there is no well-defined line between gross and detailed phenotypes, but there sure is a distinct line between phenotype and genotype.

At the end of requirements specification, we have defined the detailed phenotype of the system to be constructed or otherwise procured.

SUMMARY

This essay has drawn parallels between phenotypes in genetics and requirements in system development. The parallels are many:

- The phenotype of an organism and the requirement of a system describe externally observable characteristics.
- The phenotype of an organism and the requirement of a system do not uniquely define a genotype or a design, but in both cases, serious limitations are placed on the possible genotypes and designs.
- Until geneticists learned the difference between the genotype and phenotype, they were confused by how two red-eyed fruit flies could breed and produce a

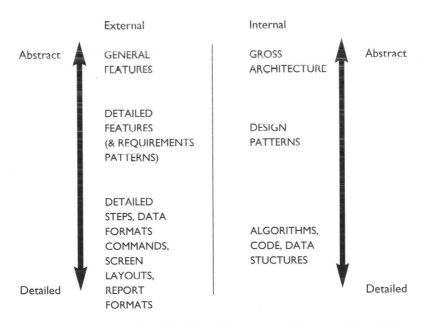

Figure 21.2. No Well-Defined Line Exists Between Abstract and Detailed.

black eyed fruit fly. Until system developers learn the difference between requirements and design, they will continue to have emotional arguments and mass confusion.

Although there are many parallels, there are also some differences. Chief among the differences is,

- In the case of genetics, the phenotype is the external manifestation of the genotype (so, in some strange way, we can think of the genotype as coming first). In the case of system development, the designer's goal is to construct a system's genotype so that it exhibits the behavior defined in its phenotype (so, the phenotype has come first).

In summary, understanding the role phenotypes play in genetics may assist system developers in understanding the role requirements play in system development.

SEEDS FOR DEBATE

1. In a January 19, 2004 email, Dale R. Sinclair wrote, "There is one difference between genotype/phenotype and requirement/design that you didn't list, but which may be of importance in some cases. The genotype of an organism not only defines how it behaves, but also what it is, i.e. the genotype contains the information necessary to build the organism." This is another major difference between phenotypes and requirements. Make a list of more. Do these differences strengthen or weaken the analogy?

The Missing Piece of
Software Development*

A. DAVIS AND A. ZWEIG

In the beginning, we coded in assembler. We liked the code. But after a while we found it impossible to maintain the code.

On the second day, we invented higher level languages and we coded in them. We liked the code. But after a while, we found our code was inefficient. It wasted memory. It was slow.

On the third day, we invented design. We liked design. But after a while, we found that designers disagreed about what the system was supposed to do. And the system often failed to meet customer expectations.

On the fourth day, we invented requirements. We liked requirements. But after a while, we found that we were still building systems that failed to meet customer needs. And the resulting systems could not be sold. And the resulting systems could not be built on budget, on schedule, or without incredible risk.

It is now the dawn of the fifth day. It is time to fix this problem. It is time to start building the *right* systems. According to the Standish Group, 29% of all software development efforts are canceled prior to completion, and another 42% are completed but never used by their intended customers. Clearly, all our efforts to write requirements well are not paying off. We are apparently building to the wrong requirements. We are building the wrong systems! We are not *planning* our software products. See the product life cycle [in Figure 22.1].

Software product planning is the activity of selecting *which* product you should build. The subsequent activities of requirements specification, design and coding are primarily *technical* activities; software product planning requires the highest levels of understanding of both *technology* and *business*. All software life cycle models to date have omitted this important activity. The net result of omitting this activity is that we end up constructing very efficient defect-free software that nobody wants to use or buy. The net result of applying sensible software product planning is the

---

*Reprinted from *Journal of Systems and Software* 53, 3 (September 2000), pp. 205–206, © 2000, with permission from Elsevier.

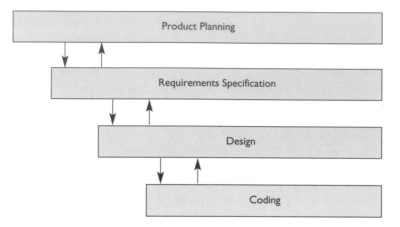

Figure 22.1. Role of Product Planning .

construction of the "right" product, and thus the achievement of improved return on investment, expanded market share, and increased customer satisfaction.

Marketing and development typically take adversarial roles during product planning. In a typical scenario, marketing reports, "We must add these three features, or we will be unable to sell the product." And development responds with an equally absolute position, "With the current schedule and resources, we cannot possibly develop the system with these features." Both of these individuals are taking a strong advocacy position for their "own side." Unfortunately (or perhaps fortunately), it is impossible for one side to "win" and the other side to "lose": both parties lose if the product cannot be sold, and both parties lose when the product is delivered a year late. Thus the only possible results are win-win and lose-lose. The trick is for all parties to comprehend this, and understand the implications of all decisions. This is difficult because so many factors* influence the selection of the right answer. For example, [see Figure 22.2]:

- Demand by customers (perhaps conflicting demands from multiple customers).
- Time to market (the more features, the later the system will be delivered; the fewer features, the less demand).
- Development cost (the more features, the more development will cost).
- Development risk (how difficult are the features to be implemented).
- Market size (how does feature selection affect the number of customers who will buy or use the product. This applies to both products and to systems used internally).
- Price (and how does price relate to feature selection and customer demand).

*We have isolated approximately 100 factors.

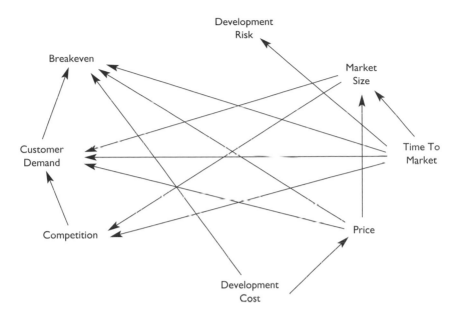

Figure 22.2. Complex Relationships Drive Product Planning.

- Competition (with respect to functionality, price, and availability)
- Breakeven (the more development costs, the later breakeven will occur; the less use or fewer sales, the later breakeven will occur).

Looking at just this short list of factors, [Figure 22.2] shows how making a change to any factor has an effect on other factors.

We have a difficult time performing software product planning because it is so interdisciplinary. Our educational institutions are notoriously poor at educating us in interdisciplinary arenas. Students of engineering learn engineering and are rarely exposed to finance or marketing. Students of marketing learn marketing and are rarely exposed to finance or engineering. Most of us become specialists in just one area. To complicate matters, few of us meet interdisciplinary people in the work force, so there are few role models to mimic. Yet, software product planning is critical to product development success and absolutely requires knowledge of multiple disciplines.

Key to being successful at software product planning is having at our disposal the concept of a "level playing field." In other words, we need the ability to see current assumptions and current expectations in every one of the many variables involved. Each side needs to understand its own factors as well as the other side's factors, and will thus be able to understand the myriad implications of every decision. For example, we should be able to examine current expected market along with expected market penetration, current price analysis (including average price, components of costs allocated to each sale, and margin), current development risks (contrasting resources and time allocated to the project with resources and time that *should* be allocated to the project), and current breakeven. By seeing all these factors simultaneously, we can have a chance at understanding the ramifications of every critical software product planning decision. Thus, when we want to delete a feature, we should fully understand how it affects development cost and risk as well as how it affects delivery date and customer satisfaction.

Until we start thinking like *product* builders instead of systems or software builders, we will continue to perpetuate an industry that has a reputation for being unresponsive to its customers.

SEEDS FOR DEBATE

1. Although many of the essays I write receive many email reactions from readers, this one produced not a one. Is the reason (a) it had nothing to say, (b) it was so wrong that nobody cared to waste his or her time writing to me, or (c) nobody read it?

2. This essay seems to argue for product planning being a separate activity, somewhat divorced from the other more traditional phases of software development. Present an argument for why product planning is not part of the software development life cycle at all. Present another argument for why product planning is simply one of the parts of the requirements phase (e.g., requirements triage as described on pages 150–151).

Object-Oriented Analysis to Object-Oriented Design: An Easy Transition?*

In the past 10 years, numerous treatises have been written on both object-oriented requirements techniques and object-oriented design techniques. With our ever-growing thirst for simple solutions to our software productivity problems, many proponents of object orientation are describing the transition between object-oriented requirements and object oriented design as straightforward. The purpose of this article is to analyze the incredible differences between object-oriented requirements and object-oriented design, explain why the transition between them is not and should not be easy, and provide guidance concerning how the transition should be made.

INTRODUCTION

Object-orientation (OO) was originally proposed in the 1960's as a programming technique. At programming time, an *object* was (and is) a data abstraction, i.e., an encapsulation of protected data (and its structure) along with procedures/techniques/processes/functions privileged to create, manipulate, and destroy that data. In addition, OO simply implies the existence of classes and inheritance. A *class* is a generic set of objects or other classes. The objects or other classes are *members* of that class. All members of a class *inherit* the data structures and the associated procedures that are defined as part of the class. By the late 1980's, a wide variety of object-oriented programming (OOP) languages were developed to make optimal use of OOP concepts. In the mid 1980's, design techniques were developed that brought the basic concepts of OOP to the design community. Many object oriented design (OOD) techniques were developed and documented. Because the principles of OOP and OOD are so similar, most of the OOD techniques were based on the features of specific OOP languages, e.g., Booch (1986) on Ada, Cox (1986) on Objective-C, Meyer (1988) on Eiffel.

In the late 1980s, requirements techniques were developed that brought many of the basic concepts of OOP and OOD to the requirements community.

*Reprinted from *Journal of Systems and Software*, 30, 1 & 2 (July–August 1995), pp. 151–159. © 1995, with permission from Elsevier.

Great Software Debates. By Alan M. Davis
ISBN 0-471-649880 © 2004 Institute of Electrical and Electronics Engineers.

The following two [sub-]sections provide details on object-oriented requirements (OOR) and OOD with particular emphasis on what they are and why they are done.

Object-Oriented Requirements

The purpose of any software requirements technique is to understand and document the needs of the user and the external behavior of the solution. Requirements engineering includes two primary groups of activities*: problem analysis and requirements specification. *Problem analysis* is the activity of learning all aspects of the problem domain so as to determine how best to solve a specific set of user needs. Problem analysis is essential for any system development for which the problem being solved is not totally self-evident. *Requirements specification* is the activity of documenting in a software requirements specification (SRS) (Davis, 1993) the expected external behavior and external characteristics of a system that solves the problem. An SRS is critical to software development in the large. It must be unambiguous, consistent, and as complete as possible. A project is flying blind (and without instruments) without an SRS. It defines what is going to be built, so all developers are aiming for the same goal and that goal is the same one the customer expects. "Expected external behavior" means a description of all inputs to the system, all outputs from the system, and all possible mapping relationships between the inputs and outputs (e.g., which light goes on when I push this button?).

An object-oriented problem analysis technique uses objects and inheritance to help the analyst learn more about the problem domain. An object-oriented requirements specification technique uses objects and inheritance to help the SRS writer described expected external software system behavior. None of the OOR techniques the author is familiar with is effective at describing eternal system behavior or its external characteristics.** They are, however, quite helpful in describing the problem (i.e., real world) domain. They are thus all object-oriented problem analysis techniques.

Object-Oriented Design

The purpose of any software design technique is to transform a set of software requirements into as close to an optimal*** configuration (i.e., architecture) of software as is feasible. What makes a design optimal is implied by the content of the SRS. It is the SRS that will determine if an "optimal" design is one that is testable, maintainable, enhanceable, [reusable,] reliable, or fine-tuned to meet strict performance or security requirements.

---

*See Davis (2004) and Davis and Zweig (2000) for more up-to-date views of what requirements activities are.

**This should not be a surprise. An object-oriented view is *not* an external view of a system. Note that Jacobson (1992) has proposed augmenting the OO view with another non-OO view, i.e., user scenarios.

***It is acknowledged that for most applications, achievement of 100% optimality is neither feasible nor possible, and in such cases, optimal means "constructible and good enough given requirements and available resources."

The purpose of an object-oriented design is to optimize maintainability, reusability, enhanceability, and reliability through the effective use of [encapsulation]. Because OOD based designs encapsulate data and its privileged procedures, errors are less likely to occur (because data is well protected). Errors that do occur are easier to detect (because incorrect data can only be caused by an error in the procedures defined to access that data, i.e., high cohesion is the rule), and changes are less likely to induce errors (because low coupling is inherent . . .).

OOR vs. OOD

As mentioned before, the purpose of OOD is to optimize maintainability, reusability, enhanceability, and reliability, i.e., to generate an "optimally performing" and constructible product. No matter what application is being developed, the primary purpose of any requirements technique (including OOR) is to optimize understandability. Secondary purposes might be to increase correctness, consistency, completeness, etc., but the concept of an "optimally performing" SRS makes no sense. The definition of an object for OOR must therefore be different than for OOD. The most commonly acceptable definition of an object at requirements time is:

- It must represent some real-world entity
- It encapsulates attributes or states of that entity
- It encapsulates the services or operations provided by that entity for other entities
- It inherits attributes and services of the class(es) of which it is a member

The most commonly accepted definition of an object at design time is:

- It encapsulates attributes or states of (or data associated with) an entity
- It encapsulates the services or operations (or methods) provided by that entity for other entities
- It inherits attributes and services of the class(es) of which it is a member

Notice that aside from terminology, the primary difference is that in OOR an object represents some real-world entity. The second big difference is that objects are selected in OOR to optimize understandability, whereas in OOD it is to optimize performance or maintainability.

OOR techniques seem to fall into four categories (Davis 1993: pp. 59–61):

- *From object-oriented design.* Some OOR techniques evolved from OOD. An object at requirements time is the same as an object at design. The only difference is the level of detail.
- *From database design.* Some OOR techniques evolved from entity relation (ER) modeling. ER diagrams have been used for years by database designers

to capture data about real-world entities (which become records in a database), relations between entities (which become [foreign keys]), and often attributes of entities (which become fields within the records). Functions or processes that act upon the entities are usually downplayed or completely ignored.

- *From the requirements analysis world.* Some object-oriented problem analysis techniques evolved from standard requirements (systems) analysis. Their proponents have been analyzing problems using a variety of informal techniques. Their primary driver has been the understanding of the problem by analyzing entities in the real world. These OOR techniques emphasize . . . objects that are exclusively in the problem domain. . . .

- *From structured analysis (SA).* A number of recently published techniques claim to be object-oriented simply because object orientation is *hot*. The proponents usually call their techniques something like "object-oriented structured. . . ." All they have done is taken data-flow diagrams, changed the shapes of transforms from circles to rectangles, and declared themselves to be object oriented.

TRANSITIONING: STATE-OF-THE-ART

This section will provide a brief survey of what major proponents of object-orientation say about the transition from requirements to design. In effect, their thoughts define the current state-of-the-art.

Jacobson and Embley et al. say that requirements objects and design objects are identical. In particular, Jacobson (1991: pp. 80-81) states that "object-oriented construction means that the analysis model is designed and implemented in source code. . . . The goal is that the objects identified during the analysis should also be found within the design." Embley et al. (1992: p. 287) state that "for design, we should fully formalize the information contained in the [analysis] model targeted for implementation. . . . By pushing the [analysis] model down to this 'executable' level, a formal model for [design] can be represented using the original modeling constructs of [analysis]."

Coad and Yourdon, Booch, and Rumbaugh et al. say that design follows relatively easily from the requirements objects. For example, Coad and Yourdon (1991: pp. 178, 185) state that "moving from [analysis] to [design] is a progressive expansion of the model. . . . The expansion occurs primarily with added components." That is, Coad and Yourdon teach that analysis-time objects remain in the design, but to complete the design "add details," and add "human interaction, task management, and data management." Booch (1991: pp. 191, 201) states that "the classes and objects we identify at this early stage . . . usually carry through the entire design process. . . . This means that the products of . . . analysis may be used almost directly at the start of . . . design. The . . . designer refines these products by inventing new abstractions . . . that use these classes and objects. . . ." Finally, Rumbaugh et al. (1991: pp. 199) recognize that the design can be different than the requirements but believe that the subsystems that make up the design are assemblies of objects. Thus the general shape of the design must mimic the general shape of the requirements, and no new objects may be introduced. Specifically, they state that "a subsystem is . . . a package of classes, associations, operations, events, and constraints. . . ."

Cox and Meyer provide less emphasis on the role of object orientation during requirements. Specifically, Cox (1986; pp. 5–7) sees requirements as part of a plot to freeze progress and inhibit designers from having the freedom to make decisions. He sees object-oriented programming as the way to achieve evolution and maintainability through the iterative refinement paradigm. A requirements specification simply inhibits progress. Meyer (1988: p. 4) only briefly addresses requirements by stating they are important but never returns to them.

This essay takes a position in support of Cherry, Lorenz, Shlaer and Mellor, and Wirfs-Brock et al. They acknowledge the need for a requirements document (that describes external system behaviors) after object-oriented analysis and before object-oriented design. More specifically, Cherry (1990: p. 39) states quite eloquently that when the requirements specification is written, one is able to avoid "worrying about program efficiency, portability, and reusability; . . . [The only] concern was to specify . . . expected external behavior. . . . All challenging problems beg for separating complex concerns. So, first describe . . . external behavior . . . [then] implement a program that produces this behavior correctly, efficiently, reusably, and maintainably. For complex systems, both [requirements and design] are [difficult]; why would anyone want to take them on simultaneously?" Lorenz (1993: p. 76) also provides excellent advice: "the documentation of the classes, techniques, . . . and contracts [of analysis] will carry forward to the design . . . phase as *draft* documentation. The designers are free to change the design." Shlaer and Mellor (1988) similarly acknowledge that design is difficult after object-oriented analysis and that it requires many questions/answers and much thought before arriving at an optimal design. Finally, Wirfs-Brock et al. (1990: 63) describe the "specification [as the source of] seeds for your [design] model of the system."

DIFFERENCES BETWEEN OO REQUIREMENTS AND OO DESIGN

Going from problem analysis (part of requirements) to requirements specification (also part of requirements) *is* difficult. There is nothing easy about deciding what system will be built to solve a problem. Similarly, going from requirements specification (part of requirements) to software design *is* difficult. There is nothing easy about selecting an optimal design to satisfy a particular set of external behavioral requirements. There is absolutely no reason why the transition from requirements to design should be easy regardless of the technique used. This transition is not easy in any engineering discipline. Why should it be easy in software engineering?

In short, requirements and design are very different. Let us look as the specific differences of these two activities when using OO.

1. Different objects. The selection criteria for an object during OOR is very simple: Is this entity an important part of the problem domain? In other words, is the understanding of the real-world entity corresponding to this object critical to our understanding of the problem to be solved? If it is important, it must be included. If it is not important, it must be excluded. What other criterion can there be for requirements-time objects? The selection criteria for an object during OOD is also simple: Can we construct it and does the inclusion of this object make effective use of data abstractions (e.g., make good use of data hiding and procedural hiding)? In other words, does the inclusion of this object in the design increase the software's quality? What other criterion can there be for design-time objects?*

   An example will illustrate how different problem analysis-time, requirements specification-time, and design-time objects are. Let us look at an elevator control system. At problem analysis-time, one critical object is the *passenger*. In fact, what entity in the real world could possibly be as important to model in our problem analysis? To better understand this object, we would include *weight* as one of its attributes and static relationships (i.e., instance connections) with *floor* objects to record the fact that every passenger starts out and terminates on exactly one floor. At requirements specification-time and at design-time, there is absolutely no need to model a passenger object. Any instance of a passenger (or its weight) is irrelevant. On the other hand, a very important object to capture during design *floor requests*. This data abstraction would encapsulate all requests for floors whether they be generated by potential passengers on floors or existing passengers on elevators. Encapsulated with this data would be all the various procedures/techniques that may modify the floor requests. Notice that the *passenger* object would exist at requirements but not design-time, and the *floor requests* object would exist at design but not requirements-time.

2. The System Object. The absence of a system object appears to be uniform across phases but for different reasons. During problem analysis, one would never model the software system itself as an object because the problem domain does *not* include the solution system. During requirements specification and design, one would also never model the software system itself as an object because the object model being built *is* the software system.

3. Aggregation. At requirements-time, it is important to record whole-part relationships between objects to better understand those objects. For example, it

---

*Some readers may argue that another valid criterion is potential reuse. This may be the case, but it does not weaken the argument presented here. Other readers may argue that another valid criterion is minimization of "intellectual distance" (Fairley, 1985). Such an argument would state that a good design should mimic the real world as closely as possible. Although this is certainly true, the position of moderation states that a good design should mimic the *relevant* real world. Since analysis occurs prior to a design of what should be automated, the design should be expected to have fewer objects than analysis and even simpler structure (Lindvall, 1994). For another counter argument, see (Siddiqi, 1994) where Siddiqi points out that different humans perceive different structures of the real world and thus a design that mimics one person's "real world" may not mimic another's.

might be helpful in the elevator control system to consider the floor request buttons, the emergency button, the open/close door buttons, and the light on/off switch to be parts of the elevator cab's control panel. Their whole-part relationship must be recorded because they have a whole-part relationship in the real world. At design time, it is important to record whole-part relationships for the purpose of optimal packaging of software, i.e., is there a data abstraction that will be fully encapsulated within another data abstraction to optimize protection, security, data integrity, etc.?

4. Instantiation. When specifying an object during requirements, we often assume that there can be multiple instances of it. For example, specifying a passenger object implies we have multiple real passengers, each an instance of the passenger object. There is rarely a need to worry about the conditions that create or destroy instances of an object. Because the object model is modeling the problem domain, a new passenger object is created when a new passenger appears, a customer object is created when a new customer appears, etc. There is rarely a need to worry about specific values associated with attributes or state variables of any one instance. On the other hand, at design-time, it is critical to specify the conditions that create or destroy instances of an object, and we must develop algorithms for the creation and modification of attributes, and expulsion of every instance of every object.

   There is another quality that appears to be uniform across phases: single instances. Some objects exist at requirements time that have only one instance, e.g., the shaft in a single-elevator elevator control system. Some objects at design time also have only single instances, e.g., the floor requests.

5. Different Emphasis on Techniques/Services. At problem analysis time, it should be acceptable not to detail the algorithm or behavior of services provided by an object. After all, if you understand some entity's behavior during problem analysis, why waste time describing it? Furthermore, during requirements specification the services provided by an object to other objects may not be the services (i.e., requirements) provided by the system to its environment; therefore, they too can often be overlooked. On the other hand, every service associated with a design time object must be specified in detail. This specification is the very essence of what detailed design is.

6. Genericity of Services and Dynamic Binding. In OOD and OOP, names for operations/techniques/services are often overloaded. An object within a class may have its own specific implementation of a service that shares a name with a service of the class. This is an important feature in OOD and OOP but less so during requirements. There are two basic reasons for this: First, class hierarchies are built in OOR primarily to aid in understanding, not to achieve productivity or maximize encapsulation. Second, the detailed specification, let alone implementation, of any service is rarely necessary to simply understand a problem. For the same two reasons, the issue of dynamic binding of a service request to appropriate code is irrelevant in OOR.

7. Verification and Validation. The V & V opportunities and challenges are entirely different for problem analysis, requirements specification, and design. When performing V & V for analysis, the primary goal should be to verify that the (OOR) model precisely captures the problem environment. When performing V & V for the requirements specification, the primary goal should be to verify that the system as specified satisfies the needs of the users and appropriately works in the problem domain. When performing V & V for design, the primary goal should be to verify that the (OOD) design correctly satisfies the requirements.

TRANSITIONING ADVICE

If 50 million people say a foolish thing, it is still a foolish thing.

—Anatole France

As mentioned previously, the proponents of the major OO schools generally advise that the transition from OOR to OOD is easy. This is a symptom of an industry-wide problem: The industry seems to embrace the latest fad and believe it is a panacea (Davis, 1993a). It is hard to disagree with the intuitive principle that OOD leads to better designs than more traditional techniques (although little hard evidence exists [Glass, 1994]). The trend from OOD toward OOR was inevitable; most of our techniques have started their popularity as programming techniques, then design techniques, then requirements techniques (e.g., structured, Jackson, OO). Unfortunately, although OOR "feels right," there are even fewer intuitive or scientific arguments for why we should do it. As a result, we have oversold OOR based on the popularity of OO rather than on any other argument. It was not until many people started questioning OOR's purpose that its proponents started justifying OOR as being ideal for requirements because the transition to OOD is easy.

The primary purpose of this essay is to explain why the transition from OOR to OOD is difficult. That was given in the previous section. Here is some advice on how to make the transition easier:

1. *Recognize that a software requirements specification is necessary.* Most OORs are aimed at problem analysis, not requirements specification. That is, the intent of most object-oriented techniques sold as requirements techniques is to aid in the understanding of the problem domain. They are almost useless at describing external behavior of the solution system.* It is critical to document the expected external behavior and characteristics of a system before attempt-

---

*Recent OORs have augmented their objects with detailed state-based behaviors (Rumbaugh et al. 1991: Embley et al. 1992: Jacobson, 1992). However, it is not clear how one extrapolates from a set of objects' behaviors to the goal, namely the behavior of the "system." For example, an SRS should be able to easily answer the question "when I push button A, what light will go on?" This cannot be derived easily from a model composed of a set of cooperating objects.

ing to design and implement it. Otherwise, customers and users will not know what system is being built for them until most of the development resources are expended. And the designers (who are experts at *design*) will be making critical *application* decisions. Without a software requirements specification, we are simply guessing, and the alleged solution system is unlikely to be useful in solving any real-world problem.

In an effort to make their technique more popular, many proponents of OOR techniques are teaching that after performing OOR the next step is OOD. This completely bypasses the critical middle step of specifying external behavior (See Figure 23.1 derived from [Davis, 1988a]). See Davis (1988) for a description of many of the techniques currently available for this step. One way of organizing an SRS is to organize the requirements by object. "Organizing requirements by object" means that we have separate sections of the document devoted to each primary object (Davis, 1993). Within each section we itemize and describe those system requirements that relate most closely to that object.

Note that this is *not* as simple as describing each problem object's services/methods; the services provided by a problem-domain *object* to/for *other objects* may or may not correspond to functions performed by the *system* to/for the *system's environment*. The former is the goal of most OORs; the latter is the goal of writing an SRS.

2. *Don't expect it to be easy.* Any requirements specification should be optimized for broad understandability by customers, users, and developers and should help readers comprehend the problem being solved and the externally observ

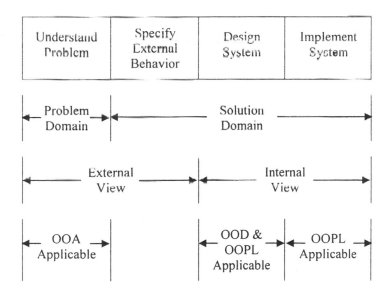

Figure 23.1. Early Activities of Software Development.

able behavior and attributes of the system that solves that problem. Any design specification should be optimized for all those traits defined *in* the requirements specification, e.g., performance, security, functionality, usability, throughput. There is no reason to expect such a major shift in emphasis to be easy. Furthermore, because most object-oriented requirements techniques address problem analysis, not external behavior specification, its objects are defined *before* a decision was made about what to automate. The decision of what to automate, and this relates closely to the issue of what exactly the problem is (Gause and Weinberg, 1990), is nontrivial.

3. *Use a system development process appropriate for your application.* Complex system applications need to be analyzed at multiple levels of abstraction. A complex system composed of hardware and software must be specified in a fashion similar to Figure 23.2 (Davis, 1993). [OO is applicable to steps 1, 3, 4, 6, and 7; the transitions from 1 to 3, and from 4 to 6 are nontrivial.] Note that we perform problem analysis at the systems level. In other words, we use some technique to comprehend the problem domain of the system. OOR is one such technique. Other approaches include structured analysis (DeMarco, 1980) and prototyping (Andriole, 1992; Davis 1992). Next we write a system-level requirements specification to describe the external behavior of the *system*. Next, we perform a *system design* to determine and document an optimal architecture that satisfies those requirements. For each element of the architecture, we repeat the above process; analyze the element (e.g., with OOR), specify its external behavior in a system-level requirements specification, perform system design on the element. This process repeats until the elements are small enough to represent a single software (or hardware) subsystem whose configuration we want to control independently of other subsystems. At this point, problem analysis is performed, and a *software* requirements specification is written for each subsystem. Next it is time to perform *software design* to create and document an optimal software design. Here, OOD be-

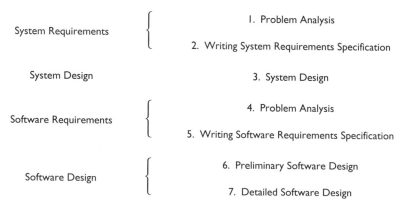

Figure 23.2. System Development Life Cycle.

comes the likely candidate for the technique of choice but not necessarily the only one.

4. *Use OOR-created objects as starting points.* Some objects described when using an OOR technique are occasionally good candidates for objects at design time. Examine each one and determine its suitability as a design object. The most important criterion is whether the selection of this analysis-time object as a design time object will aid in the maintainability, functionality, or other quality of the product. This is not easy. Many objects will not transition. See the earlier section on **Differences Between Requirements and Design** [starting on page 133] for specific examples of objects that should not transition.

5. *Add other objects from the SRS.* The software requirements specification captures the result of the decisions concerning what to automate. It also describes the interfaces to all external "systems" (including people, other hardware, other software). From it, one can determine the precise environment in which the system resides and the content of all information received and generated by the system. This it can serve as an orchard from which a designer can select additional object candidates. It is not as simple as "searching for nouns." It requires careful reading and derivation of object concepts. Consider all the design constraints implied by the SRS. Consider the maintainability, functionality, and performance requirements. Can all these be met optimally by selecting this object? If not, don't use it.

6. *Design!* A few general books on software design exist (Peters, 1981; Budgen, 1993; Witt et al. 1994; Shaw and Garlan, 1995), but most design books (Constantine and Yourdon, 1979; Booch, 1991; Coad and Yourdon, 1991a; Gomaa, 1993; Sanden, 1994) favor specific approaches. Creating an optimal architecture with a chance to satisfy all requirements is *not* easy. Once an architecture is selected and verified, there are many data abstractions that make sense at design time although these may not correspond to real-world entities. These are excellent candidates to be additional design-time objects to enhance maintainability, reusability, functionality, and performance. Many of the classic academic examples of data abstractions and/or reusable objects fall into this category, e.g., stacks, queues.

SUMMARY

This article puts forth the unpopular position that the transition from object-oriented requirements to object-oriented design is nontrivial; more importantly, that transition should be difficult. Trivial attempts to make the transition appear easy in the name of cost reduction or productivity are counterproductive at best. Going from requirements to design is a major change in emphasis, content, and goal, regardless of notation or paradigm. As Turski* said, "To every complex problem, there exists a simple solution . . . and it's wrong!"

*Words spoken at IFIPS Congress '80, Tokyo, October 1980.

Stated another way, analysis of a difficult problem *is* hard. Specification of the external behavior of a complex system *is* hard. And design of an optimal architecture for a complex system *is* hard. And to insinuate that any of these three tasks can be made easier by simply using the solution derived from one of the other two is fallacious.

A sensible development process is one that performs problem analysis (using OOR or another problem analysis technique) until the problem is well understood, determines what system will be built to solve that problem, writes a software requirements specification to describe that system's external behavior (organized by any of myriad ways, but OGA is useless), and then creates an optimal architecture (using OOD or another design technique).

ACKNOWLEDGMENTS

I wish to thank Dr. Hassan Gomaa of George Mason University for participating in some very early discussions on this subject with me, Mr. Tsuyoshi Nakajima for a critical review from an OO viewpoint, and Ms. Kerry Baugh for assuring that this article looks like a professional product.

REFERENCES

Andriole, S., *Rapid Application Prototyping.* Wellesley, MA: QED Publishers, 1992.

Booch, G., "Object Oriented Development," *IEEE Transactions on Software Engineering, 12,* 2 (February 1986), pp. 211–221.

Booch, G., *Object Oriented Design,* Redwood City, CA: Benjamin Cummings, 1991.

Budgen, D., *Software Design,* Reading, MA: Addison-Wesley, 1993.

Cherry, G., *Software Construction by Object-Oriented Pictures,* Canadaigua, NY: Thought Tools, 1990.

Coad, P., and E. Yourdon, *Object-Oriented Analysis,* Englewood Cliffs, NJ: Yourdon Press, 1991.

Coad, P., and E. Yourdon, *Object-Oriented Design,* Englewood Cliffs, NJ: Yourdon Press. 1991a.

Constantine, L., and E. Yourdon, *Structured Design,* Upper Saddle River, NJ: Prentice-Hall, 1979.

Cox, B., *Object Oriented Programming,* Reading, MA: Addison-Wesley, 1986.

Davis, A., "A Comparison of Techniques for the Specification of External System Behavior," *Communications of the ACM, 31,* 9 (September 1988), pp. 1098–1115.

Davis, A., "A Taxonomy for the Early Stages of the Software Development Life Cycle," *Journal of Systems and Software, 8,* 4 (September 1988a), pp. 297–311.

Davis, A., "Operational Prototyping: A New Development Approach," *IEEE Software, 9,* 5 (September 1992), pp. 70–78.

Davis A., *Software Requirements: Objects, Functions and States,* Upper Saddle River. NJ: Prentice-Hall, 1993.

Davis, A., "Software Lemmingineering," *IEEE Software*, 10, 5 (September 1993a), pp. 79–84; reprinted in current book as "Software Lemmings" on page 3.

Davis, A., and Z. Zweig, "Requirements Management Made Easy," *PM Network Magazine*, December 2000, pp. 61–63; reprinted in current book on page 155.

Davis, A., *Just Enough Requirements Management*, New York: Dorset House, 2004.

[DeMarco T., *Structured Analysis and System Specification*, Upper Saddle River, NJ: Prentice-Hall, 1980.]

Embley, D., et al., *Object-Oriented Systems Analysis*, Upper Saddle River, NJ: Prentice-Hall, 1992.

Fairley, R., *Software Engineering Concepts*, New York: McGraw-Hill, 1985.

Gause, D., and J. Weinberg, *Are Your Lights On?*, New York: Dorset House, 1990.

Glass, R., "Editor's Corner: Object Orientation: Theory and Practice," *Journal of Systems and Software*, 24, 2 (February 1994), pp. 91–93.

Gomaa, H., *Software Design Methods for Concurrent and Real-Time Systems*, Reading, MA: Addison-Wesley, 1993.

Jacobson, I., *Object-Oriented Software Engineering*. Reading, MA: Addison-Wesley, 1992.

Lindvall, M., "Object-Oriented Modeling in Practice," *The Software Practitioner*, 4, 3 (May June 1994), pp. 7–8.

Lorenz, M., *Object-Oriented Software Development*, Upper Saddle River, NJ: Prentice-Hall, 1993.

Meyer, B., *Object Oriented Software Construction*, New York: Prentice-Hall International, 1988.

Peters, T., *Software Design*, Upper Saddle River, NJ: Prentice-Hall, 1981.

Rumbaugh, J., et al., *Object-Oriented Modeling and Design*, Upper Saddle River, NJ: Prentice-Hall, 1991.

Sanden, B., *Software Systems Construction with Examples in Ada*, Upper Saddle River, NJ: Prentice-Hall, 1994.

Shaw, M., and D. Garlan, *An Introduction to Software Architecture*, Upper Saddle River, NJ: Prentice-Hall, 1995

Shlaer, S., and S. Mellor, *Object-Oriented Systems Analysis*, Upper Saddle River, NJ: Prentice-Hall, 1988.

Siddiqi, J., et al., "Challenging Universal Truths of Requirements Engineering," *IEEE Software*, 11, 2 (March 1994).

Wirfs-Brock, R., et al., *Designing Object-Oriented Software*, Upper Saddle River, NJ: Prentice-Hall, 1990.

Witt, B., et al., *Software Architecture and Design*, New York: Van Nostrand Reinhold, 1994.

EPILOGUE

The object-oriented community has since figured out for themselves that object-oriented analysis made little sense. In its place, the community has adopted use cases (or scenarios) as the "standard" way of defining requirements prior to performing object-oriented design. The irony of the use case fad is that there is nothing object-oriented about it. Scenarios have been used extensively since the early

1970's for writing requirements, regardless of the design method used subsequently. Scenarios are good. Object-oriented design is good. They are certainly compatible. But there should still be nothing easy about the transition from requirements to design.

Of the four categories of OOR techniques (starting on page 131) that existed when this paper was originally written, only the first still exists.

SEEDS FOR DEBATE

1. Present an argument for why the Rational Unified Process (RUP) obsoletes this essay, i.e., that RUP makes the transition from OOA to OOD easy and seamless.
2. Take the completely opposite point of view of this essay. That is, argue that one of the justifications for object-orientation is that the transition from requirements to design becomes easy.
3. If everybody were to take the position that "the organization of the requirements should become the software architecture," what will happen?
4. Can object orientation support all classic software architecture types?

Achieving Quality in Software Requirements*

INTRODUCTION

Many publications (Booch 1994; Coad and Yourdon 1991; Marca and McGowan 1998; Yourdon 1989) have been written to proclaim how this tool or that method will help companies achieve more effective requirements specification. In particular, Booch's and Coad's books herald the usefulness of object orientation during the early phases of software development. Marca and McGowan's book, *SADT*, does the same for structured analysis and design techniques, and Yourdon's does the same for modern structured analysis. Many authors (Bickerton 1992; Davis 1993; Kotonya and Sommerville 1998; Loucopoulos and Karakostas 1995; Sommerville and Sawyer 1997; Thayer and Dorfman 1997; Wieringa 1996) have written books that survey requirements tools and methods, and some even survey the best practices of requirements specification. But little has been done to compile the best practices of requirements specification independent of tools or methods and in the context of the business needs that requirements must fill. Use of these practices provides the highest likelihood that the requirements specification will exhibit maximum quality.

Measuring quality of requirements in the business context is different from measuring the quality of a product. It requires measuring the following:

- The number of requirements (or features) being addressed and their complexity
- Which requirements will be satisfied
- Whether the requirements are the ones the customers and users want
- The percentage of the customers' problems being solved
- The cost (in time and resources) to develop the system
- The risk being undertaken by development to address requirements
- The cost of system maintenance

*Originally published in *Software Quality Professional,* 1, 3 (June 1999), pp. 37–44. © 1999 Alan M. Davis. Reprinted with permission.

- The revenue that will be generated by selling the solution system or the savings that will occur as a result of using the solution system
- When the breakeven point will occur (that is, how long it will take for accumulated revenues or savings to exceed accumulated expense)

Some traditional quality professionals might question many of these quality measures. They might prefer to see quality in terms of numbers of defects and their impact. The author contends that quality can only be measured as a quantification of the true merit of the software (using the aforementioned measures). Software that has many defects but addresses real problems and achieves real goals is better than defect-free software that fails to satisfy needs. Thus, the preceding are the primary measures.

The remainder of this article is organized into sections that correspond to each of the activities that comprise requirements management:

- Collecting and refining the understanding of user needs (often called requirements elicitation)
- Creating a list of potential features for a solution system (often called feature specification)
- Deciding which features should be incorporated to achieve maximal results (often called requirements triage)
- The detailing of the external behavior of those features selected for inclusion (often called requirements specification)

Figure 24.1 shows the relationships among these activities.

REQUIREMENTS ELICITATION

Elicitation is the set of activities that extracts needs from customers and users and helps the solution provider to better understand the problem. For elicitation, like for all complex activities, the art is primarily one of thinking and being human rather than the rote application of standard methods (Dörner 1989; Davis 1998). A good elicitor should know a variety of elicitation techniques and understand how subtle changes in the environment, the project, and the application dictate radical changes to how elicitation proceeds. At best, poor or ineffective elicitation results in the creation of systems that fail to satisfy user needs. Optimally, a good elicitor employs multiple techniques and uses the right ones for the right aspects of the problem and situation.

Elicitation techniques include

- *Interviews.* Asking relevant questions to stakeholders about the problem to be solved and/or their needs and listening to their responses (Gause and Weinberg 1989)

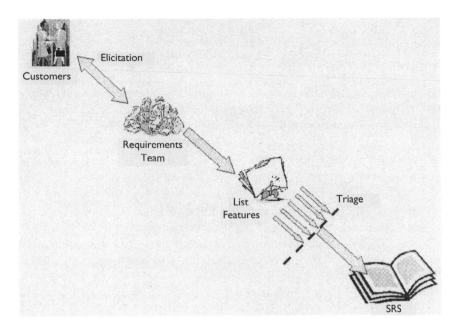

Figure 24.1. Requirements Activities

- *Questionnaires.* Distributing predefined questions to a statistically significant and representative sample of stakeholders and tallying the results
- *Ethnomethodological studies.* Observing potential users in their natural environment. This has resulted in significantly more accurate perceptions of the problem space than asking users what they do (Goguen and Jirotka 1994)
- *Brainstorming.* Assembling stakeholders in one location, establishing an environment that encourages participation, allowing all ideas to be stated out loud (so others can leverage off them) and written (so they are not lost) (Couger 1995)
- *Problem-domain storyboarding.* Using physical media (such as paper, cardboard or felt) to represent sequential states of the problem environment (Andriole 1992). Scenarios and use cases, in their many representations, can be used to represent the same information (Jacobson 1992)
- *Prototyping.* Constructing a partial implementation of a system in a quick-and-dirty manner to gain feedback for the requirements process, and then discarding the prototype (Davis 1995)
- *Reading.* Visiting the library or surfing the Web to locate information about experts' views of the problem or its potential solutions
- *Research.* Conducting experiments, exploring technology, developing new technology, and applying solutions for one problem to new problems

- *Evolutionary development.* Constructing a system that satisfies only the most understood requirements with the expectation that once customers start using it, they will think of many new requirements (Arthur 1992)

Each of these techniques can be useful in uncovering requirements, yet they are not interchangeable. Specific project conditions dictate which techniques will be most effective on the project. Following are some of those conditions:

- *Interviews.* Interviews are useful when some stakeholders hold most of the subject-matter expertise, are accessible, and are willing to spend time being interviewed. An expert interviewer is needed to be most effective.
- *Questionnaires.* Questionnaires are useful when the population of stakeholders is extremely large. Since it assumes that all questions can be predetermined, it works most effectively to ascertain opinion trends about specific (and already well-defined) requirements. Expertise in questionnaire formulation and statistical analysis is necessary.
- *Ethnomethodological studies.* Ethnomethodological studies are useful when trying to provide automation support to an existing less-automated or non-automated function, particularly when the parties are accessible by trained observers with no preconceived notions of the problem or its solution.
- *Brainstorming.* Brainstorming is particularly effective when many stakeholders each hold a modicum of knowledge about some aspect of the problem. The hope is that if 10 people each holds 5 percent of the requisite knowledge, they can leverage each other's knowledge into a full picture (that is, the whole exceeds the sum of the parts).
- *Problem-domain storyboarding.* Like brainstorming, storyboarding presupposes some knowledge of the problem. Thus, storyboarding assumes one can start someplace. Storyboarding is unlikely to be effective if it starts with blank slates and no ideas.
- *Prototyping.* Prototyping reduces the risk associated with inadvertently building the wrong system. It is a means of converting poorly understood requirements into well-understood requirements. Thus, prototyping can be effective only when people can enumerate fuzzy (that is, poorly understood) requirements.
- *Reading.* Obviously, reading works when some individuals understand something already and have written about it, and other people lack that knowledge.
- *Research.* Inventing or discovering new ideas is effective when the individuals are innovative, and it is appropriate when the ideas do not yet exist.
- *Evolutionary development.* Evolutionary development works when there are well-understood requirements. Evolutionary development also requires the belief that once customers see some functionality, they will think of more functions they would like to see (this latter condition is almost always true (Lehman 1991)).

FEATURE SPECIFICATION

As people perform elicitation, they will learn aspects of the stakeholders' problems and needs. For example, they may learn that: "Hotel guests need to communicate with parties in the local community." But they will also likely envision pieces of possible solutions. Many requirements textbooks argue that solutions during the requirements phase should be avoided. Thinking of solutions during requirements analysis is normal and good. It is important to record candidate features for the solution system as one thinks of them. This lowers the probability that they will be forgotten later. In fact, if individuals ascertain pure needs from the stakeholders, they will need to translate them into features of potential solutions anyway. Thus, for example, hotel guests' need to communicate with parties in the local community will be translated into a potential feature such as: "The system shall provide local phone service."

Prior to system construction, individuals will need to state the features in more detail to ensure that all designers, implementers, and testers are envisioning the same system. These detailed descriptions are called requirements and will look something like:

TO PROVIDE LOCAL PHONE CALL SERVICE:

- HOTEL GUEST LIFTS AN IDLE PHONE.
- WITHIN TWO SECONDS, SYSTEM SHALL GENERATE DIAL TONE.
- HOTEL GUEST DIALS "9."
- WITHIN ONE SECOND, SYSTEM SHALL GENERATE DISTINCTIVE DIAL TONE.
- HOTEL GUEST DIALS SEVEN-DIGIT LOCAL NUMBER
- WITHIN .5 SECONDS OF FIRST OF SEVEN DIGITS, SYSTEM SHALL STOP ALL TONES
- WITHIN 3 SECONDS OF SEVENTH DIGIT, . . . and so on.

But expressing requirements at this level of detail is time consuming. Such detail should be deferred until after one decides which features he or she will really attempt to satisfy.

Although it is not important to specify these features precisely or unambiguously at this stage, it is helpful to store them in a database. Storing features in a database makes it easier to annotate them with supplementary information that is critical to the triage process.

Figure 24.2 shows what a list of features might look like. Before moving on to triage, annotate the features with the following information:

- *Importance.* On a scale from zero (unimportant) to 10 (critical), record how important this feature is to stakeholders. Importance will be used during the triage process to decide which features should be included and which should be omitted or delayed to a later version.

Requirement Number	Requirement
1	System shall display up to eight simultaneous graphs.
2	System shall display expected sales by quarter.
3	System shall display internal rate of return as a function of time.
4	System shall allow users to change algorithm to convert function points to person-months.
5	System shall show relationship of optimal schedule vs. desired schedule.
6	System shall display list of requirements along with priority, difficulty, and risk.
7	System shall allow users to delete existing requirements or add new requirements.
8	System shall display the degree of market penetration by market segment.
9	When users make a change to any view, all views shall be updated simultaneously.
10	System shall allow any mouse command to be made with menu options.
11	System shall display 18 views as hot buttons on right side of screen.
12	When users select a hot button, system shall tile that view with existing views.
13	System shall allow users to add developers and maintainers.
14	All graphical items shall be selectable and editable.

Figure 24.2. Example List of Features.

- *Volatility.* On a scale from 0 percent (will not change) to 100 percent (guaranteed to change), record how likely this feature is to change in the near future. Volatility will be used during the triage process to decide which features should be included and which should be omitted or delayed to a later version.
- *Estimate of cost.* Although it is impossible to be accurate because of the inherent ambiguity of the feature specification, one needs to record a ballpark estimate of effort. Do this in units of person-months, person-hours, dollars, or function points. Estimate of cost will be used during the triage process to decide how many features can be included in the product.
- *Use-dependency relationship among features.* Record when a feature makes no sense without another feature. For example, it makes no sense to have billing in place for a new system function if the function itself is not available. This dependency will be used during the triage process to ensure that the included features make sense as a whole.
- *Risk.* On a scale from 0 percent to 100 percent, record the probability one would fail to satisfy this feature if he or she tries. Risk will be used during the triage process to decide which features will be included in the product to achieve acceptable levels of development risk.

- *Development-dependency relationship among features.* Record when building a feature requires another feature to be built. For example, printing an accounts-receivable report is not possible unless the printer-interface software is available. This dependency will be used during the triage process to generate more accurate estimates of the development cost associated with the features selected for inclusion.
- *Inclusion flag.* Use this switch to record the decision to include or exclude this feature from the product. Do not just delete the feature's record from the database.

Figure 24.3 shows the list of features annotated with some of these.

Reqt Number	Requirement	Importance	Cost (Person-Hours)	Risk	Inclusion
1	System shall display up to eight simultaneous graphs.	HI	120	MED	X
2	System shall display expected sales by quarter.	MED	400	MED	
3	System shall display internal rate of return as a function of time.	HI	750	HI	
4	System shall allow users to change algorithm to convert function points to person-months.	MED	220	MED	
5	System shall show relationship of optimal schedule vs. desired schedule.	HI	600	LO	X
6	System shall display list of requirements along with priority, difficulty, and risk.	HI	800	LO	X
7	System shall allow users to delete existing requirements or add new requirements.	LO	200	LO	X
8	System shall display the degree of market penetration by market segment.	MED	700	LO	X
9	When users make a change to any view, all views shall be updated simultaneously.	HI	1,200	HI	X
10	System shall allow any mouse command to be made with menu options.	LO	140	MED	
11	System shall display 18 views as hot buttons on right side of screen.	LO	100	MED	X
12	When users select a hot button, system shall tile that view with existing views.	LO	200	HI	X
13	System shall allow users to add developers and maintainers.	HI	450	MED	X
14	All graphical items shall be selectable and editable.	HI	1,300	HI	X

Figure 24.3. Example Annotated List of Features.

REQUIREMENTS TRIAGE

Requirements triage is the process of deciding which features will be included in and which will be excluded from the current product. Triage should be done using the features, not detailed requirements. Triage cannot be mechanical; for example, one cannot produce a formula that is a function of the annotations listed previously and have some program produce a list of *the* features to be included. Instead, triage requires mature knowledge of technology, finance, project management, sales, and marketing. Since very few people have all this expertise, triage is generally a group decision. Some of the factors to consider are:

1. If a mass-market product, when is the market window's beginning, plateau, and end (Moore 1991)? If a customized product, when is the product needed?

2. If a mass-market product, when is competition expected to enter the market window?

3. If a mass-market product, what is the expected level of market share? If a customized product, what percentage of transactions will use the new system?

4. If a product for sale, what are the expected revenues? If a product for internal use, what are the expected revenue impacts or cost savings?

5. If a mass-market product, what is the relationship between market entry (that is, delivery date) and market capture (Reinertsen 1997)?

6. If a mass-market product, what is the relationship between feature mix (that is which requirements will the company endeavor to satisfy) and market capture? If a customized product, what is the relationship between feature mix (that is which requirements will the company endeavor to satisfy) and effect?

7. What effect will the selection of features have on delivery date?

8. What effect will the selection of features have on development cost?

9. What effect will the selection of features have on development risk?

10. If a mass-market product, given an expected market entry date, the resultant degree of market capture, and the expected price, how much development cost can be tolerated? If a custom product, given an expected delivery date, and the resultant degree of business effect, how much development cost can be tolerated?

One of the greatest ironies of triage is how the forces of development and marketing work against each other. To maximize revenues, marketing generally pushes for early market entry and many features. Development wants to reduce its risk, so it generally wants to reduce the feature mix and/or demand a longer development schedule. Both of these reduce revenues. Reduced revenue projections mean the company has fewer development dollars available, thus exacerbating the situation for both development and marketing.

In any case, the goal is to arrive at an optimal set of product features that is compatible with (1) a development schedule and cost; (2) tolerable levels of development risk; (3) the market window, entry date, and expected sales, (4) acceptable levels of quality; and (5) desired margins. All of this should be done with abstract, not detailed, solution-domain requirements.

REQUIREMENTS SPECIFICATION

Once specific features are selected for inclusion as a result of triage, it is time to elaborate on those features. Do not waste time elaborating on features whose satisfaction is being deferred. This step tends to be somewhat political because it is in a domain that both requirements writers and designers claim as their own. Requirements writers claim that such details describe external behavior of the solution system and therefore is in their domain. Designers claim that such details describe how the system works and should therefore be in their domain. Neither position is wrong. The author recommends that individuals agree that such detailed description of external behavior should follow feature description and precede definition of the software's internal architecture. Once individuals agree when they should do it, all that is left is agreeing on who will do it. Here, the best solution is often an interdisciplinary team. Some team members need profound knowledge of users and their needs; some members need profound knowledge of technology capabilities.

Two ways of recording requirements are to write them in a requirements specification or maintain them in a database. A *requirements specification* is a document (and the act of producing that document) that records all externally observable behaviors of a system to be built. These behaviors include specification of: (1) all the inputs from the environment into the system; (2) all the outputs from the system into its environment; (3) all features and functions of the system; (4) performance constraints on the system (like response time, reliability, maintainability, and so on); and (5) characteristics of the system's intended environment that might impact the system. The term "system" is used here to indicate any product to be built, regardless of whether it includes software, electronic hardware, mechanical devices, and so on. A *software requirements specification* is a requirements specification that describes a system composed exclusively of software (IEEE 1998). A *hardware requirements specification* describes a system composed exclusively of hardware, and a *system requirements specification* addresses hardware, software, and any other media, including human processes.

If the database route is selected, open a new database and then populate it with detailed requirements expanded from the abstract features that were selected for inclusion during triage. Either way, the individual requirements should exhibit a set of quality traits (Davis 1993):

- Unambiguous
- Correct
- Understandable
- Verifiable

- Concise
- Annotated by relative importance
- Annotated by relative stability
- Annotated by relative cost
- Annotated by relative risk
- At the right level of detail
- Precise
- Traced
- Cross-referenced

The collection of requirements (whether in a database or a document) should also exhibit these traits (Davis 1993):

- Complete
- Understandable
- Internally consistent
- Externally consistent
- Achievable
- Concise
- Design independent
- Traceable
- Modifiable
- Not redundant
- Organized

CONCLUSION

Requirements quality can be defined meaningfully only in the context of the role requirements play in the business. Any other definitions of requirements quality are myopic and ignore the primary reason for the existence of requirements. Measuring quality of requirements in terms of measures unrelated to business objectives is like measuring quality of a novel based on its grammar and spelling. The only way to judge a novel is to determine its effect on the readers; the only way to judge requirements is to determine their effect on the business.

Thus, the quality of requirements is actually the degree to which they are consistent with the company's strategic objectives, the degree to which they describe a system that can be built in the desired time frame with the desired resources, and the degree to which they satisfy customer needs.

REFERENCES

Andriole, S. 1992. *Rapid Application Prototyping.* Boston: QED Publishers.
Arthur, L. 1992. *Rapid Evolutionary Development.* New York: John Wiley and Sons.

Bickerton, M. 1992. *A Practitioner's Handbook of Requirements Engineering Methods*. Oxford, U.K.: Oxford University Press.

Booch, G. 1994. *Object-Oriented Analysis and Design*. Redwood City, Calif.: Benjamin/ Cummings.

Coad, P., and E. Yourdon. 1991. *Object-Oriented Analysis*. Englewood Cliffs, N.J.: Yourdon Press.

Couger, D. 1995. *Creative and Innovation in Information Systems*. London: International Thomson.

Davis, A. 1993. *Software Requirements*. Englewood Cliffs, N.J.: Prentice-Hall.

Davis, A., et al. 1993. Identifying and measuring quality in software requirements specification. *IEEE International Software Metrics Symposium*. Los Alamitos, Calif: IEEE Computer Press.

Davis, A. 1995. Software prototyping. *Advances in Computers* 10:39–63.

Davis, A. 1998. Software rechoirments. *IEEE Software* 15 (March/April): pp. 6, 8: reprinted in current book on page 115.

Dörner, D. 1989. *The Logic of Failure*, Reading, Mass.: Addison-Wesley.

Gause, D., and G. Weinberg. 1989. *Exploring Requirements*. New York: Dorset House.

Goguen, J., and M. Jirotka. 1994. *Requirements Engineering*. Boston, Mass.: Academic Press.

Institute for Electrical and Electronics Engineers. 1998. *IEEE Standard 830-1998. A Recommended Practice for Software Requirements Specification*. Piscataway, N.J.: IEEE.

Jacobson, I 1992. *Object-Oriented Software Engineering*. Reading, Mass.: Addison-Wesley.

Kotonya, G., and I. Sommerville. 1998 *Requirements Engineering: Processes and Techniques*. New York: John Wiley and Sons

Lehman, M. 1991. Software engineering: The software process and their support. *Software Engineering Journal 6*, no. 5 (September): 243–258.

Loucopoulos, P., and V. Karakostas. 1995. *System Requirements Engineering*. New York: McGraw Hill.

Marca, D., and G. McGowan. 1988. *SADT*. New York: McGraw Hill.

Moore, G. 1991. *Crossing the Chasm*. New York: Harper Collins.

Reinertsen, D. 1997. *Managing the Design Factory. A Product Developer's Toolkit*. New York: The Free Press.

Sommerville, I., and P. Sawyer. 1997. *Requirements Engineering: A Good Practice Guide*. New York: John Wiley and Sons.

Thayer, R., and M. Dorfman. 1997. *Software Requirements Engineering*. Los Alamitos, Calif: IEEE Computer Society Press.

Wieringa, R. 1996. *Requirements Engineering*. New York: John Wiley and Sons.

Yourdon, E. 1989. *Modern Structured Analysis*. Englewood Cliffs, N.J.: Yourdon Press.

SEEDS FOR DEBATE

1. Some requirements experts argue that you should avoid discussing any solutions during requirements elicitation. Others argue that discussing solutions during requirements elicitation should be encouraged. Take one of these po-

sitions and argue for why it is best. Then take the other and argue for why it is best.

2. Some requirements experts argue that you should document requirements as an annotated list. Others argue that they should be documented in "book" format, i.e., with chapters, paragraphs, and so on. Take one of these positions and argue for why it is best. Then take the other and argue for why it is best.

3. Some requirements experts argue that you should not do explicit requirements gathering (after all, when the customers see the product, they'll give you plenty of feedback!). Others argue that documenting requirements before building the system is essential. Take one of these positions and argue for why it is best. Then take the other and argue for why it is best.

4. How do the 24 attributes of a well-written requirements document starting on page 151 relate to the 9 key measures of quality starting on page 143?

Requirements Management Made Easy*

A. DAVIS AND A. ZWEIG

Requirements management has been discussed for at least 15 years. As a discipline and as a practice, it has become more and more complex. We have lost sight of the fact that requirements management was created to *simplify* product development, to reduce its cost, and reduce the inherent risk associated with building systems and software. Instead, requirements management has become yet one more chore, one more error-prone activity.

Requirements are those externally observable characteristics of a system that a user, buyer, customer, or other stakeholder desires to have present in the system. Requirements management is the set of activities encompassing the collection, control, analysis, filtering, and documentation of a system's requirements. Requirements management consists of three activities:

- *Requirements elicitation* is the art of understanding the needs of stakeholders, and collecting them in a repository for future analysis. The needs can be expressed quite abstractly and in terms of the problem; for example, "I want to reduce my billing error rates by at least 35 percent." And the needs can be expressed quite specifically and in terms of a solution; for example, "I want there to be a large red button on the operator's console." In all cases, these needs are called features.

- *Requirements triage* is the art of deciding which features are the appropriate features to include in the product. Rarely is it possible to satisfy every requested feature gathered from every stakeholder during the elicitation activity. Disparate priorities, limited resources, time-to-market demands, and risk intolerance are but a few reasons for this. Triage takes into consideration all the painful realities of the marketplace and makes the decision of which features we will build now, which will be built in the next release, and which will be deferred until even later.

*Originally published in *PM Network Magazine*, December 2000, pp. 61–63. © Project Management Institute. Inc., 2000, and all rights reserved. Reproduced with the permission of PMI.

Great Software Debates. By Alan M. Davis
ISBN 0-471-649880 © 2004 Institute of Electrical and Electronics Engineers.

- *Requirements specification* is the art of detailing the exact external behavior of a system that will address the features selected during the triage process. The level of detail of these requirements depends greatly on the situation. For example, if specifying a hand-held remote mouse, it might be sufficient to state, "The system shall contain three programmable buttons, corresponding to the three buttons on a standard three-button mouse." However, if the device were to be mounted in a holster and controlled by robotic fingers instead of being hand-held, then the statement of requirements for the buttons would need to be considerably more detailed.

According to the *Chaos Report* of the Standish Group (see Figure 25.1), 71 percent of all software development projects result in complete failure (that is, premature cancellation or shelfware upon completion). As reported by Capers Jones (*Patterns of Software Failure and Success,* International Thomson Press, 1996) and Steve McConnell (*Rapid Development: Taming Wild Software Schedules,* Microsoft Press, 1996), poor requirements management is generally considered to be one of the ma-

---

For a thourough analysis of the current state of the practice in software development, visit the Standish Group at *www.standishgroup.com/visitor* and read the *CHAOS Report.*

For access to many on-line resources on requirements management, visit The Requirements Place at *www.rmplace.org** or the Requirements Engineering Specialist Group, British Computer Society, *www.cs.york.ac.uk/bcs/resg/sites.*

To read about tools to support requirements management, visit the vendors:

- Requirements elicitation tools of GroupSystems.com, such as GroupSystems Meeting Room, can be found at [*www.groupsystems.com*].
- Requirements management and requirements triage tools of Omni-Vista Inc., such as OnYourMark Pro, can be found at *www.Omni-Vista.com.*[†]
- Requirements management tools of Quality Systems and Software Inc., such as DOORS and TechPlan, can be found at *www.qssinc.com.*[‡]
- Requirements management tools of Rational Software Corp., such as RequisitePro, can be found at *www.rational.com.*[**]
- Requirements management tools of Technology Builders, Inc., such as Caliber and Monte Carlo, can be found at *www.tbi.com/products/asq.*[§]

Online polling tools can be found at *www.app3.vanta.genet.com.*

[*Since this paper was written, the Requirements Place (a service of Omni-Vista, Inc., a now dissolved corporation) his closed. The best on-line bibliography for requirements management is at *web.uccs.edu/adavis/uccs/reqbib.htm.* At the time of this writing, the IEEE Computer Society was in the process of creating a new on-line portal for requirements management. Check *www.computer.org* to see if it is available now.]
[†Now closed. See history of company starting on page 81.]
[‡Since acquired by Telelogic, Inc. See *www.telelogic.com.*]
[**Since acquired by IBM. Inc. See either *www.rational.com* or *www.ibm.com.*]
[§Since acquired by Starbase. Inc., and subsequently acquired by Borland, Inc. See either *www.starbase.com* or *www borland.com.*]

Figure 25.1. Additional Resources for Requirements Management.

jor causes for product failure. After all, if we do a poor job of understanding our customers' needs, if we do a poor job of deciding the right features to build, and if we do a poor job of writing down what we think we want out of a system, how can we possibly expect a successful project? All the development techniques and tools and whatever level of process maturity you have achieved will be of no use to you if you are not building the "right" product.

REQUIREMENTS ELICITATION

Requirements elicitation is the art of determining all possible features that you might want to include in your next product. This is the time to be broad and inclusive. The candidates may come from potential customers, existing customers, customers of customers, users, marketing, sales win/loss reports, change requests, trouble reports, features rejected from earlier releases, internal development personnel, inventors/innovators within the company, management, and so on. We will use the term *stakeholder* to identify any of these sources of candidate features.

The techniques of requirements elicitation vary considerably depending on the situation. For example, if you have identified a set of key stakeholders that are committed to mutual success and are willing to help you help them, you might seriously consider facilitated group sessions (brainstorming). To conduct one of these sessions, assemble key stakeholders in a room with plenty of wall space. Announce the purpose of the meeting, to learn potential features for version x of product y. Advise participants that the goal is to synthesize the largest possible list of candidate features. To do so, participants should encourage each other as much as possible, and not criticize any idea. In many cases, the seemingly most outrageous idea can become the catalyst for the creation of the best ideas.

For another approach, especially useful when you are unable to isolate such stakeholders in one place, you might consider an analysis of needs, pains, and solutions in Michael Bosworth's *Solution Selling: Creating Buyers in Difficult Selling Markets* (McGraw Hill Professional Publishing, 1995). In this approach, the target customers are analyzed in detail. Their activities are modeled, their pains identified, the impacts of those pains explored, current solutions to those problems delineated, and the features that could alleviate those pains most effectively are listed. Obviously, the more information you can gather from "real" potential customers the better. But in any case, the idea of deriving candidate features from a thorough understanding of customers and their pains is difficult to argue with.

Other elicitation techniques include interviewing, as explored by Donald C. Gause and Gerald M. Weinberg (*Exploring Requirements: Quality Before Design*, Dorset House. 1989); ethnomethodological studies, as explored by Marina Jirotka [and] Joseph Goguen . . . (editors) (*Requirements Engineering. Social and Technical Issues (Computers and People)*, Academic Press, 1994); surveys; and requirements workshops, as explored by Dean Leffingwell [and] Don Widrig . . . (*Managing Software Requirements: A Unified Approach*, Addison-Wesley, 1999).

Interviewing is ideal when you have identified a reasonable-sized set of representative stakeholders and it is feasible to meet them each individually. It is also helpful when competitive, logistic, or political issues make it impractical to gather stakeholders in one place for brainstorming. Ethnomethodological studies try to eliminate preconceived notions of problems and solutions to those problems. The objective third-party observer in these studies eliminates the bias inherent in interviewing and brainstorming. Surveys work especially well when the population of representative stakeholders is too large to assemble in one place or too large to be interviewed. However, they only work well when you have very specific questions that you want answered. They eliminate the spontaneity inherent in interviews or brainstorming. Requirements workshops are a special case of brainstorming.

Tools are available to assist in a variety of elicitation techniques. For example, computer-assisted cooperative work (CSCW) tools such as those provided by GroupSystems.com (see Figure 25.1) can facilitate brainstorming sessions whether the stakeholders are co-located or are physically distributed (Kathy Spurr, Paul Layzell, Leslie Jennison, and Neil Richards, *Computer Support for Co-operative Work*, John Wiley and Sons, 1994). Forms such as Bosworth's pain sheet (while not automated, to our knowledge) can be used easily to organize and analyze pains, impacts, competition, and remedies. Online polling tools such as those by VantageNet (see Figure 25.1) can gather opinions of many stakeholders and be useful aids to performing surveys.

Requirements elicitation is the most difficult of the three requirements management activities because you are creating something from nothing.

The result of elicitation is a list of candidate features, each annotated with relative technical risk, an estimate of effort required to address the feature, and a relative priority or measure of importance from the customers' perspective. Tools exist to record this result. These range from basic tools such as word processors, spreadsheets, and databases, to simple requirements-specific repositories such as those by Omni-Vista, to more complex requirements management tools such as those by Rational, QSS, and Technology Builders, Inc. (see Figure 25.1 to find out where to learn more about these tools).

REQUIREMENTS TRIAGE

Requirements triage is the process of deciding precisely which product is to be built.

From a purely development manager's perspective, triage is quite simple. Development managers estimate the effort and time required to satisfy the stated features. They compare these with the budgets and schedules given to them. If they are not compatible, the development manager simply removes features until the work involved is compatible with the given schedule and budget! Presto! Triage is complete. Just one problem, however, removing features may have a positive effect on development risk, but this logic completely ignores impacts on market, price, revenue, and profit. See Donald Reinertsen's *Managing the Design Factory: The Product Developer's Toolkit* (Free Press, 1997) for a discussion of this phenomenon.

Thus, requirements triage *must* consider marketing, financial, *and* development factors.

The goal of requirements triage is quite straightforward:

- A set of features
- Which can be implemented using available resources and with acceptable levels of risk
- Which can be sold at an acceptable price to a known market
- In sufficient quantities to achieve
- Acceptable levels of revenue and profit
- And thus achieve a reasonable return on investment.

You will note that the naïve development manager's view of triage previously explained considers only the first two bullets.

These variables are at the disposal of the team performing triage:

- Add, delete, or change a feature
- Make the delivery date earlier or later
- Increase or decrease the resources applied to development
- Increase or decrease the price
- Increase or decrease costs of goods sold
- Increase or decrease the resources devoted to marketing and sales.

Triage, then, is the process of altering assumptions about these six variables until the results are acceptable. Once you arrive at an acceptable set of values for the variables, most companies produce a product plan. A *product plan* (also called a "business case") details.

- Which features are to be included
- Which market is to be addressed (or for internal developments, what internal problem or opportunity is to be addressed)
- What percentage of that market is likely to be successfully sold (or for internal developments, what percentage of potential users will actually use it)
- How many resources (and over what time frame) are required for development
- How much risk exists for development, sales, meeting the schedule, meeting the development budget
- How many units will be sold and at what price (or for internal developments, how many times will the system be used)
- How much revenue will be generated (or for internal developments, how much savings or revenue or reduction in cost or reduction in errors will result)

- What is the organization's return on investment

Tools are available to assist in some aspects of requirements triage. For example, tools by Omni-Vista* allow users to decide which requirements will enable the project to complete on schedule and within budget. Other Omni-Vista tools allow users to witness the effects of features, resources, and costs of goods sold on revenue, risk, profit, and return on investment. Primavera** has a tool that allows users to simulate over time the effects of making key product planning decisions. And QSS*** has a tool that allows users to compare the effects of decisions on technology, risk, and marketing.

REQUIREMENTS SPECIFICATION

Requirements specification is the task of documenting the precise external behavior of the system that is to be built. It takes the features selected during requirements triage and expands them into considerable detail. The primary purpose of this is to ensure that customers and developers have the same understanding of what is to be built; all developers have identical understanding of what is to be built; testers are testing for the same qualities that developers are building; and management is applying resources to the same set of tasks that the developers are performing. Traditionally, requirements have been documented in a requirements specification. More recently, they are being maintained in a database or repository of discrete requirements, rather than a formal document.

Numerous textbooks have been written to teach how to properly document requirements. For example, Dean Leffingwell [and Don Widrig] (as mentioned above), Alan Davis, *Software Requirements: Objects, Functions, and States* (Prentice Hall, 1993); and Ian Sommerville and Gerald Kotonya, *Requirements Engineering: Processes and Techniques* (John Wiley and Sons, 1998).

According to Alan Davis, et al., in "Identifying and Measuring Quality in Software Requirements Specification," (*IEEE International Software Metrics Symposium*, May 1993; reprinted in Dorfman and Thayer's *Software Requirements Engineering*, Second Edition, IEEE Computer Society Press, 1997), every documented requirement should be at least:

- Correct, in that it describes something the stakeholders want
- Consistent, in that it does not conflict with other requirements
- Unambiguous, in that it has only one possible interpretation
- Verifiable, in that there must exist some means by which we can check that the final system meets this requirement.

[*Now closed. See history of company starting on page 53.]
[**I believe that Primavera is no longer selling this particular tool. See www.primavera.com.]
[***Since acquired by Telelogic, Inc. See *www.telelogic.com*. Also, I believe that this particular tool is no longer available.]

Most requirements tools allow you to record the annotated requirements.

SUMMARY

Requirements management has somehow grown over the years to be more and more complex. In actuality, it is a straightforward set of activities. Performing each of these activities is quite simple. The most complex aspect of requirements management is doing the background investigation (for example, learning what effect on sales will occur when a feature is eliminated). However, these investigations must be done whether or not you perform requirements management; otherwise you embark on a risky business route. You invite your company to become a statistic, to become part of the 71 percent of projects that are never completed or become shelfware.

SEEDS FOR DEBATE

1. This essay organizes requirements management into three sets of activities: elicitation, triage, and specification. This is by no means universal. Find in the literature at least 5 other ways to organize requirements management*, and argue for why each of them is superior to the one given here.
2. Some readers will oppose my suggestion that doing requirements elicitation is anything like selling. I agree that there is little similarity to what most of us consider traditional selling. But read Michael Bosworth's *Solution Selling* for yourself. Then structure an argument for why the two are entirely different. Then construct another for why they are quite similar.
3. What happens if you try and change the variables listed in the center of page 159 and still cannot reach an acceptable decision?

---

*Or requirements engineering. You see, some authors (including my own earlier books and papers) use the term "requirements engineering" as the overall encompassing term, and requirements management is just one of the activities within the domain.

Elicitation: How Do the Experts Do It?*

A. DAVIS AND A. HICKEY

ABSTRACT

Requirements elicitation techniques are methods used by analysts to determine the needs of customers and users, so that systems can be built with a high probability of satisfying those needs. Analysts with extensive experience seem to be more successful than less experienced analysts in uncovering the user needs. Less experienced analysts often select a technique based on one of two reasons: (a) it is the only one they know, or (b) they think that a technique that worked well last time must surely be appropriate this time. This essay reports on the results of in-depth interviews with some of the world's most experienced analysts and careful analyses of the most recently published requirements books. These results demonstrate how expert analysts select elicitation techniques based on a variety of situational assessments.

INTRODUCTION

The success or failure of a system development effort depends heavily on the quality of the requirements [1]. The quality of the requirements is greatly influenced by techniques employed during requirements elicitation [2] because elicitation is all about learning the needs of user communities, and communicating those needs to system builders. How we select an appropriate elicitation technique out of the plethora of available techniques greatly affects the success or failure of requirements elicitation [2]. Meanwhile, we believe that requirements analysts who have extensive experience (and are considered to be masters of elicitation by most of us) seem to have the ability to select appropriate elicitation techniques on a regular basis. Since most practicing requirements analysts have less experience and are more journeyman than master, it is no surprise that over half the products created by the software industry fail to satisfy users' needs [3]. If we could improve the

---

*Adapted from Hickey, A., and A. Davis, "Elicitation and Technique Selection: How Do Experts Do It?" *International Conference on Requirements Engineering (RE03),* Los Alamitos, CA: IEEE Computer Society Press, 2003.

average analyst's ability to select elicitation techniques, we would most likely improve our record of successful products. Our industry should find ways of transferring these experts' knowledge of elicitation technique selection to the less experienced. This essay's mission is to begin that process by assembling and reporting in one place the elicitation technique selection processes employed by some of the experts.

Before beginning that process, however, it is important to recognize that unsatisfactory performance by practicing analysts could be caused by a variety of conditions. The poor performance could be (1) unrelated to elicitation techniques, (2) caused by lack of effective elicitation techniques [4], or (3) a result of poor use of available, effective elicitation techniques. If the latter is true, and effective elicitation techniques do in fact exist, then our product failures may be attributable to the skills of the practicing analysts. For example, perhaps technology transfer has not been taking place with the fault lying with the researchers, or techniques' inherent complexity, or insufficient time, or analysts' lack of interest in new techniques [5]. Or perhaps, analysts do really know the existence of elicitation techniques, but do not know how to apply them, or perhaps, analysts know *how* to apply the techniques, but fail to understand *when* to apply them. In all likelihood, it is a combination of all these conditions that cause projects to fail. Furthermore, some projects probably fail due to some subset of the conditions and others fail due to another subset of conditions. This essay applies when analysts do not know how or when to apply elicitation techniques. In particular, given that appropriate elicitation techniques are available, given that we believe that the best analysts are likely to be innovators or early adopters [6] with respect to these techniques, and given that we believe that more experienced analysts are more successful, what is it that these analysts are doing that can be captured and conveyed to less experienced analysts to improve their records of performance?

RELATED RESEARCH

Many articles [7, 8, 9] and books [10, 11, 12, 13, 14] have been written that describe a way to perform requirements elicitation. This is logical since so many practitioners are looking for a simple recipe for success—the *silver bullet* [15]—that will make all their elicitation problems go away. However, consensus already exists that one requirements elicitation technique cannot work for all situations [4, 16, 17, 18, 19, 20, 21, 22]. Almost all general requirements textbooks [11, 16, 17, 23, 24, 25, 26, 27] and some articles [28, 29. 30] enumerate and describe multiple requirements elicitation techniques.

Some writings, e.g., [16, 17, 23, 25, 26, 27, 31, 32], provide limited insight into *when* an elicitation technique might or might not be applicable. Maiden and Rugg [18] have performed the most extensive research concerning the relationship between conditions and elicitation techniques. In [18], the number of elicitation techniques analyzed was quite limited, and no attempt was made to assemble the collective wisdom of the most experienced analysts.

As far as we know, no research has been done to date concerning how experts actually select elicitation techniques. And no author has tried to compare and contrast the advice from experts using common terminology.

THE STATE OF REQUIREMENTS ELICITATION

Requirements elicitation is an iterative process [33]. At any moment, conditions cause the analyst to perform a specific step using a specific elicitation technique. The use of that technique changes the conditions, and thus at the very next moment, the analyst may want to do something else using a different technique. The result of elicitation is either a list of candidate requirements, or some kind of model of the solution system, or both.

Requirements elicitation is conducted today in a variety of contexts. For example, organizations that create software for sale to a mass-market, perform elicitation while doing market research [34]. Meanwhile, the responsibility of elicitation in organizations that either create custom software, or customize a base of software for sale to a single client, tends to fall on an interdisciplinary team representing the customer and developer. Finally, in IT organizations that build custom software (or procure off-the-shelf systems and produce glueware) for use within the same company, analysts serve as a bridge between the company's IT and operating divisions. In all cases, the responsibility of the individual doing elicitation is the same: to fully understand the needs of users and translate them into terminology understood by IT

Elicitation can be performed in a wide variety of ways, e.g., interviewing [35] collaborative workshops [36], prototyping [7, 37], modeling [10, 23, 24, 38], and observation [32]. It is the relationship between detailed characteristics of situations and elicitation technique selection that we are concerned with in this paper.

The requirements elicitation field has benefited from the presence of many expert consultants, who have had extensive experience in many projects, and who make themselves available to organizations endeavoring on a new or continuing systems effort. These individuals bring with them both successful and unsuccessful experience on previous projects, and either help perform elicitation, or advise the analysts on how they should perform elicitation. If involvement by individuals like those described above does improve a project's likelihood of success (a conjecture that we and their customers believe, but that has not necessarily been proven to be true), then it would behoove us all to better understand how such people approach elicitation.

RESEARCH METHOD

We are gathering expert opinions about how situational characteristics affect the selection of elicitation techniques using three methods:

1. *Participation in the Setting.* In some cases, our own experience, based on a combined total of 40+ years leading and participating in requirements elicita-

tion in industry, has shown repeatedly that certain situations demand the use of certain techniques. For example, when we as analysts have little experience in a domain, we tend to start by seeking knowledge from a subject matter expert.

2. *Document Analysis.* We have found preliminary information about how situations affect the selection of elicitation techniques from books written by Beck [39], Bray [21], Conger [40], Gause and Weinberg [35], Gottesdiener [36], Hay [41], Hoffer, et al. [42], Hooks and Farry [43], Hull, et al. [44], Kotonya and Sommerville [16], Laueson [25], Leffingwell and Widrig [26], Macauley [17], Robertson and Robertson [22], Sommerville and Sawyer [45], Wiegers [27], Windle and Abreo [46], and Young [47], as well as articles written by Goguen and Linde [32], Hudlicka [28], and Maiden and Rugg [18].

3. *In-Depth Interviews with Experts.* In-depth interviewing is ideally suited for gaining understanding of people's behavior, its context, and the meaning they make of that behavior [48, 49]. Johnson [50] states that it is likely the best approach "where the knowledge sought is often taken for granted and not readily articulated by most" [p. 105] as it is in this case where experts rely on tacit [51] knowledge when selecting elicitation techniques.

Based on the information gathered from these sources, we plan to develop a set of tentative relationships among situational characteristics and techniques. We then plan to validate these relationships through further interviews and surveys, and finally capture the results in a tool, which can be used by less-experienced analysts who wish to behave more like experts.

This paper reports on the results of

1. interviews with eleven experts*, Grady Booch, Larry Constantine, Tom DeMarco, Don Gause, Ellen Gottesdiener, Tim Lister, Lucy Lockwood, Don Reifer, Suzanne Robertson, Karl Wiegers, and Ed Yourdon; and

2. extraction of key recommendations from fifteen requirements-related books written by Beck [39], Bray [21], Conger [40], Gottesdiener [36], Hay [41], Hoffer, et al. [42], Hull, et al. [44], Kotonya and Sommerville [16], Laueson [25], Leffingwell and Widrig [26], Robertson and Robertson [22], Sommerville and Sawyer [45], Wiegers [27], Windle and Abreo [46], and Young [47].

In the remainder of this paper, we will not associate specific opinions with any individual or book**. We will also refer to any of the twenty-six sources as that from all "expert" or "expert analyst" without regard to whether the source of information

*Most practitioners and researchers consider these individuals to be representative of elicitation experts. However, almost every one of the eleven refused to acknowledge that they were indeed *experts*. They agreed they had much experience, but felt that they were also learning every day how to perform elicitation effectively.
**As part of this, we have used the pronoun "he" for all references to the analysts or their authored works. We do not mean to imply the genders of the individuals.

was an interview or a book. You will note that in three cases, an individual was interviewed who was also an author of an analyzed book. We do not believe that this leads to inaccurate or biased results because our interviews with these individuals explicitly avoided asking questions for which we could extract answers from their books.

INTERVIEW DETAILS

The interview subjects represent a subset of the list of thirty experts we assembled using the following criteria (a) at least five year's experience performing analysis or elicitation in industry as a consultant or employee, and (b) author of a major book or many articles on requirements. Combined, the eleven individuals have over 285 years experience analyzing requirements on more than 700 projects. Eight of the experts provided more detailed information for approximately 300 of their projects. These projects spanned many domains: 14% were embedded systems, 56% were business information systems, 14% were government systems, and 16% were systems software. Of these projects, 33% were intended for external sale, 64% were intended for internal use, and 3% unknown. Finally, 88% were mostly custom development, 8% were primarily commercial off-the-shelf, and 4% unknown. All considered themselves to be primarily "doers" as opposed to "thinkers" or "researchers." All have had extensive elicitation experience in multiple countries.

The interview goal was to understand how each expert performs elicitation. Interviews were held from August 2002 through June 2003. Each expert completed a brief pre-interview questionnaire summarizing their elicitation experience, the types of projects on which they had worked and the elicitation techniques they were familiar with and had used. Recommended by Seidman [48], these "focused life histories" enabled us to compare our interviewees to our desired sample. The expert's responses also served as the basis for follow-up questions. Each interview started the same way:

1. A short period of informal social discussion.
2. A brief introduction to our research goals, definitions, research approach, and interview style.
3. An open-ended query to the interviewee along the line of "so, can you tell us how you perform elicitation?"

What ensued differed significantly from interview to interview. In response to our open-ended question, some of the experts told us "stories" of how they performed elicitation in a variety of situations. Others told us *the* way they always performed elicitation. And still others responded with a description of the conditions they consider when deciding upon an optimal approach.

- When the interviewee told us stories, we carefully listened for aspects of the stories that might trigger particular elicitation paths. When we suspected this, we asked the interviewee for verification by either asking directly, "Was it *this* situation that inspired you to do that?" or the contrapositive, "If *this* situation were not true, would you still have chosen to do that?"

- When the interviewee told us *the* way he always performed elicitation, we would listen and take careful notes. Then we'd carefully pose variations to the assumptions that the interviewee made, and invariably his response would be something like, "Of course if *that* were true, I wouldn't do elicitation the same way." We thus discovered that although some experts think of themselves as practitioners of just *one* means of performing elicitation, they really have a *default* means of doing elicitation, and anomalous conditions result in alternative approaches.

- When interviewees told us conditions under which they would take one route or another, we listened carefully and took notes.

To ensure that we received some normalized data from the interviews, we also posed the same "situations" to all the interviewees, and asked them to describe how they would approach the situation.

We independently analyzed the interview results. An open coding method [52, 53] was used; every elicitation technique and situation mentioned by the experts was coded. We then compared our respective analyses to validate our observations. Finally, we developed a comprehensive set of lessons learned from the expert interviews. These results are reported later in this paper.

BOOK DETAILS

The books were selected based on the following criteria: (a) must contain explicit advice concerning elicitation technique selection, (b) must be recognized as a major requirements book, (c) should be a book written by individuals who were not interviewed, but we allowed selected exceptions when there was insufficient time during the interview to explore all the facets of elicitation technique selection covered in the books.

Both authors analyzed the fifteen books independently. Whenever we detected an implication that an elicitation technique was applicable in specific circumstances, we coded the data in a simple four-column format: (a) author, (b) book title, (b) conditions under which a technique was applicable, and (d) the name of the technique. To ensure accuracy, we verified consistency between our independently extracted results.

LESSONS LEARNED

This section summarizes guidance explicitly stated by the experts on when to use elicitation techniques. Whenever counts are provided (e.g., "five of twenty-six"), the reader should assume the other experts did not mention or write about that technique, not that they necessarily disagreed with the others.

Collaborative Sessions. Most of the experts stressed the effectiveness of gathering multiple stakeholders in a single room to conduct a collaborative session. Nine stated that collaborative sessions should always be conducted. Many others expressed the conditions under which they would use collaborative sessions. For example,

- Two when there is general belief that "missed opportunities" exist.
- One when there is conflict.
- Two when inventing new, complex products.
- One when no current system exists.

And one *avoids* group meetings when turf wars or heavy politics are present. In general, it appears that collaborative sessions are seen by most to be a standard or default approach for eliciting requirements.

Interviewing. Seventeen of the experts reported that they regularly (four said always) sit down with one or more key stakeholders to ask questions. Others expressed the conditions under which they would use interviews. For example,

- One when heavy politics are present.
- One in the presence of conflict.
- One when senior management has a dream, and employees consider him crazy.
- Two when there are relatively few stakeholders.
- One on "small projects" only.
- One when no current system exists.
- One prior to collaborative sessions.

Another said that interviewing should never be relied upon as the primary elicitation technique due to the ever-presence of tacit knowledge. In general, interviews appear to be widely used, primarily to surface new information, or to uncover conflicts or politics.

Ethnography. Many of the experts highlighted ethnographic techniques, such as observation of users, as extremely effective. However, all added caveats:

- Four when there is an existing system.
- One when users are too busy to be involved in interviews, group sessions, or questionnaires.
- One to assess political and power relationships.
- One when a relatively small number of stakeholders exist.
- Two when tasks within an existing system have become routine.
- Three when trying to uncover discrepancies between "as defined" processes and "as performed" processes.

Another recommended that analysts take a temporary assignment (also called "apprenticeship") as the user/customer rather than just observing. All in all, many of the analysts seemed to acknowledge that stakeholders should be observed when feasible.

Models. Almost all of the experts mentioned the critical role played by models, such as data flow diagrams (DFD) [10], statecharts [54], or the Unified Modeling Language (UML) [55], in elicitation.
    Nine of the experts had favorite models; for example,

- Three always used time-ordered sequences of events to capture a typical interaction between the system and the systems or people it interfaces with,*
- One always used data flow diagrams,
- Three *usually* used data flow diagrams (of these, two tended to model the current business rules, while the other tended to model the new or proposed system),
- One constructed user role models and task models, and
- Two always created models of the current situation—one using data flow diagrams and scenarios, and the other using use cases, scenarios, or stories.

Six emphasized the need to employ multiple models as a means to better understand customers' problems. One of the analysts cautioned to use only those models that the stakeholders find palatable. Three of the analysts were able to state conditions under which they would use certain approaches. In particular:

- One builds a data model, probably ER diagrams [56], for database-intensive applications or systems to be implemented using object-oriented approaches.
- Another uses data dictionaries whenever there are multiple, diverse, and autonomous stakeholders.
- Another likes to model (using storyboards) when few requirements are known, or when users do not know what they want.
- One models the viewpoints of each stakeholder separately and then integrates them. In addition, he constructs mathematical models to capture the modes of a system.
- Yet another models using scenarios, but only after the basic requirements are understood.
- And the last uses scenarios when there is a desire to stay practical.

In summary, analysts seem to rely on models in almost every situation. Although historically, modeling was used as *the* elicitation technique, more and more analysts

---

*Many terms are used to represent this concept, or to represent examples of this concept, including use cases, scenarios, stories, stimulus-response sequences, storyboards, and so on.

are now seeing modeling as a means to (a) facilitate communication, (b) uncover missing information, (c) organize information gathered from other elicitation techniques, and (d) uncover inconsistencies.

Issues List.* Four of the experts emphasized the need to maintain a list of outstanding issues on the side (so that the issues are not forgotten and can be re-surfaced later). Regardless of what technique is being used, new issues are simply appended to the list as they arise. This enables the team to stay focused and not follow the tangent induced by the new issue. Two of these recommended that every meeting end with the assignment of open issues to members of the team. Although only four mentioned issues lists per se, we suspect that most of the analysts actually employ them. We will need more data to verify this.

Questionnaires. Only seven of the twenty-six experts mentioned questionnaires or surveys. All added caveats:

- One when dealing with a fairly concrete problem.
- One for market research.
- One when questions could be well-established in advance.
- One when there are a very large number of stakeholders.
- Two more emphasized the need to use interviews and questionnaires together, but differed in the recommended order; one uses questionnaires exclusively to validate the results of previously conducted interviews, while the other uses interviews with key stakeholders to validate the results of the questionnaires.

Prototyping. Thirteen of the experts see prototyping as an elicitation technique. Eleven were strong supporters of the important role that prototyping plays in helping to uncover requirements. Two expressed concerns:

- One warned not to do rapid prototyping unless you really believe it would be rapid.
- The other suggested prototyping only when there is mutual trust.

Extreme Programming. Extreme Programming [57] calls for little up-front explicit elicitation, and replaces it with an omni-present customer, co-located with the development team, who can answer questions that arise during development. Only two analysts recommended this approach, with one adding the caveat that it be used when the domain is undergoing enormous and constant flux. Another emphasized the need to have at least monthly builds in order to contain the risk of incorrect or changing requirements; this is not as "extreme" as extreme programming.

*Also called a "parking lot"

DISCUSSION

Overall, the expert interviews and book reviews resulted in an extremely rich source of information about requirements elicitation and technique selection. The structure and flow of the interviews also provided information, since they were a form of elicitation as well. For example, when asked how they performed elicitation, many of the experts told stories about their elicitation projects. This demonstrates the power of stories (i.e., scenarios, use cases) in elicitation. However, it is also interesting to note, that the stories the experts chose to tell us always described their standard, default elicitation approach. While this may have been a result of our specific question, it may also be an indicator that individuals tend to choose common stories and must be prompted for exceptions. Finally, while the focus of our research is on technique selection, the experts were just as likely to describe the information they were seeking as the specific technique they would use. From this we can conclude that elicitation technique selection is not only a function of situational characteristics, but is also a function of what information (requirements) is still needed [33].

Even though we have interviewed only a small sample of experts and reviewed only fifteen books, some general theories of elicitation technique selection, grounded in the data [52, 53] have already emerged:

- Some expert analysts work best with their default technique, and only vary from it under extenuating circumstances. Instead of changing techniques under less stringent circumstances, they tend to simply make small mid-course corrections to their default technique when and where appropriate.
- For each elicitation technique, there exists a specific, unique, small set of predicates concerning situational characteristics that drive experts to seriously consider that technique. We call these "Major Drivers," as shown in Figure 26.1. For driving a car, an example is a green light. For collaborative sessions, major drivers are multiple stakeholders, disparate needs, and a demand to reach consensus before proceeding.
- For each elicitation technique, there exists a set of additional predicates which if true cause experts to alter their primary choice. We call these "Anomalies," as shown in Figure 26.1. For driving a car, this includes an ambulance in the intersection. For collaborative sessions, anomalies include stakeholders who cannot know of each other's existence, geographical distribution of stakeholders or no suitable venue (and no distributed meeting technology available), and not enough time to adequately prepare for the session.
- For each elicitation technique, there exists a set of basic analyst skills that must be present or the technique will not be effective. If not present, the analyst will once again need to alter the prevailing tendency to select the original technique indicated by the major drivers. We call these "Prerequisite Skills," as shown in Figure 26.1. For driving a car, this includes the ability to

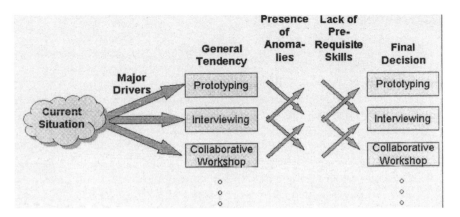

Figure 26.1. Drivers of Elicitation Techniques.

press the accelerator and brake pedals. For collaborative sessions, the prerequisite skills include communication, leadership, and the ability to facilitate meetings.

- For each elicitation technique, there exists a set of additional skills that are not universally needed, but that come into play during the technique's execution without pro knowledge. We call these skills "Success Enhancers." For driving a car, this includes defensive driving. For collaborative sessions, these include modeling, conflict resolution, and creativity skills.

LIMITATIONS

The research reported herein has some limitations:

- These interviews of eleven experts and analyses of fifteen books may not (a) be representative of all expert analyst opinions, (b) capture all their expertise, or (c) provide sufficient coverage of all situations and techniques. We feel that we have not yet reached the point of "theoretical saturation" [53] where we have learned all we need, so we are planning additional interviews.
- Although we are both very experienced interviewers, our style of interviewing and previous experience may have biased the responses given by the subjects. We have tried to limit this bias through use of the interview protocol [21], delaying hypotheses formulation until after the interviews [52, 53], and following research-based interviewing guidelines.
- A difference may exist between what these experts *say* they do, and what they actually *do* do. The best way to determine this is to observe experts doing elicitation rather than just asking them what they would do.

FUTURE RESEARCH

The study reported in this essay represents the results from eleven interviews and fifteen books. Plans are underway to extend this work to include additional interviews and readings. Because of the preeminence of the eleven analysts interviewed, we felt it important to report their unique and insightful comments. Other research that can be performed based on this paper include:

- Integrate the results of these interviews and book reviews with (a) recommendations made by key articles, and (b) our own experiences as analysts.
- More fully understand the full range of situational characteristics that could affect technique selection. This work has begun [58].
- Create a more complete faceted classification of elicitation techniques. This work has also begun [58].
- Pivot the results reported in this essay, i.e., rather than discuss the conditions necessary to drive an elicitation technique, we need to discuss the technique alternatives that make sense under sets of conditions.
- Creation of a tool that uses the knowledge of the experts to map situational characteristics into the set of appropriate elicitation techniques.

CONCLUSIONS AND CONTRIBUTIONS

We can reach the following conclusions about the use of elicitation techniques:

- Many expert analysts have a standard technique that they have used for many years. For many, this works fine because they tend to work in the same domains with similar situations repeatedly.
- When faced with new situations or new domains, many of the expert analysts simply alter their standard approach (while still maintaining its name) to accommodate the situation rather than conscript an alternate technique. This phenomenon might cause the casual observer to conclude incorrectly that these experts think that "one size fits all."
- Almost all the experts concur that collaborative workshops and interviewing are the two key techniques.
- Most of the experts are more motivated by "producing *this* model" than "following *this* technique" to produce this model.
- Creation of models (perhaps multiple models) seems to aid analysts in fully comprehending a situation and in communicating with stakeholders. Almost all the analysts use them.
- For the experts (but probably not for less experienced analysts), selecting a modeling notation that they are most comfortable with appears to be a good choice, but that notation must be palatable to the users.

- Many experts assess early the immediate gaps in knowledge among the stakeholders, and deliberately direct the elicitation toward achieving these intermediate goals. Examples might include particular non-behavioral requirements, user interfaces, and database contents. This often drives the expert analyst toward specific modeling notations to supplement the elicitation technique.

While the state of our research has not allowed us to reach definitive conclusions on all situations and techniques, this essay is an important contribution to understanding the techniques that experts use during elicitation and the situational factors they consider when choosing those techniques.

REFERENCES

[1] Jones, C., *Patterns of Software Failure and Success,* Boston: International Thomson Comp Press, 1996.

[2] Hickey, A., and A. Davis, "The Role of Requirements Elicitation Techniques in Achieving Software Quality," *Reqts Eng Workshop: Foundations for Software Quality (REFSQ),* 2002.

[3] The Standish Group, "The Chaos Report," 1995, and "Chaos: A Recipe for Success." 1999, www.standishgroup.com.

[4] Davis, A., and A. Hickey, "Requirements Researchers: Do We Practice What We Preach," *Req Eng J 2002;* 7, pp. 107–111; reprinted in current book on page 199.

[5] Hickey, A., and A. Davis, "Requirements Elicitation Techniques: Analyzing the Gap Between Technology Availability and Technology Use," *Journal of Comparative Technology Transfer and Society, 1,* 3 (December 2003), pp. 279–304.

[6] Moore, G., *Crossing the Chasm,* New York: HarperCollins, 1991.

[7] Davis, A., "Operational Prototyping: A New Development Approach," *IEEE Software, 9,* 5(September 1992), pp. 70–78.

[8] Ross, D., "Structured Analysis (SA): A Language for Communicating Ideas," *IEEE Trans on Software Eng, 3,* 1 (January 1977), pp. 16–34.

[9] Heninger, K., "Specifying Software Requirements for Complex Systems: New Techniques and their Application," *IEEE Trans on Soft Eng, 6,* 1 (January 1980), pp. 2–12.

[10] DeMarco, T., *Structured Analysis and System Specification,* Upper Saddle River, NJ: Prentice-Hall, 1979.

[11] Gause, D., and G. Weinberg, *Are Your Lights On?,* New York: Dorset House, 1990.

[12] Wood, J., and D. Silver, *Joint Application Development,* New York: John Wiley, 1995.

[13] Jackson, M., *Problem Frames,* Reading, MA: Addison-Wesley, 2001.

[14] Booch, G., *Object-Oriented Analysis and Design.* Redwood City, CA: Benjamin/Cummings Publishing Co., 1994.

[15] Brooks, F., "No Silver Bullet—Essence and Accidents of Software Engineering," *Computer, 20,* 4 (April 1987), pp. 10–19.

[16] Kotonya, G., and I. Sommerville, *Requirements Engineering,* New York: John Wiley, 1998.

[17] Macaulay, L., *Requirements Engineering*, New York: Springer, 1996.

[18] Maiden, N., and G. Rugg, "ACRE: Selecting Methods for Requirements Acquisition," *Software Eng J, 11*, 5 (May 1996), pp. 183–192.

[19] Glass, R., "Searching for the Holy Grail of Software Engineering," *Comm ACM, 45*, 5 (May 2002), pp. 15–16.

[20] Yadav, S., et al. "Comparison of Analysis Techniques for Information Requirements Determination," *Comm ACM, 31*, 9 (September 1988), pp. 1090–1097.

[21] Bray, I., *Introduction to Requirements Engineering*, Harlow, UK: Addison Wesley, 2002.

[22] Robertson, S., and J. Robertson, *Mastering the Requirements Process*, Harlow, UK: Addison-Wesley, 1999.

[23] Davis, A., *Software Requirements: Objects, Functions and States*, Upper Saddle River, NJ: Prentice-Hall, 1993.

[24] Wieringa, R., *Requirements Engineering*. New York: John Wiley, 1996.

[25] Lauesen, S., *Software Requirements: Styles and Techniques*. Harlow, UK: Addison-Wesley, 2002.

[26] Leffingwell, D., and D. Widrig, *Managing Software Requirements*, Reading, MA: Addison-Wesley, 2000.

[27] Wiegers, K., *Software Requirements*. Redmond, WA: Microsoft Press, 1999.

[28] Hudlicka, E., "Requirements Elicitation with Indirect Knowledge Elicitation Techniques: Comparison of Three Methods," *Intl Conf on Req Eng (ICRE)*, Los Alamitos, CA: IEEE CS Press, 1996, pp. 4–11.

[29] Byrd, T., et al., "A Synthesis of Research on Requirements Analysis and Knowledge Acquisition Techniques," *MIS Quarterly, 16*, 1 (January 1992), pp. 117–138.

[30] Couger, D., "Evolution of Business System Analysis Techniques," *ACM Comp Surv, 5*, 3 (March 1973), pp. 167–198.

[31] Davis, A., "A Taxonomy for the Early Stages of the Software Development Life Cycle," *J of Sys and Software, 8*, 4 (April 1988), pp. 297–311.

[32] Goguen, J., and C. Linde, "Software Requirements Analysis and Specification in Europe: An Overview," *First Intl Symp on Req Eng*, Los Alamitos, CA: IEEE Comp Soc Press, 1993, pp. 152–164.

[33] Hickey, A., and A. Davis, "A Unified Model of Requirements Elicitation," *Journal of Management Information Systems, 20*, 4 (Spring 2004), pp. 65–85.

[34] McDaniel, C., and R. Gates, *Marketing Research Essentials*. St. Paul, MN: West Publishing, 1998.

[35] Gause, D., and G. Weinberg, *Exploring Requirements: Quality before Design*. New York: Dorset House, 1989.

[36] Gottesdiener, E., *Requirements by Collaboration*. Reading, MA: Addison-Wesley, 2002.

[37] Davis, A., "Software Prototyping," *Advances in Computers, 40* (1995), New York: Academic Press, pp. 39–63.

[38] Kowal, J., *Behavior Models*. Upper Saddle River, NJ: Prentice-Hall 1992

[39] Beck, K., *Extreme Programming Explained*. Reading, MA: Addison Wesley, 2000.

[40] Conger, S., *The New Software Engineering*. Belmont, CA: Wadsworth, 1994.

[41] Hay, D., *Requirements Analysis: From Business Views to Architecture*. Upper Saddle River, NJ: Prentice-Hall, 2003.

[42] Hoffer, J., et al., *Modern Systems Analysis and Design*. Upper Saddle River, NJ: Prentice-Hall, 2002.

[43] Hooks, I., and K. Farry, *Customer-Centered Products: Creating Successful Products through Smart Requirements Management*. New York: AMACOM, 2001.

[44] Hull, E., et al., *Requirements Engineering*. Berlin: Springer Verlag, 2002.

[45] Sommerville, I., and P. Sawyer, *Requirements Engineering: A Good Practice Guide*. New York: John Wiley, 1997.

[46] Windle, D., and L. Abreo, *Software Requirements Using the Unified Process*. Upper Saddle River, NJ: Prentice-Hall, 2003.

[47] Young, R., *Effective Requirements Practices*. Reading, MA: Addison Wesley, 2001.

[48] Seidman, I., *Interviewing as Qualitative Research: A Guide for Researchers' in Education and the Social Sciences*, 2nd edition. New York: Teachers College Press, 1998.

[49] Warren, C., "Qualitative Interviewing," in J. Gubrium and J. Holstein (eds.), *Handbook of Interview Research: Context and Method*. Thousand Oaks, CA: Sage, 2002, pp. 83–101.

[50] Johnson, J., "In-Depth Interviewing," in J. Gubrium and J. Holstein (eds.), *Handbook of Interview Research: Context and Method*. Thousand Oaks, CA: Sage, 2002, pp. 103–119.

[51] Polanyi, M., *Tacit Dimension*. New York: Doubleday, 1966.

[52] Strauss, A., and J. Corbin, *Basics of Qualitative Research*, 2nd edition. Thousand Oaks, CA: Sage, 1998.

[53] Glaser. B., and A. Strauss, *The Discovery of Grounded Theory: Strategies for Qualitative Research*. New York: Aldine, 1967.

[54] Harel, D., "Statecharts: A Visual Formalism for Complex Systems," *Sci of Comp Prog*, 8 (1987), pp. 231–274.

[55] Rational Software Corporation, *UML Summary*, Jan 1997.

[56] Chen, P., "The Entity-Relationship Model: Toward a Unifying View of Data," *ACM Trans on Database Sys, 1,* 1 (1977), pp. 9–36.

[57] Beck, K., *Extreme Programming Explained*. Reading, MA: Addison Wesley 2000.

[58] Hickey, Ann, and A. Davis, "A Tale of Two Ontologies: A Basis for Systems Analysis Technique Selection," *Americas Conf on Info Sys (AMCIS)*, 2003.

SEEDS FOR DEBATE

1. Argue the position that understanding how expert analysts perform elicitation in various situations is essential for the success of less experienced analysts. Next argue that it is irrelevant.

2. Assemble an argument in favor of "There are *so many* factors that influence the success and failure of a project that the choice of elicitation technique is in the noise." Then argue in favor of the statement "If a project does not start out on the right foot, it cannot possibly succeed. Since a project starts with elicitation technique selection, and it is responsible for determining *what* the system will do, a project can succeed only when an appropriate elicitation technique is selected."

3. Argue for why you believe the data collection method used in this essay is flawed. Now defend it.

4. Very few of the experts seemed to think that the requirements techniques espoused by XP were effective. Why do you think that is the case? Is it because the wrong experts were interviewed? Are they just from a different school? Are the all too old to appreciate better ways of doing things?

5. Many of the experts seem to have a standard default elicitation technique. Will that work for us less experienced analysts?

6. What is it about models that make them so universally applicable?

7. Can you enumerate other caveats that should be stated for any of the elicitation techniques?

Requirements Are But a Snapshot in Time

THE ELUSIVE BASELINE

On most software development projects, an attempt is made to "baseline" the requirements prior to design. A baseline is defined as a "specification . . . that has been formally reviewed and agreed upon, that thereafter serves as the basis for further development, and that can be changed only through formal change control procedures." [1] Creating a requirements baseline is a worthwhile goal, and one to which all projects should aspire. However, once the baseline is signed off, it is almost impossible to make changes to it without a major confrontation. In company after company, I have witnessed some variation of the following dialog:

MARKETING: "We need to add these three new requirements."

DEVELOPMENT: "Sorry, but we can't do it. It is impossible unless we extend the delivery date."

MARKETING: "But the date is fixed. The customers expect the product on time. Our company's reputation is on the line."

DEVELOPMENT: "Then we cannot add the requirements!"

MARKETING: "How about if we remove these five other requirements from the baseline?"

DEVELOPMENT: "If we add the three requirements, the product will be a few weeks late. But if we add the three requirements *and* try to remove those other five, the product will be even later."

The end result is that each party learns to distrust the other party. Development feels that marketing is "always changing the requirements," and marketing feels that development "can never be counted on to deliver on time."

The root of this problem lies way back in the way that we agree to requirements in the first place.

Great Software Debates. By Alan M. Davis
ISBN 0-471-649880 © 2004 Institute of Electrical and Electronics Engineers.

CHANGING REQUIREMENTS

The real customer's real needs are in constant flux. Marketing departments know this. Perhaps the reason that developers fail to recognize this is that we always model requirements activities as a *phase* in a process model. In reality, it is ongoing, as shown in Figure 27.1. Regardless of whether software is being constructed in one large release (as shown in the figure) or in a series of iterations (where the figure represents just one iteration), an organization cannot afford to ever stop eliciting requirements from the customers. This is not an option. Customers' needs change. Our perceptions of their needs change. The problems that customers face are changing. We cannot stop the hands of time. Burying our heads in the sands dooms us to failure. If we ignore the changes we will end up building a useless system. And building a useless system is worse than building no system at all.

Let's differentiate for a minute between the customers' actual needs and the documented requirements. As shown in Figure 27.2, the needs are in constant flux (i.e., $t_0, t_1 \ldots$) [2]. If we use our original knowledge of those needs (t_0) to document the requirements at the beginning of the project, and do not allow them to change, we guarantee that the as-built product will fail to satisfy the customers current needs (t_i). The fact that it satisfies the as-documented requirements is a source of satisfaction for some, especially those driven by the "letter of the law" rather than the "spirit of the law." After all, you cannot be sued (at least not successfully) by customers if you meet the as-documented requirements and the contract stipulates that you must do so. However, customers are likely to be more excited with a system that meets their needs than one that prevents them from suing the development group. So what do we do?

If we allow the documented requirements to change every time the needs change, as shown in Figure 27.3, we have anarchy, and the product will never be completed, let alone on time. So neither extreme is useful. The right answer is

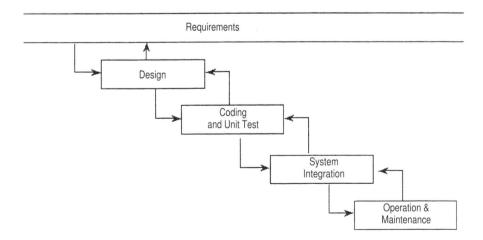

Figure 27.1. Requirements Activities Are Ongoing.

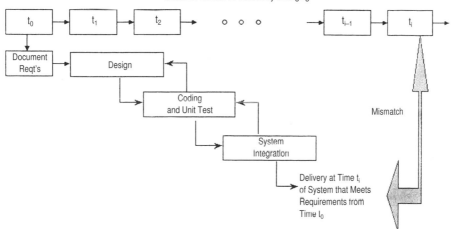

Figure 27.2. Requirements Mismatch.

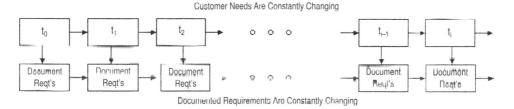

Figure 27.3. We Cannot Change Requirements Every Time Needs Change.

moderation, understanding, mutual respect, and common sense. As a guide, Young [3] suggests that requirements change be limited to less than ½% per month (or 6% per year).

AGREEING TO REQUIREMENTS

When requirements are documented, there is usually an official event. When software is being built for a specific customer (internal or external), both the customer and the development organizations participate. When software is being built for mass sale to a market, representatives of marketing and development participate. In many companies, the parties are required to sign the document. In some companies, no signatures are required, but the parties are agreeing via a handshake. After projects go awry, I am occasionally hired as a consultant to uncover the causes of the disaster and to recommend solutions. On many occasions, I have discovered that the signature page (if any) in the requirements document simply contains a set of signatures, period. The best I can determine, these signatures mean, "The following parties hereby agree that they have signed this document." What does that mean? Absolutely nothing!

I recommend that parties signing the document agree to a specific set of terms and conditions. For example,

- Development agrees to deliver a product satisfying all these requirements with sufficient quality on this date: _____.
- Finance and/or management agrees to not reduce total funding/staffing of this project below _____.
- We agree that the requirements documented herein represent the best set of requirements for which we can now agree to, and represents the best balance* between requirements, schedule, and resources.
- We agree that if changes to these requirements are necessary prior to product delivery, schedules and/or resources will be changed accordingly so that we once again achieve the best balance between requirements, schedule, and resources.
- We agree that if changes to either budget/staffing or desired product delivery date are necessary, requirements will be changed accordingly so that we once again achieve the best balance between requirements, schedule, and resources.

The advantages of such an agreement are that all parties will acknowledge before the project begins that (a) requirements as documented are not perfect and that changes are inevitable, and (b) when requirements change, schedule and/or budget will need to be revisited. This prevents development from getting surprised by changes, and prevents marketing and/or customers from expecting to be able to add new requirements without significant implications.

WHEN CHANGES OCCUR

Some requirements changes increase entropy, and others decrease entropy. Pohl [5] has written an excellent treatise concerning how requirements converge through time toward decreased entropy. Specifically, he describes three dimensions of that convergence: degree of specification (i.e., how much has been recorded), degree of representation (i.e., how formally is it described), and degree of agreement (i.e., how much of it is agreed to by all stakeholders). In response to changing user needs, the position of a requirement along the axis of agreement may increase while moving the overall baseline toward increasing entropy. The trick is to recognize that needs change, that requirements that were correct yesterday may no longer be correct today and that we must recover in a constructive fashion.

*See [4] for a description of how the balance is reached.

When a need (or our perception of a need) changes, we have a few alternatives:

- Accept the change for the current release and delay its planned delivery date.
- Accept the change for a future release and maintain the current release's planned delivery date.
- Accept the change for the current release, maintain its planned delivery date, but everybody now understands that the probability of a successful delivery on schedule is lower than before. The exact percentage loss of success likelihood should be plotted using a cumulative probability curve [4].
- Accept the change for the current release, delete other less important requirements,* and maintain its planned delivery date.

The following is *not* an alternative unless the goal is to alienate the developers and guarantee failure:

- Intimidate the development organization into accepting the change for the current release while maintaining the planned delivery date.

Of course, if this is your purpose, you should not be in software management (although you will certainly have lots of company).

REFERENCES

[1] Institute for Electrical and Electronic Engineers (IEEE), *IEEE Standard Glossary of Software Engineering Terminology*, New York: IEEE Press, 1997.

[2] Davis, A., et al., "A Strategy for Comparing Alternative Software Development Life Cycle Models," *IEEE Transactions on Software Engineering*, 14, 10 (October 1988), pp. 1453–1461.

[3] Young, R., *Effective Requirements Practices*, Boston, Massachusetts: Addison Wesley, 2001.

[4] Davis, A., "The Art of Requirements Triage," *IEEE Computer*, 36, 3 (March 2003), pp 42–29.

[5] Pohl, K., "The Three Dimensions of Requirements Engineering: A Framework and Its Application," *Information Systems*, 3, 19 (June 1994), pp. 243–258.

SEEDS FOR DEBATE

1. Some companies do not update the requirements document during development. Instead they maintain the changes on bits of paper and store them in a

---

*Of course the benefit of deleting a requirement is directly proportional to how much work has already been invested in satisfying that requirement. In some cases, deleting a requirement may actually *lengthen* the schedule because of the additional effort needed to remove that which has already been included.

"change pocket" in the back inside cover of the requirements document. Then, when the project is over, they update the document. Argue for why this may be sufficient. Now, argue for why it is too dangerous to use.

2. In some environments, the customer demands that requirements be signed off by all parties, and agreed to as the requirements (forever!). Argue for why this is ludicrous. Now, argue for why it makes complete business sense.

3. Read Klaus Pohl's paper called "The Three Dimensions of Requirements Engineering: A Framework and its Application." [5] Can you think of any more dimensions that could be valuable?

4. My colleague, Ann Zweig, has criticized the words I use in my baseline agreement on page 182 as too strongly worded. Can you soften the words?

SOFTWARE RESEARCH AND ACADEME

Although I have spent many years in academe, and have accumulated many publications, I am not considered to be a great researcher in software. Basically, I select research topics to pursue because they are fun, challenging, and (I think) important to practitioners. As a result, I am not and have never been at the *forefront* of what academics consider to be leading-edge research. This has resulted in me developing an attitude of "looking in" to the research community, not being part of it. This has resulted perhaps in somewhat of a bias, and perhaps a jaundiced view of software research and academe. In Homer's *Odyssey*, Odysseus travels from foreign land to foreign land, until finally returning home. In the first essay of this section, *Between Scylla and Charybdis*, I describe my own career as such a voyage. The reader may gain some insight into the differences between academic and industrial careers.

Essay 30, *Why Industry Often Says "No Thanks" To Research* explores the huge gap that exists between what practitioners need and what researchers think they need. It is the story told from two perspectives: first from a researcher's viewpoint, and then from a practitioner's. It traces my career change from a researcher trying to solve a specific organization's software problems to becoming part of that very organization.

The next essay, *Requirements Researchers: Do We Practice What We Preach?*, expresses some significant frustration with requirements researchers. Requirements people are supposed to be *the* experts in understanding somebody's needs. If that is the case, then why do requirements researchers fail so miserably at solving requirements practitioners' problems?

I don't want the reader to believe that I am the only contrarian. Essay 31, titled *From Wonderland to the Real Problem*, is authored by a fellow contrarian, Bob Glass. I think you will find his essay insightful and fun.

I have mixed feelings about the title of the last essay, *Practitioner, Heal Thyself*. On one hand, I like it because it is controversial and does capture the spirit of what I think most software development personnel think, i.e., that the problem is the customer's, not theirs. On the other hand, the title seems to imply that I think that practitioners should fix their own problems—and that is quite the opposite of what I believe. That said, this essay describes how miserably we train our new software personnel, and pleads for a new model of education, which could enable us to actually solve some of the problems that we and our customers experience.

Between Scylla and Charybdis*

After spending approximately half my career in industry and half in academe, I recently asked my wife, "Am I an academic or an industry person?" She answered matter-of-factly, "Well, of course you're an academic."

It wasn't the answer I wanted. I would rather have heard "a blend of both."

Academic and industrial jobs have little in common. Common to my two career lives is that I have always been considered an outsider. Throughout my career in industry, mostly in middle and senior management positions, my peers considered me to be too idealistic, too dreamy, too theoretical—perhaps I should say too *academic*. Throughout my career in academe, as an assistant and then full professor, my peers have considered me to be too practical, too interested in solving real problems, too entrepreneurial—perhaps I should say too *industrial*. Like Odysseus, I am a man wandering between foreign shores, always a stranger. Yet, as a somewhat detached observer of both worlds, I find it enlightening to compare and contrast the two realms.

POLITICS

I am often asked where the politics are worse. I believe it is in academe. Perhaps because there are so few resources to fight over, academics fight over everything: policies, procedures, teaching loads, students, all-too-scarce funding, salary increases, space, course subject matter, and so on. Everything is fair dinkum, as they say in Australia.

In industry, although corporate politics are real and you must always watch your back, you can usually predict where the knife will come from; not so in academe. Perhaps the backbiting in industrial politics is muzzled—or directed outward at the competition—to better serve the common goal of corporate success.

*Originally published in *IEEE Software, 14,* 5 (September/October 1997), pp. 4–6.

Great Software Debates. By Alan M. Davis
ISBN 0-471-649880 © 2004 Institute of Electrical and Electronics Engineers.

FREEDOM

In 1988, soon after I moved from industry to academe, I asked the department chair how to obtain permission for a day off so that I could spend time with my family. He laughed, then explained that anytime I wanted to take a day off, I need only do so. Nobody would care as long as I fulfilled department expectations for teaching, research, and service by the end of the year. The degree of freedom in academe is remarkable. Not only can you take a day off whenever the whim hits you, but nobody really cares what work you do. You can do research in any subject you desire as long as you publish the results in an approved journal. You can start your own business on the side as long as it consumes no more than one day per week. You can pursue any professional activity you desire, such as serving as editor-in-chief for a publication like *IEEE Software*. In short, you have the freedom to do what you want when you want. Nobody "owns" your time but you. Of course, individuals who need direction, who thrive on excelling at duties assigned to them, will fail miserably in academe.

As a technical contributor in industry, you tend to be assigned one or more tasks. You are expected to devote your full attention to these tasks except when you receive approval for a vacation day. As a manager in industry, you are swallowed in action: You plan, budget, put out fires, produce a plethora of reports for others, talk to customers, tend to your people, and on and on. The pressures of the job give you little freedom and less free time.

SECURITY

In industry, you can always be dismissed, terminated, fired, laid off, RIFed (from reduction in force), retired early, and so on—the variety of terms available to describe your involuntary departure reveals just how often the phenomenon occurs.

In academe, you can't beat the security attained once you earn tenure. Short of committing a heinous crime, or the institution closing your department, your job is practically guaranteed. I appreciate having tenure because it affords me the opportunity to stand up to the Dean for a cause I believe in without [fear of] serious retribution. Yet I believe the practice of tenure is inappropriate. In theory, tenure is given to faculty who have demonstrated excellence and have the potential to maintain that level of performance in the future. Yet, if they do so, they'll keep their jobs anyway. And if they don't maintain a high performance level, they *should* be given their walking papers.

TEN-YEAR, NOT TENURE?

What would happen to this system if we replaced tenure with a 10-year contract? Ten years of guaranteed employment is much better than any other occupation offers. If a faculty member decides to relax once tenure is earned, the university knows that it doesn't have to keep the employee until he or she dies! Meanwhile, responsible faculty members will get their 10-year contract renewed as long as they perform. What could be fairer than that? The usual argument for tenure is to give faculty freedom to think, freedom from retaliation if they express unpopular beliefs, and so forth. Although I endorse these freedoms, faculty should be protected only while they continue to demonstrate excellence in the key categories of teaching, research, and service. While it is true that politics may occasionally force the loss of an otherwise great faculty member at the end of 10 years, this would he overshadowed by the windfall of eliminating nonperforming faculty. More importantly, truly great faculty will always find another job elsewhere and thus don't need the protection of tenure.

IMPACT

Whether you work in industry or academe, you choose how profoundly you affect your field. The type of impact you will have, however, and the accompanying rewards, will differ greatly. In industry, you either solve a real problem or you help create wealth. You experience a wonderful feeling of success when *your* efforts help to protect a nation, streamline a process, let people live longer, improve people's quality of life, and so on. Likewise, helping to create products, make decisions, and provide services is incredibly rewarding when you can see the impact of these activities on company revenues, profits, and valuation—especially when you own a piece of the corporate pie.

An academic's rewards, on the other hand, tend to be more subtle, more personal if you will. The successful academic affects individuals, usually students. As a teacher and mentor, you can experience a wonderful sense of accomplishment when you see your students excel, acquire appreciation of a technology, mature as a public speaker, gain self-confidence, or land a lucrative job.

RETROSPECTIVE

Although profoundly different in nature, with strongly contrasting values, drawbacks, and rewards, both industry and academe can offer you opportunities to make meaningful contributions. Each world can also learn from the other. I've been uncommonly fortunate in that I have moved freely between the two and, looking over my diverse career, I have no regrets. Every experience has provided me with new insights, new knowledge, new friends. My travels have taken me all over the world; my jobs have provided me with new and never-ending challenges. Perhaps my ship will someday encounter Odysseus's and we can exchange stories about what a rich, beautiful, diverse, and wonderful world we live in.

EPILOGUE

Since this article was published in 1997, I have continued my ongoing voyage: in 1998 back to industry, and in 2001 back to academe.

SEEDS FOR DEBATE

1. Present an argument for why politics in industry are much worse than academe. Then present an argument for why politics in academe are much worse than industry.
2. Contrast the personality attributes that would make one an ideal employee of an academic institution vs. a corporation.
3. As I indicated in the essay, I think tenure is a travesty. Describe what has happened in the past 800 years that makes the tenure policies of the Middle Ages no longer appropriate.
4. Argue for why tenure is essential in today's world.

Why Industry Often Says "No Thanks" to Research*

I spent the first nine years of my career in research institutions: universities and corporate research jobs. During this time, I did all the things expected of researchers and research managers: I acquired grants, and I published results in prestigious journals. In 1983, I entered the trenches for the first time when I became director of a division of 140 software and hardware engineers, all doing "real" work.

This is the story of how different research results look from the diverse perspectives of the researcher and practitioner.

PERCEIVED NEEDS

As a researcher, I read lots of papers on requirements specification and software testing, all written by fellow researchers. As a result, I developed what I thought was a very keen view of the actual problems of requirements writing and software testing. What I had really gained was a very keen view of what researchers *thought* were the problems of requirements writing and software testing. I learned that

• After systems are built, they rarely satisfy the needs of the users. Clearly we must do a better job of writing requirements.

• Systems are shipped to customers without sufficient testing because of schedule crunches. Clearly we must find more time-efficient ways of testing.

• Even after apparently thorough testing, systems still suffered from numerous failures after shipment. Clearly we must do a more thorough job of defining the tests.

On the basis of these observations, my research center proceeded to develop software tools, write papers, and present results. By research standards, we accomplished a lot: During 1982 alone, our group published 22 papers.

We also developed a tool called the Requirements Language Processor. The RLP let requirements writers specify their requirements in any one of myriad applica-

*Originally published in *IEEE Software*, 9, 6 (November 1992), pp. 97–99.

Great Software Debates. By Alan M. Davis
ISBN 0-471-649880 © 2004 Institute of Electrical and Electronics Engineers.

tion-oriented languages. The applications orientation of the specification languages guaranteed that the requirements would be easy to write and easy to read by systems engineers expert in specific application areas. The RLP checked the requirements for ambiguities (if they violated the language's lexical. syntactical, or semantic rules) and inconsistencies (if two independently written requirements conflicted) and created a single requirements database. It was hard to believe that developers with unsatisfied customers would not flock to use the RLP.

We developed a second tool called the Test Plan Generator. The TPG accepted as input the requirements database produced by RLP and a set of test-coverage criteria. Using these criteria, TPG generated a set of test plans. When the test plans were applied to the actual product as built, their successful (or unsuccessful) execution would indicate a correct (or incorrect) implementation. It was hard to believe that developers with a history of poorly tested software would not flock to use the TPG.

We developed a third tool called the Automatic Test Executor. It accepted as input the test plans generated by the TPG. Connected by a customized harness to the actual system, it would follow the test plans, exercise the system, and report the success or failure of the system. It was hard to believe that developers with insufficient time to test would not flock to use the ATE.

NO NEED

So here we were, living in our dream world, developing tools that we believed were perfect for system developers in our corporation.

Meanwhile, I had the responsibility to transfer this obviously great technology to the corporate operating divisions. The division managers and directors were polite when I described our "great" tools, but their tone of voice clearly said, "Thanks, but no thanks."

Many dozens of phone calls and meetings later, I finally found out how they really felt. They were happy to keep sending us money to develop tools because it kept us out of trouble and out of their hair. They saw our results as interesting, but definitely not useful.

Naturally, I concluded that I must be smarter than they were. I understood how these tools could revolutionize product development. If they couldn't see it, that was their problem. I grew increasingly frustrated with the apparent incompetence of my colleagues in the "real world."

In early 1983, I was having a beer with Paul (not his real name) from one of the company's major operating divisions. He confided in me that he was to be promoted to division vice president of research and development within the next two months. He was disappointed with how the division had been managed in the past and wanted to see big changes. He asked if I would join his team as director of one of his major development groups.

I realized at once that this was my opportunity to make a big difference. I would be on the receiving end of the technology from the research lab. With my (self-assessed) superior knowledge of the technology and of the tools available from the laboratory, I could make the division considerably more successful at specifying requirements, generating tests, and system testing. And I could help the research lab transfer technology successfully. Everything seemed perfect.

Two months later, I started my new job. My 140 software and hardware engineers were responsible for the operating systems, diagnostics and recovery software, and part of the digital circuit design for our large (about one million lines of code) Pascal-based system. We were responsible for all enhancements, ongoing maintenance, and new developments within the product family. There were three or four major versions of the product already released and in operation. There were three or four major new versions with considerable enhancements under simultaneous development, and there were three or four additional versions with yet more enhancements being specified.

The products in the field were experiencing major problems. Service outages at important customer sites occurred weekly. Whenever one of these systems crashed, Paul would be in my office to demand that I send 10 of my very best engineers to the customer site. Being new in the trenches, I complied; after all, Paul had been in this division for many years and knew what was expected.

The new versions were grossly late because the best engineers were constantly being called on to put out fires in the field. Yet marketing continued to promise new deliveries of systems with still more features. A corporate hiring freeze made it impossible to hire any new talent to replace the traveling engineers. Of course, even if we could have hired more people, we would have had great difficulty training them—when the good engineers came off the road, they had so much work to do on the new versions they had no time to train new employees.

REAL NEEDS

So the problems we faced were (not necessarily in order of importance):
- An unstable installed base.
- Senior management's insistence on looking as if we were solving problems rather than actually solving them.
- Insufficient personnel.
- Inability to hire new personnel.
- Marketing's delivery promises that could not be satisfied.

Right in the middle of this mess, I received a phone call from the research lab. They had just finished some part of the RLP-TPG-ATE system and wanted to know if we were interested in applying it to our product development. The researchers were expecting to get a positive answer from me because they considered me to be one of their kind. But what I told them was, "The last thing I need right now is some automated tool. I've got real problems here."

After I hung up, I began analyzing what we did need to get out of our quagmire. After they hung up, the research lab folks began to analyze what had happened to me, their onetime colleague. Why had I abandoned them? What automated tools could they develop next that would be acceptable to Davis and his group?

I decided that we were clearly thrashing, in the same way that an operating system thrashes. We were reallocating scarce resources so often that nothing got done. We appeared to be doing a lot, but we were definitely experiencing deadlock. Nothing was happening, even though we were all running around like crazy. What we did need was for management and senior engineers to define and document a process model for our software development.

This process needed to include both technical and management issues, including procedures for

- putting out field fires (including how many key personnel to send),
- analyzing, costing, scheduling, implementing, and documenting enhancements to existing software,
- prioritizing new customer needs by marketing and development personnel,
- pairing junior engineers with senior engineers on all activities (including fire-fighting) to provide on-the-job training,
- open forums to discuss the effects of fire-fighting on delivery schedules.

We also needed to

- establish communication channels among engineers and between engineers and managers,
- reassess the current schedules for versions in process, and
- hang a large graph on the wall that charted the number of field-generated trouble reports so that we could all easily see if our problems were getting better or worse.

After I compiled my list of problem areas and their potential solutions, it was clear why the call from the lab was so unwelcome. They were offering technology solutions to technology problems. We had management problems. We had process problems. We probably had technology problems, too, but they were heavily masked by the first two problems. We needed time. We needed enforced process and procedures. We needed more people. We needed a training plan.

For some time thereafter, the lab tried to "reach" me. But they kept offering solutions to problems I did not have. When they asked me to explain what types of technology development would be useful, I told them "nothing, absolutely nothing." To my ex-colleagues in the lab, I had become as incompetent as my predecessors!

NEEDS HIERARCHY

Seeing the technology-transfer problem from both sides gave me insight into how big a challenge it is. Providing me and my organization with innovative technological solutions to technological problems was like giving a starving child a bicycle.

I began to think of the problem in terms of Maslow's hierarchy, which depicts the relative ranking of human needs in a pyramid, shown in Figure 29.1A. The needs at the base of the pyramid must be satisfied first; attempts to satisfy the need for love will fail unless the need for safety is already satisfied. Figure 29.1B shows my hierarchy for software-development needs.

The most basic need is a task—we can't do much unless we have something to do. Once we have a task to perform, we next need resources:

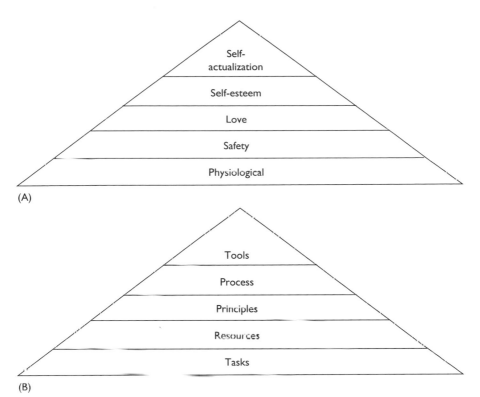

(A)

(B)

Figure 29.1. Software development in terms of Maslow's hierarchy of needs. (A) The psychologist Maslow depicted the relative ranking of human needs in a pyramid; the needs at the base must be satisfied before those at the top can be met. (B) In software development, some needs must be satisfied before tools can be used effectively.

- personnel (systems analysts, designers, coders, testers, quality-assurance experts, leaders),
- financial (funds sufficient for the task), and
- time (reasonable schedules).

Once resources are in place we need principles. It is only with a thorough understanding of underlying rules or oracles that we can possibly create process. We must understand the software-engineering processes to be used by engineers, quality-assurance experts, and managers. Only after we have all four needs met can we hope to use tools effectively. This hierarchy applies to all "building" activities. For example, I cannot build a piece of furniture until I know what it is. Once I know what I'm building, I need money to buy raw materials and time to work on it. Next I need to understand the basic principles of wood: its strength, durability, pliability. Next I must know how to build furniture—I must be familiar with appropriate procedures that will let me transform a pile of wood into a work of utilitarian art. Only then can I hope to use lathes, saws, screwdrivers, and so on to produce the piece of furniture.

In software engineering, it is true that knowledge of processes and tools will influence the amount of resources that will be sufficient. But it is still the case that you need the resources before you can use either process or tools.

In the case of my original predicament, my development organization was suffering from gross lack of process, principles, and resources. That's why we could not effectively use the really great tools being offered to us.

The solution was first to establish new reasonable deadlines, hire more personnel, and establish and document a modern software-engineering process based on understood principles. Most likely, the process would help us start meeting schedules and quality objectives. This would release some resources (people) to examine the tools, which would probably result in a reassessment and probable modification of the process to optimize the tools. Finally, after all this is done, we would be in a position to incorporate the tools in our division, successfully transferring technology from research to practice.

Flushed with new insight, I gave Paul my assessment of the situation. His reaction was not what I had expected: "Problems? We don't have problems here. We don't need principles or process or tools. All we need is for you to find a way to make your people work harder and with more devotion to the company."

I started looking for a job that day. A few months after I left, the division was sold to another corporation.

SEEDS FOR DEBATE

1. Which is more important for a researcher: To create innovative ideas or useful ideas?

2. How can researchers identify real problems in the world, so they can direct their research accordingly?

3. Dozens of scholarly papers were written in the 1980's concerning the RLP-TPG-ATE suite of tools. And yet, today nobody references those ideas. Does that mean the research was a waste of time? For naught? Or just forgotten? Today, you can read many papers being written that describe tools virtually identical to those three tools. Does that mean that the original research was a waste of time? Does that mean that the new research is a waste of time? Take opposing views for all these questions.

4. In the part of this essay titled "No Need," I describe a problem of developing multiple simultaneous releases. Is that problem present whenever multiple simultaneous releases are being worked on, or was it some other characteristic of our environment or product that made the problem so bad?

5. How can you prevent the problems of developing multiple simultaneous releases when doing iterative development?

6. Colin Potts wrote a masterful article in 1993 on the problems of technology transfer (See "Software Engineering Research Revisited," *IEEE Software, 10,* 5

(September 1993), pp. 19-28). Describe how his ideas could have been applied to the two divisions I described in the essay to enable the research division to really help the operating division.

7. In the last two paragraphs of the essay, I described Paul's reaction to my recommendations. How could I have altered the presentation of my recommendations so that Paul would have responded more positively? If you were Paul, what would your response have been?

Requirements Researchers:
Do We Practice What We Preach?*

A. DAVIS AND A. HICKEY

INTRODUCTION

All researchers have a responsibility to thoroughly understand the current research literature *and* the current state-of-the-practice. If they fail to understand the former, they risk repeating work that has already been done and their research will be for naught. If they fail to understand the latter, they risk creating new knowledge that has no practical value. Researchers in the field of requirements engineering are no exception. They must understand both how requirements engineering is practiced and what research has been performed in the past. This paper argues that many requirements engineering researchers fail to understand current practices. The paper also argues that requirements engineering researchers, more than any other type of researcher, have little excuse for failing in this regard. This is true because by its very nature, requirements engineering is the investigation of how people do things currently. Thus, these individuals are not just irresponsible researchers, they are also poor requirements engineers. They seem to not understand the first rule of requirements engineering: *Know Thy Customer*. This begs the question: Do we as requirements researchers practice what we preach?

WHAT DO WE PREACH?

As researchers and as educators we preach that requirements engineering practitioners should thoroughly understand the problem domain in which we are trying to solve a problem. After all, practicing requirements engineers** have five primary

---

*Originally published in *The Requirements Engineering Journal*, 7, 2 (July 2002), pp. 107–111 © 2002 Springer-Verlag GmbH & Co., Reprinted with permission,

**We are *not* trying to debate the subtle differences between requirements engineering, requirements management, and requirements analysis. For the purposes of this article, we are considering them to be identical.

Great Software Debates. By Alan M. Davis
ISBN 0-471-649880 © 2004 Institute of Electrical and Electronics Engineers.

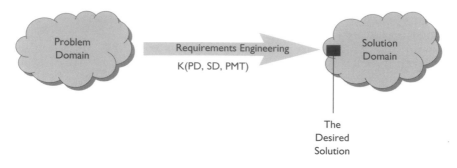

Figure 30.1. The Practice of Requirements Engineering.

purposes: (1) determining what needs exist, (2) determining which needs are to be addressed*, (3) selecting an appropriate solution** from a variety of possible solutions, (4) documenting the intended external behavior of the system*** to be offered (built or purchased), and (5) managing the ongoing evolution of the needs and the solution's intended external behavior. Thus, requirements engineering maps problems from a problem domain into a proposed solution from the solution domain, as shown in Figure 30.1.

To be effective as a requirements engineer, the individual must be capable of utilizing knowledge to synthesize effective solutions. In the traditional view of requirements engineering, the knowledge required includes the items appearing just below the requirements engineering arrow, i.e., (1) knowledge of the problem domain [K(PD)], (2) knowledge of existing solutions within the solution domain [K(SD)], and (3) knowledge of processes, tools, and methods of the practice of requirements engineering [K(PMT)]. And only recently, we have begun to recognize the need for a fourth area of knowledge: (4) knowledge of how to decide which processes, tools, and methods make most sense as a function of certain aspects of the problem domain, the specific problem being addressed, the people involved, and so on. Figure 30.2 shows how the knowledge of these domains interact. Note that requirements engineers cannot do their jobs without understanding both the problem/application domains and the world of available process, tools, and methods. And they need to understand the meta-processes necessary to determine which processes, tools, and methods are appropriate for which applications and problems.

---

*Often termed triage [13]

**We intend to imply that one task of a requirements engineer is to propose alternative external behaviors to customers (e.g., via prototyping), and eventually select one. We are *not* implying that the requirements engineer selects data structures, algorithms, and the like.

***We use the term *system* in the broadest possible manner. It could be any subset of software, hardware, people, and procedures.

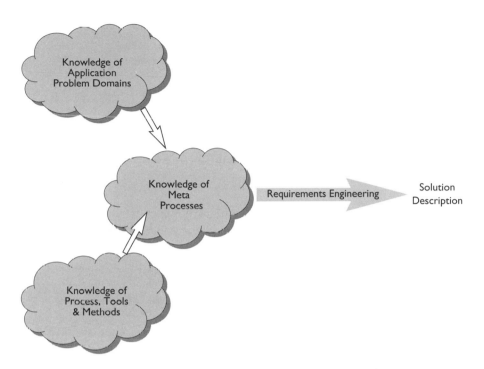

Figure 30.2. Areas of Knowledge for a Requirements Engineer.

WHAT DO PRACTITIONERS DO?

The final test of whether a requirements engineer has been successful is to determine how successful the resulting system is in the eyes of intended customers. If the intended customers are basically satisfied with the resulting system, then we could conclude the requirements engineering process was successful. If the intended customers are unsatisfied with the resulting system, then the requirements engineering process may have been at fault. According to the Standish Group [12], 31% of systems built today are never delivered, and another 15% had fewer than half of the intended customers' needs satisfied. This clearly demonstrates the failure of requirements engineers.

Many researchers blame practitioners for being unwilling to accept new ways of doing requirements engineering, that they insist on doing things the same old way. Our opinion is somewhat different. The most problematic requirements-related difficulties that companies face are related to the inherent difficulty of right-brained activities [3]. For example, here are scenarios we have seen often in industry:

1. Engineering/Development has its view of what the customers' needs are and proceeds to satisfy those needs in direct opposition to the views of marketing (or the customer).

2. A development organization thinks it knows the problems of the customer better than the customer does [6].

3. Multiple customer groups have different, and in some cases conflicting, needs.

4. Marketing has no idea how the inclusion of certain requirements relates to likelihood of successful use.

5. Needs of customers are in constant flux.

6. The customers really have little idea of what they need. What they do have is a fuzzy perception of a need for a solution to some ill-defined problem.

7. Market windows demand product delivery in a timeframe in which development/engineering cannot possibly deliver.

8. Development/Engineering think that the solution to all requirements problems is to document requirements using a notation that the customers cannot possibly understand.

9. No respect exists between development/engineering and marketing (or customer). Insults regularly fly in both directions, e.g., "You have no idea of what the needs are. If you did, you wouldn't be changing them all the time." And "You couldn't meet a delivery schedule no matter when it was."

10. Naïve practitioners grasp repeatedly at left-brained panaceas to solve their right-brained problems. Examples include Structured Analysis, Object-Oriented Analysis, Use Cases, CASE tools, and so on.

WHAT DO RESEARCHERS DO?

In most fields, the purpose of performing research is to synthesize new knowledge that can be either (1) put into practice, or (2) used by other researchers to help them perform research. As shown in Figure 30.3, the responsible researcher needs to thoroughly understand two domains: the domain of practice (so the research results—or the results of subsequent research based on the current research results—can be applied to that practice), and previous research (so the research results do not simply duplicate previous research . . . resulting in no new knowledge). Researchers who fail to understand this basic concept are doomed to producing results that are never used by anybody in the "real world."

Every responsible requirements engineering researcher must at least identify (a) how their research compares and contrasts with existing research (in our opinion, this is not generally a problem), and (b) how it can be used practically in the real world. Part of this might be for the researcher to recognize to which of the three clouds in Figure 30.2 the new research applies. Another would be for the researcher to understand the technical, political, and social barriers to effective technology transfer and change the research to make it more assimilable. Since Figure 30.2 defines the requisite knowledge of requirements engineering, we can embed Figure 30.2 inside the "Domain of Practice" cloud of Figure 30.3 to see how and where in the real world any practical requirements research can be applied.

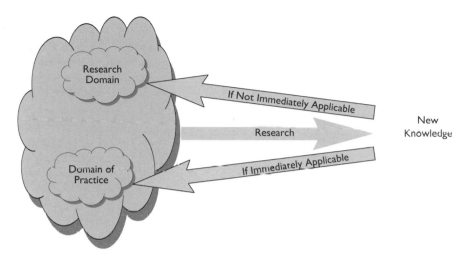

Figure 30.3. The Role of Research.

We believe that the process by which requirements engineering researchers perform research is broken.

Many requirements researchers complain that something is wrong with practicing requirements engineers because they don't adopt the "latest and most terrific" research results. Some papers [4, 8] have suggested that we need to improve communication between researchers and practitioners so that the practitioners will better understand the research. We believe that we need to improve the communication between researchers and practitioners so that the researchers will better understand the practice.

If a company produces a product and nobody buys it, is it the market's fault or the company's? We contend that only the company can be blamed. If a researcher performs research with the intent for it to be adopted into practice immediately and nobody chooses to use it, is it the practitioner's fault or the researcher's? We contend that only the researcher can be blamed.

THE CHALLENGE

Most requirements research to date has not been used by its intended customers, i.e., the requirements engineers—and we *cannot* blame the customers. It is time to stop talking about how ill-informed the requirements engineers are, and start talking about how ill-informed requirements researchers are. If requirements engineering researchers would follow the first rule of any requirements engineer, i.e., Know Thy Customer, more of the research would prove to be helpful in practice. The research that needs to be done may not be fun or popular, but it is what needs to be done if we as researchers want to help our customers. Some of the more fruitful areas may include:

- *Scenarios,* as one of many approaches to talking in terms of the customer. As stated so well by the Robertsons [10], "scenarios work well because they look like the stakeholders' world" not because there is some technical magic in some arbitrary notation to represent scenarios.

- *Situational research* [7], so we better learn *when* various requirements approaches work most effectively.

- *Conflict resolution, mutual respect,* and *collaboration* [4]. Analysis of how to improve the ways that humans communicate.

- *Flux-sensitive architecture.* Requirements do change. Instead of talking about how requirements creep adversely affects our development, we should talk about how our development needs to change to accommodate requirements creep.

- Practical requirements *organization* techniques, including both the use of lists and the use of word processed documents [1, 10].

- Techniques that increase *alignment* between marketing and requirements engineering.

The challenge to researchers in requirements engineering is to either acknowledge that their research is purely theoretical (and stop lamenting its lack of use), or to study current practice carefully. Studying current practice is tantamount to performing requirements analysis of the current practice, something we should be very good at! Note that studying current practice is not just doing a survey, any more than performing requirements analysis is just doing a survey. Analysis is all about thinking, experiencing, observing, listening, feeling, understanding pains, and so on. Also, a practicing requirements engineer has a responsibility to produce feasible solutions, where feasibility includes sensitivity to political, operational, economic, schedule, and technical issues. If the practitioner will use a new system only if it reflects a small change from current practice, the requirements engineer must make only small changes . . . or they will fail. Researchers have a similar challenge: understand not only how requirements engineers do their job, but also understand all the political, operational, economic, schedule, and technical issues affecting their ability to adopt new ideas.

This discussion would not be complete without acknowledging the presence of systemic issues that interfere with our ability to produce research results ready for common practice. These include (1) emphasis on publishing, rather than technology transfer, in universities, (2) disincentives to leave the university for periods of time to work in industry, (3) emphasis on more theoretical journals for "credit" toward tenure and/or promotion, (4) disincentives (e.g.. low academic salaries) for individuals with extensive real-world experience from entering academia, (5) lack of reading by practitioners of journals in which researchers publish* (unlike physicians who *do* read the Journal of the American Medical Association), and (6) a learning

---

*Of course this will only come to pass when researchers learn to write for practitioners, and not just for other researchers.

environment in which (unlike medical school) students are taught by professors with little or no experience in the "real world," and who have learned everything they know from yet other professors who have learned everything they know from yet other professors, and so on [2].

CONCLUSION

When we as requirements researchers lament that technology transfer takes a whopping 15 years [9], perhaps we should look no further than ourselves.

As requirements engineering researchers we should be *experts* (not just "knowledgeable") in how requirements engineers ply their trade. But even more importantly, we must be able to practice sound requirements engineering principles *while* we are doing research. Practicing requirements engineers use the acceptance of the resulting system by its intended users as the primary judge of whether they did a good job. We must use the same notion for our research: Requirements engineer researchers should use the acceptance of the resulting research by its intended users, practicing requirements engineers, as the primary judge of whether they did a good job. We also need to collectively work on diminishing the systemic problems described at the end of the previous section, not use the systemic problems as an excuse for our own inadequacy. Let's start practicing what we preach.

REFERENCES

1. Davis, A., "Achieving Quality in Software Requirements," *Software Quality Professional, 1*, 3 (June 1999); reprinted in current book on page 143.
2. Davis, A., "Practitioner, Heal Thyself," *IEEE Software, 13*, 3 (May 1996), pp. 4–5: reprinted in the current book on page 215
3. Davis, A., "The Harmony in Rechoirments," *IEEE Software, 15*, 2 (March/April 1998), pp. 6–8, reprinted in current book on page 115.
4. Dean, et al., "Enabling the Effective Involvement of Multiple Users: Methods and Tools for Collaborative Software Engineering," *Journal of Management Information Systems, 14*, 3 (Winter 1997 1998), pp. 179–222.
5. Debou, C., et al., "Selling Believable Technology," *IEEE Software, 10*, 6 (November 1993), pp. 22–27.
6. Gause, D., and G. Weinberg, *Are Your Lights On?*, New York: Dorset House, 1990.
7. Jackson, M., *Problem Frames*, Reading, Massachusetts: Addison-Wesley, 2001.
8. Potts, C., "Software Engineering Revisited," *IEEE Software 10*, 5 (September 1993), pp. 19–28.
9. Redwine, S., and W. Riddle, "Software Technology Maturity," *IEEE Eighth International Conference on Software Engineering*, 1985, pp. 189–200.
10. Robertson, J., and S. Robertson, *Mastering the Requirements Process*, Reading, Massachusetts: Addison-Wesley, 1999.

11. Robertson, J., and S. Robertson, "Requirements Management: A Cinderella Story," *Requirements Engineering Journal 5* (2000), pp. 134–136.

12. Standish Group, The Chaos Report, *www.standishgroup.com,* 1995.

13. Yourdon, E., *Death March,* Englewood Cliffs, New Jersey: Prentice Hall, 1997.

SEEDS FOR DEBATE

1. One could argue that academe is one of the very few places where original thoughts can be conceived. To create truly innovative results, one needs to think thoroughly out of the box, and not be restricted to the world of practicality. It is only through such a process that thousands of ideas can be generated. And it is only with such volume, that real progress will be made. Take this position, and argue that the gap described in this essay is not only good, it is essential.

2. Characterize a publication that academics would want to publish in and that practitioners would want to read.

From Wonderland to
the Real Problem*

ROBERT GLASS

In somewhat of a departure from our usual column, Robert Glass, editor and publisher of a newsletter for software practitioners, offers his view on the real problems in software development. Hint: It isn't the software crisis. His views are somewhat "contrary," as he himself notes, and I follow them with my own counterpoints. The action takes place in Wonderland, where the Practitioners are attempting to get back to reality, but the Others (management, vendors, and researchers) are thwarting their every move. Who will ultimately win out?

Alan Davis

I consider this a contrary article because I'm not taking a popular position. Most people see the software crisis as a reality in software development. I disagree. I believe that long ago the software world moved through the looking glass into Wonderland, in which proposed breakthrough solutions resemble the conversations at the Mad Hatter's tea party. What we should be doing is finding our way back to the other side, where the real solutions are, yet we seem content to wander from technique to technique looking for one that will make us just the right size to fit through the keyhole.

THE PROBLEM

The first thing to do in an article like this is, of course, to define "the problem." Easier said than done. If you ask most people, the problem is some sort of variation on the software crisis, usually "software is always over budget, behind schedule, and unreliable."

But—and here's the essence of my contrary view—I don't believe that's the problem at all. First of all, the only evidence for such a problem is largely anecdotal (Bruce Blum pretty soundly debunked the only "data"; see "Some Very Famous Sta-

*Originally published in *IEEE Software*, 11, 3 (May 1994), pp. 90–92.

Great Software Debates. By Alan M. Davis
ISBN 0-471-649880 © 2004 Institute of Electrical and Electronics Engineers.

tistics," *The Software Practitioner,* Mar. 1991). Second, even those who cry "crisis" must admit that software is everywhere, *and* it is almost always doing the job we expect it to do, sometimes spectacularly, and rarely with a fuss.

No, I believe the real problem is a near total disconnection of Practitioners— those who build and maintain the product—and Others—the managers, vendors, and researchers who perpetuate the idea of a crisis and advise Practitioners how to handle it. In this Wonderland, there is more than one Cheshire Cat. The result is that solutions become the problems.

Moreover (and this is *really* contrary), I believe the Practitioners are generally closer to the truth than the Others. I think the misinformation chain starts with researchers, who advocate rather than evaluate new concepts. Vendors of products, services, and methodologies, who use and elaborate that unfounded advocacy, add more links to the chain. Finally, managers bind Practitioners to the misinformed practices advocated and elaborated by those earlier in the chain.

CRISIS PERSONIFIED

To Put this difference of opinion into perspective, let me share a story. Five or so years ago, Westpac, an Australian bank, launched a project to build an all-new, all-encompassing banking system. The project, CS90 (Core Systems Redevelopment), was expected to set the software world on its ear and all Wetpac's problems to right. Westpac—with the aid of several contractors, including IBM—announced it would use all the latest technology. As A. Boynton and colleagues wrote in their description of CS90, "Westpac managers ignored conventional wisdom and sought out a new wisdom . . . a completely new systems development and operational environment." ("New Competitive Strategies: Challenges to Organizations and Information Technology," *IBM Systems J.,* No. 1, 1993). As each announcement of CS90's goals and methods was made, the list of technological advances grew longer. This was to be paragon of software advances for some time to come.

The bitter end came all too quickly. Far from being the breakthrough success its advocates had claimed, CS90 became the epitome of failure, software crisis personified. It cost the bank $150 million with no result, and it joined other negative factors in tilting Westpac's books so far southward that it is still trying to recover.

You would think the lessons learned from such a fiasco would be clear. Advanced technologies alone simply cannot make a success out of an otherwise ill-conceived project, and, taken to extreme, as in CS90, can guarantee its failure.

Now you may be thinking that CS90 is an argument in favor of the software crisis. You'd be right, except for two reasons:

1. Usually those who cry "crisis" offer technology as the solution to the problem. In this case advanced technology, to a large extent, *was* the problem.

2. The participants in CS90 apparently refused to learn obvious lessons. In the same article in which they described the project, Boynton and colleagues maintain that the approaches taken will be the way of the future. And they take this position more than a year after the project died from taking those very approaches!

DISCONNECTION

The Westpac anecdote is a good example of the disconnection I referred to earlier. It shows what happens when Practitioner beliefs are ignored and the Others have total control of setting project directions. In this case, the Others, believing that breakthrough technology was either available or imminent, and that only the historic stubbornness of the Practitioners had prevented them from achieving it thus far, moved blindly ahead into a Wonderland that was, in fact, a minefield. The supposed breakthroughs were at best unproved, unevaluated concepts and at worse malicious, counterproductive mischief—the mines that eventually blew the project (and its Wonderland) to pieces.

Now I am not saying that new technological concepts are without benefit. What I *am* saying is that no one has taken the responsibility for determining if these new technologies have benefit and, if so, how much. (Instead, benefits are proclaimed and off with the heads of the doubters!) A close examination of the evaluative research in the literature—what little there is—reveals that there was no basis in reality for the Westpac Others to conclude that the technological breakthroughs they sought were achievable.

Lest I be accused of presenting my own brand of unsupported claims, is there any evidence that the disconnection exists? Yes!

• There is an epidemic of lying to management in the software field. Those who confess to lying say they do it because management doesn't want to hear or won't listen to the truth.

• One of the underlying, if not overt, reasons for outsourcing is that management believes so little in its employees that they would rather have their work taken over by an outside firm.

• Programmer stress is beginning to be recognized as a major problem in our ability to build software (see Y. Fujigaki, "Stress Analysis: A New Perspective on Peopleware," *American Programmer*, July 1993). That stress is caused by what I call "management by schedule," the current management practice in which schedule is given higher management priority than either product quality or project cost.

• There is also evidence that programmer morale is dropping alarmingly, which correlates with the previous point.

TRUTHSAYERS

As I said earlier, I believe Practitioners are closer to the truth than Others. Consider this. There are major flip-flops in the Others' belief about the process of building software. Beginning 20 years ago, and continuing until somewhat recently, many Others believed in an interpretation of the waterfall approach that required the steps be done in just the "right" sequence with no iteration or backtracking.

Once that approach was debunked, Others hurried to embrace a new concept, concurrent engineering. In this approach, not only do you iterate among the life-cycle steps, but you intentionally plan to conduct them in parallel. The dangers in this approach are so obvious that I wonder what its advocates can be thinking. Meanwhile, Practitioners have quietly continued to use the only process approach that really works, the spiral (iterative) life cycle, *in spite of* what Others are advising them to do.

If that isn't enough to make you lose faith in the Others, consider their one-size-fits-all approach to software. The Capability Maturity Model put forth by the Software Engineering Institute advocates one process for all projects, vendors advocate one methodology for enterprise-wide use, and researchers advocate such concepts as object orientation without defining the circumstances under which they might be most useful.

There is mounting evidence that this attitude leads to weaker solutions than more focused alternatives. For example, the cognitive fit notion that Iris Vessey and Dennis Galletta describe ("Cognitive Fit: An Empirical Study of Information Acquisition, *Information Systems Research,* Mar. 1991) suggests that optimum problem-solving occurs when the tool is chosen to match the task. But with the one-size approach, the task is bent to match the tool.

The final nail in the Others' coffin is that Total Quality Management (which at its best is about employee empowerment to achieve customer satisfaction) is repeatedly distorted by traditional managers into old-fashioned quality control. Management Others direct and Practitioners obey. Researcher Others reinforce this approach by advocating disciplined and formal approaches, words defined by some higher authority, perhaps even mandated by law. TQM, which promised to be a solution, has thus been revised into a reinforcement of the problem.

COMPLEXITY: THE ROOT CAUSE

There is in all this contrary discussion a key point that Fred Brooks has told us in many forums and on many occasions: Software is the most complex task humanity has ever undertaken. All the Others listen intently, intellectualize what Brooks has said, and then proceed to follow all the old ways. They continue to believe that the practice of software can be automated, obliterated, or given to users, ignoring the essence of the Brooks message. The few who really take Brooks to heart, and search for evolutionary improvements to our ability to mold and craft this complex product (instead of silver bullets), are overrun by the thundering masses of Others who continue to proclaim breakthrough after breakthrough, despite the two-decade litany of broken promises.

GETTING HOME

If we are ever to get back through the looking glass to the real world, the others will have to acknowledge that management is in fact the ultimate problem, because they have the power to stop the flow of misinformation, but don't. The solution is a new, enlightened kind of management that

- Searches for the best of practice among its practitioners, and gives those findings at least equal weight with those of vendors and researchers. Begins to believe that practitioners may, at heart, know how to do their job. Learns the *real* lessons of TQM.
- Urges vendors, researchers, and research funders to adopt evaluative approaches so that managers, vendors, and researchers will have some understanding of whether their new ideas have value in a practical setting, and if so, how much. Is skeptical of breakthroughs that offer no such support.
- Learns the lessons of cognitive fit, and begins to find solution approaches that match the task at hand. Urges researchers to learn the same lessons.
- Recognizes that management by schedule has failed (the schedules themselves are usually wrong or impossible) and that attempts to continue its use are doomed to more failures, increased programmer stress, and ruined morale.
- Begins to move past management by schedule alone, and turns to management of process and issues.

As long as we remain in our present Wonderland, where problems masquerade as solutions and those who tend to be wrong prevail over those who tend to be right, nothing can change the status of software productivity and quality. Even Alice had to wake up eventually.

COUNTERPOINT: THERE ARE NO BAD GUYS, AND NO ONE HAS THE "TRUTH"
Alan Davis

I agree in principle with this message, but I disagree with many of the details and the supposition that the disconnection of Practitioners and Others is the primary problem in the software industry today.

I do support the notion of disconnection. As I pointed out in my November 1992 column ("Why Industry Often Says 'No Thanks' to Research," reprinted in the current book on page 191), as each new wave of so-called technology arrives, practitioners are bombarded with marketing hype that tries to convince them of incredibly large productivity and quality payoffs and implies that anybody who ignores it is clearly not on the cutting edge.

The Problem

What I don't agree with is the characterization of such technologies as "at worst, malicious, counterproductive mischief." I object because I do not believe there is any intentional malice; researchers believe that what they are doing is useful. Also my gut feeling is that the technology behind many of the major fads that wrack this industry really could increase productivity and quality. Prototyping, for example, increases the likelihood that the eventual product will satisfy user needs. Software designed using objects is likely to be more maintainable and reliable than if it is designed with more classical approaches. CASE tools increase productivity.

The problem is not with the technology, but with the hype and misuse that surround it. Prototyping does not mean you can build software without standards, quality, or documentation and ship it to the customer as a product. Just using the syntax of C++ does not make your program object-oriented. Building objects does not mean you automatically get the rewards of software reuse. CASE tools do not shave 50 to 90 percent off your development costs, and they do not pay for themselves in six months.

Truthsayers

As far as Practitioners being the good guys, I believe just as many practitioners as researchers think they've discovered the silver bullet. More to the point, there aren't any good guys and bad guys. Everybody is just trying to make things better. It's not clear to me who ultimately has the entire truth, if there is such a thing. Who's "doing it right"?

As for management flip-flopping on approaches, I find nothing mutually exclusive about the waterfall, concurrent, and spiral development models. The waterfall model defines a series of management stages that a project goes through (just as humans go through childhood, adolescence, and adult). It says little or nothing about the activities performed during those stages. During any stage, developers can perform many activities concurrently, and of course many of the activities are performed during multiple stages.

The spiral model basically says look before you leap. It certainly doesn't advocate a one-size-fits-all approach. During any loop around the spiral, you could decide to use a waterfall model or some other kind.

Finally, TQM is no different from any other fad. It is useful, can offer great potential, just like prototyping, object orientation and CASE, and—just like other fads—it is oversold and misused.

Getting Home

I think Glass wants to shake us up, and he has succeeded. I'd like to offer some less threatening advice, however, which I gave in a recent column (see "Software Lemmingineering," reprinted as "Software Lemmings" in the current book on page 3).

- Set realistic goals.
- Don't believe the hype.
- Select a path that makes sense for you.
- Understand risks and rewards, in both degree and probability.
- Be cautious, but don't ignore every path.
- Don't forget your primary goal—to solve user needs with a reliable, maintainable, usable, safe system within budget and schedule.
- Don't follow a path just because everybody's doing it.

Maybe this is the beginning of the enlightened management solution that Glass believes will take us out of Wonderland.

SEEDS FOR DEBATE

1. One of my favorite lines from this essay is that software "solutions become the problems." What a deep but simply worded expression. Debate both sides of this statement.

2. In the CS90 case, Bob Glass states that clearly the technology was the major cause of the problem. Put together a case to argue that technology was just the scapegoat, that something else was the primary cause of failure.

3. Another quote from the essay is "one of the . . . reasons for outsourcing is that management believes so little in its employees that it would rather have their work taken over by an outside firm." Those are fighting words! So, take both sides of this argument. First, argue that this is totally preposterous, and describe why. Then, argue that this is patently obvious, and describe why.

4. Yet another great quote is "There is mounting evidence that [selecting just one process model for all a company's software projects] leads to weaker solutions than more focused alternatives." Once again, take both sides of this argument. First, argue for this statement, and provide solid (if necessary, anecdotal) evidence. Then, argue against this statement, and provide solid (if necessary, anecdotal) evidence.

Practitioner, Heal Thyself*

We do not teach software engineers how to be good software engineers. Typical degrees earned by software engineers are in computer science or, more recently, software engineering. Those who receive BS, MS, and PhD degrees in these subjects supposedly acquire with them the ability to practice software engineering at its best. They are expected to solve real problems professionally. Are they capable of doing so? Should they be trusted to work on aspects of nuclear-reactor control, commercial aircraft flight control, medical instruments, or life support systems?

No!

Software engineers trained at today's universities usually are taught by instructors who themselves have little or no practical real-life software-engineering experience. Many of those instructors attained their teaching positions not through practice but through study with other instructors who themselves had little or no practical experience. Having generations of professional educators train yet more generations of professional educators to train software engineers is unacceptable and, in the most literal sense, impractical.

PRESCRIPTION FOR DISASTER

Imagine if we trained physicians the same way we now train software engineers. Physicians would learn their profession from individuals who had never *practiced* medicine, *performed* surgery, or *prescribed* pharmaceuticals. Presumably, these instructors would be qualified to teach our future physicians based solely on their academic credentials. Would you be comfortable knowing that *your* surgeon had been taught surgery by people who themselves had never performed a single operation?

The terminal degree for software engineering should be similar in skill-building to that received from a medical school. Instructors should be drawn from the ranks of those who have practiced software development successfully (and *perhaps* have demonstrated academic excellence as well). The only exception would be that research courses could be taught by research professionals, just as medical research courses can be taught now by physicians without patient experience.

*Originally published in *IEEE Software*, 13, 3 (May 1996), pp. 4–5.

Great Software Debates. By Alan M. Davis
ISBN 0-471-649880 © 2004 Institute of Electrical and Electronics Engineers.

By this point, many of you who are software-engineering professors are no doubt enraged. I hope this is because you realize that I am right, rather than because you feel threatened. Others of you may be concerned about the impracticality of what I suggest. After all, how many qualified—by my standards—software-engineering instructors are there? I admit there are currently few. The solution is to start moving in this direction, not to continue blindly down our current path.

MEDICAL MODEL

My proposed school of software is modeled on existing schools of medicine.
- *Faculty.* Instructors must have a minimum of five and preferably 10 years of experience in real-world, professional practice. They should also have strong academic qualifications and should maintain a current professional practice while teaching.
- *Curriculum.* Like most current curricula, individual courses would cover requirements, design, implementation, testing, quality assurance and configuration management, project management, formal methods, maintenance, metrics, and so on. But unlike most current curricula, a laboratory section would accompany most courses. After all, we should strive to teach how to do things, not just how to talk about things.
- *Laboratory.* Like medical students, each software student should also be assigned a "cadaver": a large software system that either works now or worked at one time. During every regular class, students would simultaneously enroll in the "cadaver" lab, where they would perform related tasks on their assigned software.
- *Duration.* Most medical degrees require four years of study. Because so much less is known about software engineering, we can reduce this to three years of study.
- *Internship.* As in medicine, our students must complete a minimum one-year internship. Like the medical profession's interns and the apprentices of traditional trades, software interns would work in a real-world setting practicing what they've learned under an expert's watchful eye. Internships could take place in special for-profit or not-for-profit companies closely affiliated with or established by the school of software.

I am suggesting a major overhaul of our process for educating software engineers. I do not believe the transformation can occur overnight, but it sure would be nice to see two or three schools of software founded by millennium's end. For it is only through such change that the software industry can have any hope of serving society in a meaningful way.

EPILOGUE

When I originally wrote this essay in 1995, the economy was booming worldwide. There was huge demand for software development personnel. India, Taiwan, Russia, Singapore, and many other countries had thriving development shops that specialized in doing outsourced software jobs for American and European countries. Times have now changed. Economies are faltering everywhere. For the first time since the dawn of computers, software personnel are unemployed. It is probably not the right time to act on the idea of this essay. However, I am more convinced than ever that we need to re-examine how we train both our software developers and our software managers.

The industry clearly needs software schools modeled after medical schools. After this essay appeared, I received a half-dozen or so letters from various places around the world claiming that they had already created such institutions. If that is the case, it is occurring in isolated cases only; the approach certainly has not permeated the industry, nor have I met any of their graduates.

SEEDS FOR DEBATE

1. This essay suggests that our industry could be improved by utilizing a medical school model in our universities. What other alternatives can you enumerate and describe that could have an equally profound effect, but would not require such a dramatic change to society?

2. Are there disciplines other than software engineering that could benefit from using the medical school model?

LIFE AND SOFTWARE

In this section, I will take some principles, wisdom, and experience from life in general, and apply them to the field of software.

I have always been a collector of great sayings. You know, these are the words that some authors add to the beginning of their essays to add meaning to the essay, and to force the reader to think bigger thoughts. Alas, most readers skip right past them. I don't. The first two essays in this section, *Words of Wisdom* and *More Words of Wisdom,* include 29 of my favorite timeless sayings. In most cases, these words speak for themselves. In a few cases, where I think I have something to add, I append my thoughts on how the wisdom may apply to our industry specifically.

While I was editor-in-chief of *IEEE Software,* I asked one of the IEEE Computer Society staff editors, Jim Sanders, to write a piece for the magazine on how writing music and developing software are similar (or different). He wrote a wonderful piece that I am honored to be able to include in this collection. His *Product, Not Process: A Parable* is followed by a few comments by me about how writing symphonies and software are similar, and of course Jim provides similar insight into how they are different. Enjoy.

I have tremendous respect for Tom DeMarco, both as a fellow occupant of this small planet called Earth, and as a thinker. My next piece *Making a Mark on the World* is my way of saying "You're great, Tom!"

Like Bob Glass, I am proud to be a naysayer. However, I sometimes get paranoid that all I talk about is what I don't like in our industry. In Essay 37, *Rewards of Taking the Path Less Traveled,* I try to be more constructive, discussing the good things that are done (and should be done more of) in our industry.

The last essay in this section, *Miscellaneous Thoughts on Evolution,* was inspired by my recent 4-month visit to Africa. It describes how evolution and progress can only be measured relative to the environment.

Great Software Debates. By Alan M. Davis
ISBN 0-471-649880 © 2004 Institute of Electrical and Electronics Engineers.

Words of Wisdom*

Over the years, I have collected words of wisdom from many famous (and some not-so-famous) writers. I thought you might enjoy reading some of them and thinking about how they relate to our industry.

But the Emperor has nothing on at all! —Hans Christian Anderson

Although Anderson had no exposure to our industry, I find I can apply this quote often. Our industry is full of self-proclaimed experts (indeed, some might include me in their ranks) who spend much of their time declaring how everybody else's logic is severely flawed. Lo and behold, by applying identical arguments we can easily see that their own logic suffers from the same flaws.

The only Zen you find on the tops of mountains is the Zen you bring up there. —Robert Pirsig

Although they are not limited to professionals in the software industry, I regularly meet frustrated people. Many of them are unhappy with their lot in life and yearn for greener pastures: jobs with more reasonable bosses and coworkers, or universities with better faculty, better students, and more considerate colleagues. In reality, many of these people are frustrated by their own inability, not by their environment. They are in constant search, but wherever they go they find no escape.

Practicing principles matters more than proving them. —Epictetus

Our industry is obsessed with trying to prove the utility of useful practices. If we spent half as much energy "doing" as we spend trying to prove, we would all be better off. Of course, many empiricists say this is poor advice. They cite cases where some commonly believed practice was later "proven" to be false by some experiment. In many cases, however, the experiment was so flawed that the common belief actually "proves" the experiment false.

*Originally published in *IEEE Software, 14*, 3 (May/June 1997), pp. 4, 6.

Please treat me tomorrow the way I have treated others today. —Unknown

If you can honestly make this request in the evening, then perhaps you have treated your fellow humans decently that day. Which is why the preceding quote of unknown origin, is more meaningful to me than the often-cited "Do unto others as you would have them do unto you."

Be suspicious of convention. Take charge of your own thinking. Rouse yourself from the ruse of unexamined habit. —Epictetus

We are like lemmings (see essay starting on page 3) in that we follow the latest fads without question. As long as we have much company on our travels, we assume we must he doing the right thing. We also feel safe; after all, everybody's doing it. Think for yourselves. Question common practices. Decide for yourselves whether or not something works for your world.

Say one word with your mouth shut. —Zen saying

Here's a bit of advice I have too often failed to heed. Only recently have I realized how powerful silence can be. When somebody says something you think is stupid or offensive, say nothing. A few of my friends practice martial arts. I understand from them how powerful it is to step aside when attacked. Let the attackers fall as a result of their own energies; you need not counter. The Zen saying above is the verbal equivalent of stepping aside.

You can only find truth with logic if you have already found truth without it. —G. K. Chesterton

This is great advice for people driven to experiment and prove the usefulness of software technology. If something works well and feels right, then use logic and data to better understand why, not to try to disprove its value. If something doesn't work well or feels wrong, then use logic and data to better understand why not. You know what works. Don't let manipulated data convince you otherwise.

When making choices in life, do not neglect to live. —Samuel Johnson

It is good to have an end to journey toward; but it is the journey that matters, in the end. —Ursula K. LeGuin

Too many computer and software professionals live as if computers and software were all that existed. There is more in life. Smell the roses. Walk in the woods. Stroll on a beach. Sit and talk with a terminally ill patient. Attend a concert. Help somebody. Visit an art museum. Learn a new, *nonprogramming* language. Visit a nursing home. Volunteer for a local not-for-profit organization.

People need to know they are dealing with a genuine person, not someone who is managing them. —Richard Farson

As software managers, we spend a lifetime trying to perfect our "technique" as managers. True, there are some critical techniques that must be learned: planning, scheduling, tracking, and so on. But most of the techniques we try to somehow learn are those related to people skills. We cannot learn techniques to be better "people managers" any more than we can learn techniques to be better lovers. As soon as our behavior seems mechanical, as if following a prescribed technique, we are perceived as artificial. Being a good people manager requires you to be vulnerable, real, human, genuine, sincere. It is not the art of following a library of "proven techniques."

Finally, I'd like to close with a few additional words of wisdom. They speak for themselves.

When you meet a master swordsman, show him your sword. When you meet a man who is not a poet, do not show him your poem. —Lin Chi

One day Chao-Chou fell down in the snow, and called out: Help me! Help me! A monk came and lay down beside him. Chao-Chou got up and went away. —Zen koan

Teachers open the door, but you must enter by yourself. —Chinese proverb

Think of life as a banquet. When dishes are passed to you, extend your hand and help yourself to a moderate portion. If a dish should pass you by, enjoy what is already on your plate. Or if a dish hasn't been passed to you yet, wait your turn. —Epictetus

Out of clutter, find simplicity. From discord, find harmony. In the middle of difficulty, find opportunity. —Albert Einstein

SEEDS FOR DEBATE

1. For each of the following quotes, describe how it relates to the software industry:

   - There is often wisdom under a shaggy coat.
   - What one hopes for is always better than one has
   - Even monkeys fall from trees.*
   - Life is a candle before the wind.*
   - For rice cakes, go to the rice-cake maker.*
   - Put a lid on what smells bad.*
   - One may study calligraphy at eighty.*

2. Select some of your own favorites quotes, and describe how they relate to the software industry.

*From D. Galef, *"Even Monkeys Fall from Trees" and Other Japanese Proverbs*, Rutland, Vermont: Charles E. Tuttle Company, 1987.

More Words of Wisdom*

In the previous essay, I quoted words of wisdom from some famous (and some not so famous) people, and provided ideas on how these words apply to our software industry today. By popular demand, I now offer you More Words of Wisdom.

> *Raise up many students. Help them see reality for themselves; remove dependency—there is no hierarchy in true learning* —Pirkei Avot (The Sayings of the Fathers)

Those of us who are teachers, of computer science or software engineering or anything else for that matter, should take heed. Our first responsibility is to help our students be independent of us, to give them wings, to help them fly for themselves. But even more important than that is this: There is no difference between teacher and student. We all travel the same road, all striving to attain more knowledge, to better comprehend existence, to share what we've learned with others. Teaching's highest rewards accrue when we share knowledge with others. We serve as essential cogs in the plan to retain knowledge in our society, to ensure that future generations can build upon all the knowledge of past generations. May some of you grow to be teachers yourselves, and fulfill this challenging but rewarding mission.

> *The bug, that perverse and elusive malfunctioning of hardware and later software, was born in the nineteenth century. It was already accepted shop slang as early as 1878, when Thomas Edison described. . . [the process of] invention: "The first step is an intuition and it comes with a burst, then difficulties arise—this thing gives out and then that. . . . '[B]ugs' . . . show themselves, and months of intense . . . study and labor are requisite before . . . success or failure is . . . reached.—Edward Tenner*

> *If there's more than one way to do a job and one of those ways will end in disaster, then somebody will do it that way.—Captain Edward Murphy Jr.*

> *Saru mo ki kara ichinru.—Japanese proverb*

*Originally published in IEEE Software, 15, 3 (May/June 1998), pp. 6–8.

Great Software Debates. By Alan M. Davis
ISBN 0-471-649880 © 2004 Institute of Electrical and Electronics Engineers.

Literally, this last one means "Even monkeys fall from trees." None of us are so great or so smart or so wise that we cannot falter. The greatest programmer inserts bugs. The greatest tester fails to discover an error. The greatest project manager will still on occasion be late or over budget. The most mature software development organization can create a disaster. The smartest guru of the "method du jour" might be wrong. Take this advice as both a leader and a follower. As a leader, make sure your followers know you might be wrong; help them understand what is known and what is conjecture; help them better understand why you "feel" something is right, rather than just pontificating. As a follower, you have a responsibility to question. And as a human being, be modest, humble, and never be afraid to admit you made a mistake.

> *Terrible suspicion: The real reason for use of pressure and overtime [on a software project] may be to make everyone look better when the project fails. —Mr. Tomkin (from* The Deadline, *by Tom DeMarco)*

Oh, how I hope this is not the norm. But I am afraid it is. If project managers do not apply undue pressure on their personnel and the project comes in late or over budget, their managers will blame them personally because they did not do everything in their power to help the project succeed. I can hear the comments now: "You'd think you were running a summer camp; throughout the project your people were happy and content. How dare you sacrifice the company's success for personal reasons. Don't you realize we're trying to run a business here?" Obviously, the right solution is to treat people with respect, kindness, and generosity, and also to bring the project in on budget and on time and with the quality and functionality your customers expect. The key is to do things that help the project succeed rather than doing things that only make it look like you're doing things to make the project succeed.

> *If a man perform that which hath not been attempted before, he shall purchase more honour than by effecting a matter of greater difficulty or virtue, wherein he is but a follower. —Sir Francis Bacon*

> *Far better to dare mighty things, to win glorious triumphs, even though checkered by failure, than to rank with those poor spirits who neither enjoy much nor suffer much. [They] know not victory, nor defeat. —Theodore Roosevelt*

We can't all be leaders all the time. But each of us must take the baton sometime. Go the extra mile on occasion. Try something nobody has tried before. Although I believe Francis Bacon was talking about doing things that nobody has done before, this also applies to trying to do things that you personally have never done before. So try something you've never tried before. If you succeed, you will feel great, and others will have great respect for you. If you fail, at least you tried! As Bloody Mary said in *South Pacific,* "If you don't have a dream, how you gonna have a dream come true?"

Assume you will die in three years. Select five people to deliver your eulogy: one family member, one friend, one co-worker, one boss, and one from a not-for-profit (perhaps your church). Write those eulogies. Now live your life to make those eulogies accurate. —Stephen Covey

Stephen Covey's challenge is one of the most powerful I've heard. I am repeatedly disappointed by the blatantly unethical behavior exhibited by those around me. It makes me wonder, are there different ethics? Could these people think their behaviors are acceptable? Perhaps their behaviors are ethical using some other set of rules? Would they behave differently if they had written their own eulogies? I try to live as if I had taken Covey's advice. Do others see me as unethical in spite of my best efforts? I hope not, for that would clearly disorient my perception of right and wrong. So what can we do? I believe our only recourse is to do what we believe in our hearts is the right thing. Perhaps we should all start writing those eulogies and then living that life.

If we believe that we're working for just another company then we're going to be like another company.—Thomas J. Watson, Jr.

Although Watson said this to IBM employees, it is great advice for us all. In corporate America, I often hear, "But that's not how so-and-so does it." In academe, I often hear, "We can't expect excellence; we're not an excellent university." Both of these attitudes condemn our organizations to a life of either mediocrity or sameness.

The term "exceptional" has two meanings: (1) to be an exception, that is, different than others, and (2) to be great. It is not a coincidence that the same word carries both meanings. To achieve greatness, we must find new and better ways to do things. We must dare to be different, whether we are teachers, students, editors, software developers, project managers, CEOs, entrepreneurs, or employees in big companies or start-ups. Strive to be all that exceptional means.

Now let me close with a few more gems that are totally self-explanatory.

Don't bother just to be better than your contemporaries or predecessors. Try to be better than yourself. —William Faulkner

If you think about which of your organs is active as you manage, the head doesn't come into it much at all. Management is in the gut, in the heart, and in the soul. —Belinda Binda (from The Deadline, *by Tom DeMarco)*

Purpose for Incorporation: To establish a place of work where engineers can feel the joy of technological innovation, be aware of their mission to society and work to their heart's content.—James Collins and Jerry Porras

If we provide real satisfaction to real customers, we will be profitable. —John Young (Hewlett-Packard)

People are number 1. Treat them well, expect a lot, and the rest will follow.—Marriott Ideology

SEEDS FOR DEBATE

1. For each of the following quotes, describe how it relates to the software industry:

   - First there is a time when we believe everything, then for a little while we believe with discrimination, then we believe nothing whatever, and then we believe everything again—and, moreover, give reasons why we believe. —Georg Christoph Lichtenberg (1742–1799)
   - One excellent way to maintain a hypothesis indefinitely is to ignore information that does not conform to it. —Dietrich Dörner
   - Do not say "When I find time, I will study." Time is never found, only made. —Hillel
   - We find comfort among those who agree with us; growth among those who don't. —Frank A. Clark
   - In the book of life, the answers aren't in the back. —Charlie Brown

2. Select some of your own favorites quotes, and describe how they relate to the software industry.

Product Not Process: A Parable*

JAMES SANDERS

So advanced was his deafness, Ludwig van Beethoven did not notice his valet until the man tapped him gently on the shoulder. The visitor the valet announced was a neatly dressed gentleman with a satchel under one arm. Beethoven did not recognize him—nor did he care to. It was late in the summer of 1823 and he was deeply immersed in the composition of what would become his ninth symphony.

Before he could snarl a protest at being interrupted, the man crossed the study and slammed his satchel down on Beethoven's desk. "Good day, Herr Beethoven." The words came to him only faintly. The composer saw that the satchel bore the crest of the Austrian baron who was secretly underwriting his work. He must listen to this fool, then. He nodded for the man to continue.

"My employer is concerned about the slow progress of your work. He insists that you finish by the end of the year so that he can stage an exclusive premiere of your symphony at his New Year's ball."

"But of course." Beethoven knew that if the angels smiled upon him, he might complete the Ninth by next February. March was more likely. Experience had taught him never to disclose such bad news until absolutely necessary.

"But *not* of course." The man dug into his satchel and pulled out a sheaf of crinkled papers. Beethoven realized they were manuscript pages from an earlier draft of the Ninth—pages he'd discarded weeks ago. "You are taking too much time to write your symphony," the man said. "Worse, you are padding it with far too many notes. At this rate you will finish months late and deliver a work so large and ungainly no one will listen to it."

Beethoven glanced at his valet; the man would not meet his eyes. So. His manser-

---

*Originally published in *IEEE Software, 14,* 2 (March/April 1997), pp. 6–8.

Great Software Debates. By Alan M. Davis
ISBN 0-471-649880 © 2004 Institute of Electrical and Electronics Engineers.

vant had betrayed him and now the world knew what a tortured struggle each composition was for him. Did it matter that the process of creation was ugly if the finished product was beautiful, even brilliant? Apparently so. Beethoven felt strangely
exposed and, for once, had no retort.

His visitor mistook Beethoven's silence for despair and placed a comforting hand
on his shoulder. "Don't worry, friend. I have the solution to your problems." He
reached into his satchel and withdrew a stack of charts and graphs. "I have studied
your compositional procedures and although they may be excusable for a novice,
they are unforgivable for a mature composer. I've isolated several practices I think
you can improve upon. For example, look here. This section with the long cello
solo—very inefficient. The violins could play it much faster, yes?"

The visitor pulled out another chart. "Speaking of violins, why do you use the
strings and woodwinds so much, yet neglect the brass? For that matter, why don't
you write more *tutti* passages? The musicians get paid as much whether they play or
just sit, so it's most economical to have them all play at the same time, don't you
think?"

Beethoven gasped, his mouth worked, but no words would come.

"Ah, I see you're a quick-minded fellow, you grasp the implications immediately.
You'll be delighted to know that I've volunteered to spend the coming weeks at your
side, monitoring your work. Oh, those bloated passages bursting with too many
notes, those interminable crescendos, those meandering codas—just think of the in-
efficiencies we can eliminate. Why, we'll double the number of notes you write per
hour!"

Beethoven rocked back in his chair. "No!'

"Incredible, yes? But don't thank me now, it will only slow us down." The visitor flipped over another chart. "Let's jump right in, shall we? Here—you introduce
a theme and then restate it later in the movement. A fairly standard practice and
an efficient one that saves you from having to compose a new section entirely. Ah,
but here's where you go wrong: you vary the theme too much to make reusing the
notes worthwhile. All this breaking passages down and tossing them back and
forth between the violins and the oboes. . . ." The visitor paused and drew a finger
across his throat. "That's the best solution, don't you think? With this section
tightened   and   more   self-contained,   we   can   drop   it   in   here   . . .   and
here . . . and cut by almost half the time it will take you to write the entire movement."

Beethoven finally found his voice. "Who *are* you?"

The visitor drew himself to attention. "Herr Nummerich, at your service. I was
an officer m the Austrian artillery during the wars against Napoleon."

Beethoven glared at him. "And this somehow makes you an expert on music?"
Nummerich nodded emphatically. "Why? Because my tympani remind you of your
guns firing?"

"No. Because artillery is all math: the bore and length of the gun barrel, the weight
of the shot, the curve of the ball's trajectory and the force of its impact. Music is all
math too: the pitch and duration of notes, the intervals between those notes in a scale,
the timing between beats in a measure. People think of music as an art, but they're

wrong. It's a science, or it could be. Music wants to be a science. I feel that. Don't you?"

"No, you cretin. Now get out."

Nummerich made no move to leave. "I must inform you that if you refuse to accept my counsel, my employer will withdraw his support. Immediately."

"Fine. I'll find another patron."

"I doubt it. With all modesty, I confess that my ideas are much *en vogue* with Vienna's nobles. Any one of them would most likely hire first an efficient composer who costs less and produces more."

"I see." Although outwardly calm, Beethoven felt deeply shaken. The thought of spending the rest of his days an impoverished invalid held little appeal. Still, to let this fool cut the heart from his music and extinguish its fire—it was unbearable. And yet . . . what of all the charts and numbers that lay spread before him? Beethoven shuddered— maybe *he* was wrong. "Perhaps I have reacted hastily, Herr Nummerich. What else do you propose?"

Nummerich bent over the desk eagerly. "I've run some estimates. My projections indicate that your next symphony will take more than an hour to play. Ach! Mozart and Haydn never wrote such monsters. So first, we reduce the length of your composition by 41.4 percent." Beethoven winced, then nodded.

"Good." Nummerich shuffled through the papers and pulled out a rumpled page from the fourth movement. "We can start with the chorus. A chorus in a symphony? Madness! If listeners want to hear singing they can attend an opera or a chorale."

"But the Ode . . ."

"Is not part of the requirements. Really, now. Cutting the chorus reduces the composition by nearly 15 percent. Besides, you should leave such wild innovations for upstarts trying to make a name for themselves. You and your patron have a reputation to uphold and listeners to satisfy."

Beethoven would always remember that afternoon as the longest of his life. Months later, when the symphony premiered—on time—Beethoven was appalled by the audience's lukewarm applause and stifled yawns. Yawns? His works had provoked tears, laughter, even outrage, but never this. Herr Nummerich, at his side throughout the performance, asked what he thought of the premiere. "For the first time in my life," Beethoven told him, "I am happy to be deaf."

EPILOGUE

If you are a student, let me warn you that there are many Herr Nummerich's out there!

If you are in industry, you know that there are many Herr Nummerich's out there.

If you are Herr Nummerich, I am sure you are trying to help us and help your career. But please, do it someplace else.

TOP TEN REASONS WHY SYMPHONIES AND SOFTWARE ARE ALIKE
Al Davis

Of course, it seems ludicrous to apply process metrics to symphonic composition. But I think symphonies and software bear enough similarities to make us question the wisdom of applying process metrics to software.

1. The building blocks for composition are very small.
2. Measures per month (M/mo.) and lines of code per month (LOC/mo.) are both easily tracked and equally meaningless.
3. The process that creates a product is totally unimportant once that product is delivered.
4. The product reveals a great deal about its creator's beliefs and values.
5. As Christopher Alexander observed when explaining his "quality without a name" concept, great products are easily recognized—but describing exactly why they are great is difficult.
6. Not surprisingly, then, no absolute rules exist for measuring product quality.
7. User satisfaction completely drives a product's popularity and economic success.
8. The greatest works in the field have tremendous emotional impact and stylistic influence.
9. Both forms permeate our culture.
10. Preconceived requirements do not encompass all user desires. Users can be surprised and delighted by the unexpected; sometimes they learn what they want only after they experience it in a finished product.

TOP TEN REASONS WHY SYMPHONIES ARE NOT LIKE SOFTWARE
James Sanders

I agree with Al that conceptually software design and symphonic composition have much in common. But software products, given their nature and use, will inevitably benefit from a system that can codify good practice without hamstringing creativity and innovation.

1. Symphonies are not written by teams.
2. Symphonies are not revised continually in response to end-user requirements.
3. Listeners do not need a consultant to tell them which symphonies to listen to, when, or how.
4. Symphonies do not require maintenance, are never upgraded, and do not become obsolete when technology advances.
5. Symphonies are always platform-independent: the violin parts, for example, can be played by a Stradivarius, a Yamaha, or a synthesizer—the symphony doesn't care.
6. Symphonies are not application-specific. Beethoven never wrote an accounting symphony; Brahms never wrote a word processing symphony; Mozart never even wrote a Java applet.
7. Large corporations do not routinely contract with composers to write symphonies, nor must symphonies ever model a corporation's work processes.
8. Symphonies cannot be critical systems: a symphonic bug (incorrect meter, unintentional disharmony) has never caused death, injury, or business failure.
9. Symphonies—no matter how badly written or played—never crash the orchestra, even when listeners wish they would.
10. Bill Gates has no plans for controlling the direction, structure, and pricing of all symphonies . . . yet.

SEEDS FOR DEBATE

1. Have you met a Herr Nummerich in your life? If so, write about him or her in the same way that Jim Sanders did. Of course, you may want to keep the person's real name a secret, especially if you still are working with him/her.

2. Take the position that Herr Nummerich is really trying to help Beethoven. What could he do that would really be helpful?

3. Select something other than symphonies, e.g., rock music, sculpture, bridge-building, home construction, teaching a class. Make a list of ten reasons why it is like software and ten reasons why it is unlike software, just like the boxed lists on page 232.

Making a Mark on the World*

I'm sitting in a hotel room in Atlanta, contemplating the great loss of Princess Diana and Mother Teresa. Mother Teresa's selfless devotion to giving, to comforting, to extending a hand and heart to whomever was in need was truly remarkable. Her passing is of course sad, but as she herself said so many times and so eloquently, everybody must die some time. At 87, it is hard to feel like she (or humanity) was cheated. Princess Diana's humanitarianism was also truly remarkable. Her passing at such a young age and in such a senseless manner filled me—and millions of others—with great sadness. These two wonderful humans should be role models for us all.

Now, in the weeks since their passing, sadness has given way to frustration: the giving of my time, hand, and heart to others seems minuscule when compared to theirs. I have also been wondering why computer and software people in general are not great "givers." Some professions have organized their public service formally, as in medicine's Doctors Without Borders. In our industry, exceptions to a general apathy are hard to find. But they do exist. Chief among these exceptions is Tom DeMarco, the great giver among us.

DeMarco—a humble person—will of course be embarrassed by these comments; but his consistent generosity deserves mention. I am not referring solely to his technical work; his contribution extends beyond this to encompass larger issues of meaning to Earth travelers.

HONORING OUR OWN

Have you picked up your copy of *Peopleware* [co-authored with Tim Lister] recently? What a wonderful message: *People are important*. The book is chock full of insights on how to manage software people. The answer is simple: treat them like people, nothing more and nothing less.

In the 10 years since *Peopleware* was published, the software industry has largely persisted in its mistakes. We continue to use partitions and cubicles in lieu of offices. We promote the best technical people into management, though they lack

*Originally published in *IEEE Software*, 14, 6 (November/December 1997), pp. 4, 6.

Great Software Debates. By Alan M. Davis
ISBN 0-471-649880 © 2004 Institute of Electrical and Electronics Engineers.

management skills. We trade quality for schedule. We search for the magic solution to the "software productivity problem."

Isn't anybody out there listening? Perhaps I should not be surprised. AIDS and HIV continue to spread despite the tireless efforts of medical researchers and volunteers (like Diana) who work to improve the lives of those infected. Poverty and hunger continue to spread despite the efforts of those (like Mother Teresa) who work to feed and comfort the hungry. And so the software industry—like so many other industries—continues to mistreat its members, despite the work of people like DeMarco.

DIGGING DEEP

Have you read *Why Does Software Cost So Much?* If not do so! Here's another great work that raises our social consciences. *Why Does Software* complements *Peopleware* wonderfully. Where *Peopleware* suggests we look beyond titles and treat each other more humanely in the workplace, this book suggests we behave more humanely in the wider world.

In *Why Does Software,* DeMarco has as much to tell us about our world as our industry. He says that as Earth dwellers, we have a responsibility to each other. It is not enough to just manage software developers well. Nor is it enough to write great software and produce great requirements specifications. We must also help our fellow travelers. We must pick a cause and give.

When I say "give," I don't mean money (although that's okay too); I mean our hands, our hearts, our time. Help inner city youth learn about software. Volunteer time to an AIDS, Alzheimer's, or children's cancer support group. We can't say we don't have the skills; the only skill that's needed is in the heart and hand. One of DeMarco's causes is improving the quality of K-12 education in Maine. He makes a difference. We can all make a difference, too.

TRIPLE PLAY

Have you read DeMarco's latest book, *The Deadline*? This book purports to be a novel about project management and certainly is—it has intrigue, suspense, murder, spies, kidnapping, and so on. It holds your attention so well it is hard to put down. I read it in two sittings.

But housed within this "novel" is a text on project management. The experiences of Mr. Tompkin (the lead character; kin to Tom?) and the decisions he is forced to make—hiring, scheduling, risk analyzing, or trying to deal with wholly incompetent senior management—are all too real for anybody who has been there. And the messages are profound. One of the many delectable tidbits is that your primary anatomical asset as a manager is not your head: "management is in the gut, in the heart, and in the soul." Another tidbit on software projects in general: "The real reason for use of pressure and overtime may be to make everyone look better when the project fails." How powerful!

The Deadline can also be read as a gossip column. Although officially fictitious, some of the characters in the book bear some remarkable similarities to real people. It is fun to try to see if anybody you know makes an appearance.

DeMarco's trilogy—*Peopleware, Why Does Software Cost So Much?*, and *The Deadline*—should be on the shelf of every software developer and manager. In addition to empowering us, they provide profound insights into who Tom DeMarco is. Like other great individuals, his life and work offer a model for how and why we should aspire to be better managers, better developers, better professionals, and—most importantly—better human beings.

EPILOGUE

Since this article appeared, Tom DeMarco has written five more books, all of which are well worth reading:

- *Peopleware: Productive Projects and Teams*, 2nd edition (with Tim Lister), Dorset House, 1999
- *Dark Harbor House: A Novel*, Down East Books, 1999
- *Slack. Getting Past Burnout, Busywork, and the Myth of Total Efficiency*, Broadway, 2002
- *Lieutenant America and Miss Apple Pie*, Down East Books, 2002
- *Waltzing with Bears: Managing Risks on Software Projects* (with Tim Lister), Dorset House, 2003

SEEDS FOR DEBATE

1. What have you done for your fellow man lately? This is meant for you to think about, not actually write down.
2. Is there somebody that you really respect in your field? Tell them so!

Rewards of Taking the
Path Less Traveled*

In Essay 1, I painted an image of the software-engineering industry in which hordes of professionals all followed one of a half-dozen or so well-trod "lemming paths." Each path corresponds to a "technology" whose proponents have made outrageous claims that its use will result in great increases in either quality or productivity or whatever. Although the paths may lead to great results for some (or even all), nobody on the path really knows. In fact, not even the outspoken proponents know for sure. They think the technology is great, but their hypotheses have never been verified.

What should you do? If you follow the lemmings, I'll accuse you of making blind decisions. If you stay still, you'll feel weak, you'll feel alone, and worst of all, you'll feel "backward" because you're not using so-called modern technology. Actually, that's not the worst. The worst is if your customers perceive you to be backward.

You have three choices. Follow the lemmings, get an eagle-eye perspective, or take the path less traveled. I explored the problems associated with the first choice thoroughly in Essay 1. This essay examines the other two.

BIG PICTURE

The view from a helicopter is very different from that at ground level. From this eagle-eye perspective, you see the big picture. You can see forks in paths and which one leads to a chasm. You can see paths leading to box canyons. You can easily see how to avoid the potholes.

I suggest you take this perspective. Instead of following the lemmings, look at the evidence. Is there solid evidence the technology works? Is there solid evidence it will work in your environment? In your application? With your management style? If the answer to any of these questions is no, are you willing and able to take the associated risks?

*Originally published in *IEEE Software, 11,* 4 (July 1994), pp. 100–103.

Great Software Debates. By Alan M. Davis
ISBN 0-471-649880 © 2004 Institute of Electrical and Electronics Engineers.

By the way, what are the risks involved in taking the wrong path? Does it simply make your project later? Or does it make you unable to even produce a product? Talk to others on the path now. Find out what problems they had. Talk to others who have tried and abandoned the path. Every new technology has zealous supporters and equally zealous detractors. Speak to both. In short, get as much information as you can before you make your decision. Once you start on the path, keep your eyes open. Keep trying to learn from others just ahead of you.

PATH LESS TRAVELED

In [Essay 31], Bob Glass laments the misdirection of software-engineering researchers and practicing managers. He wrote that researchers produce unproven technologies and managers embrace them blindly.

It turns out that managers actually do have a choice. There is a plethora of rarely used, yet proven techniques that can be used at little or no cost, with little or no risk, to achieve small to moderate gains in quality and productivity. None of these are silver bullets. But all can help your project. None will result in incredibly large increases in quality or productivity, but then neither will fads associated with the lemmings. Table 37.1 highlights the differences between the techniques on the path less traveled and the popular "hot" fads.

The proven techniques along the path less traveled include some incredibly simple ideas:

• *Talk to your customers.* This advice is so obvious, but so often ignored—for reasons as varied as the software industry itself. Some developers are afraid to talk to their customers because they might tell them to do something other than they had planned. Guess what? If you are building system x because you think it is "neat" or "modern" or "revolutionary'" or "easy to use," and the customer really wants system y, you will end up with neat, modern, revolutionary, easy-to-use shelfware. If you build system y, you can use the profit to build system x later. And once you have loyal customers, you'll more readily sell system x.

I've given this advice before. "If a commercial developer, talk often with the

TABLE 37.1. Differences Between Fads and the Path Less Traveled

Hot fads	Path less traveled
Proponents claim incredible increases in productivity or quality.	There are few outspoken proponents.
You will possibly obtain small to moderate increases in productivity or quality.	You will possibly obtain small to moderate increases in productivity or quality.
There is significant risk.	There is little risk.
The technology is mostly unproven.	The technology is proven.
Others will see you as modern.	Others will see you as old-fashioned.

clients. Keep them involved. Sure, it is easier to develop software in a vacuum, but will the customer like the result? If a producer of shrinkwrap software, 'customers' are harder to locate during development. So instead, role play. Designate three to four individuals in your organization as prospective customers and tap them for ideas that will keep them as customers or make them happy. If a government contractor, talk often with the contracting officers, their technical representatives, and if possible, the users. People and situations change often in the government. The only way to keep up with it is communication. Ignoring the changes may make life seem easier in the short term, but the final system will not be useful." (Davis, A., *201 Principles of Software Engineering,* McGraw-Hill, 1995). Communicating with the customer increases the probability that the system you build meets your customers real needs and expectations.

- *Build prototypes.* Not every application lends itself to prototyping, but many do. A throwaway prototype is built quick and dirty, then given to customers to experiment with. Customer feedback is collected and analyzed. Features that result in positive feedback are incorporated in the requirements specification; those that don't, aren't. Once the requirements are baselined, the developer discards the prototype and builds the software from scratch, using proven, full-scale development techniques.

In short, prototyping is appropriate whenever you are unsure of the requirements. You should prototype only those features you are unsure of because otherwise the customer is likely to say OK to every feature you implement. You won't learn a thing and you will have wasted resources. In the March 1994 *IEEE Software Manager* column, ("Fast, Cheap Requirements: Prototype, or Else!" pp. 85–87), Stephen Andriole takes a more extreme position. He advocates always prototyping. Prototyping increases the probability that the system as built meets real customer needs and expectations.

- *Do trade-off analyses.* Software designers typically select an architecture according to one of five criteria: (1) it's the only one we can think of; (2) it's the "obvious" one; (3) it looks "neat"; (4) it looks like it should work; or (5) it's the one we've always used. These are not good criteria.

Instead, select three to four diverse architectures. Compare and contrast them in detail in regard to performance, throughput, maintainability, testability, simplicity, and elegance. Run simulations if necessary to determine performance and throughput. In short, gather as much information about the alternatives before you eliminate any or select the best one. Systems engineers have been doing this for years. If we want to be taken seriously as engineers, software engineers need to start making intelligent, well-informed engineering decisions. Doing trade-off analyses among design alternatives will help reduce development and maintenance costs and shorten development time.

- *Play with formal models.* One of the biggest gaps between software researchers and practitioners is the use of formal models. Many researchers claim that unless formal models are used, little can be accomplished. Many practitioners are alienated by formal models. They don't want to read them, and they certainly don't want to create them.

A very useful solution is to have practitioners "play" with such models. Here's how it works: Write the requirements specification in natural language, then select segments of the specification and try to construct a more formal model (like a finite-state machine, decision table, Petri net, Statechart, or Z notation). You do not need to complete the construction (although I am not suggesting you deliberately avoid completing it).

In the process of trying to construct a formal model, you'll expose ambiguities and incompleteness in the original specification. Fix the natural language whenever you find a problem. When you're done you can discard the formal model or incorporate it in the specification. The final disposition of the model is not as important as how you use it to reduce errors in the natural-language specification. Playing with formal models will increase the probability that the as-built system meets real customer needs and expectations, decrease development costs, and shorten schedules.

- *Review, walkthrough, and inspect.* Although there are significant differences among a technical review, a walk-through, and an inspection, they all have something in common. In all three, someone other than the developer examines a development product to uncover misconceptions or faults. In all three, the goal is to detect (and subsequently repair) errors as early as possible in the development process, to reduce rework.

Some proponents of these methods will advise you to invest large sums of money in a long course to learn the "perfect" inspection process. It's likely this will result in optimal increases in quality and productivity. However, this essay is about low-cost, low-risk alternatives that result in small to moderate gains. Thus, I recommend that you simply read a book (see Table 37.2) or take a very short course. Then start practicing intelligent reviews, walkthroughs, or inspections. The results will not be as dramatic or as predictable as if you had taken one of the proven, full-course techniques, but you will nonetheless improve quality and/or productivity.

- *Salvage.* Software reuse is the incorporation of previously used requirements, designs, code segments, test plans, or documentation into a new product. There is much research underway in characterizing potentially reusable components, cataloging and retrieving them, tailoring them, and composing systems from them. There is also much activity underway to populate reuse repositories. With all this activity, we are forgetting a very simple way to reuse: Just do it!

Salvaging means going to your colleagues and saying, "Hey, I need to build a data-fusion algorithm for a particular class of ship. Sally, didn't you do something like that two years ago?" True, salvaging does not result in the spectacular increases in productivity and quality afforded by a repository. However, it risks you nothing and costs you nothing, and it can contribute small to moderate increases in quality and productivity.

I recommend you adopt all six of these low-cost, low-risk ideas. Every one of them will have a positive effect on the quality of your product, your productivity, and your ability to satisfy your customers' needs. It is true that the effect will not be as dramatic as those claimed by the proponents of fad technologies, but how can you beat the low cost and risk?

Finally, do not misinterpret my advice as a substitute for the "hot" technologies.

Table 37.2. Simple Truths: Low-Risk, Low-Cost Learning

For more information on communicating with the customer, read D. Gause and G. Weinberg, Are Your Lights On? *Dorset House, New York, 1990.*

For more information on prototyping, read: S. Andriole. Rapid Application Prototyping, *QED, Wellesley, Mass., 1993; A. Davis, "Operational Prototyping: A New Development Approach," IEEE Software, Sept. 1992, pp. 70–78; and H. Gomaa, "Prototypes: Keep Them or Throw Them Away?" InfoTech State of the Art Report on Prototyping, Pergamon Press, Oxford, 1986.*

For more information on doing trade-off analyses on software architectures, read D. Garlan and M. Shaw, "An Introduction to Software Architecture," Advances in Software Engineering and Knowledge Engineering, *1993.*

For more information on practical use of formal models, read A. Davis, Software Requirements: Objects, Functions and States, *Prentice-Hall. Englewood Cliffs, N.J., 1993; and A. Hall, "Seven Myths of Formal Methods," IEEE Software, Sept. 1990, pp. 11–19.*

For more information on reviews, walkthroughs, and inspections, read T. Gilb and D. Graham, Software Inspections, *Addison-Wesley, Reading, Mass., 1993; and D. Freedman and G. Weinberg,* Walkthroughs, Inspections and Technical Reviews, *Little Brown, Boston, 1982.*

For more information on salvaging and reuse, read A.J. Incorvaia et al., "Case Studies in Software Reuse," Proc. Compsac, IEEE CS Press, Los Alamitos, Calif, 1990, pp. 301–306; and W. Tracz, *Tutorial: Software Reuse, IEEE CS Press, Los Alamitos, Calif, 1990.*

You owe it to yourself and your organization to carefully assess these too, and embrace those that are best for your environment.

SEEDS FOR DEBATE

1. What would be so bad if you "followed the lemmings" anyway?

2. In this essay, I recommend that you examine the evidence before you embark on a path. Considering my opinions on metrics (see "Why Build Software?" and "Eras of Software Technology Transfer" on pages 31 and 37, respectively), what evidence do you think I'm talking about?

3. Prepare a list of "hot fads" and "paths less traveled" that is valid today.

4. Why do you suppose I recommend that you just play with formal models? Construct an argument why you should do a lot more than just play with them. Now construct an argument for why you should avoid formal methods altogether.

Miscellaneous Thoughts on Evolution

I am sitting now in a reed shelter in the middle of nowhere, after driving on a 4×4 trail for 7 hours across the vast Kalahari Desert. This is the culmination of a three-week voyage that has spanned both Namibia and Botswana from their southern-most to their northernmost frontiers. For almost three weeks I have been unable to access Internet. Instead I have been most fortunate to have met many indigenous people and learned some of the ways they live in this harsh, dry land.

THE NEED FOR WESTERN-STYLE PROGRESS

I have had much time to think with a mind uncluttered with my usual day-to-day thoughts, worries, and miscellaneous meanderings. I began to worry that the Inter-net is widening the gap between the have's and the have-not's [NOR01]. After all, in the so called western world, our rate of knowledge acquisition has increased dra-matically with the advent of the Internet, while people in the so-called underdevel-oped nations know less than us and now acquire new information at an even slower relative rate. We have access to more knowledge and goods than they have, and every day we gain access to even more.

Furthermore, the educational system in the western world is likewise far superior to that of sub-Saharan Africa. Our educational process enables knowledge to be spread from person to person and from generation to generation at a far greater rate than at economically less prosperous countries.

The combination of the Internet and quality education seems to make the gap more profound, and to make it more insurmountable with every passing year.

PROGRESS IS AN ILLUSION

Then it dawned on me: Progress is but an illusion, or at least it only makes sense rel-ative to an environment. This thought came to me during a three-hour hike in the Kgalagadi Transfrontier Park with a local guide as he pointed out fresh animal tracks in the sand. He explained how to identify them as lion spoor (and in this case male lion spoor). He also taught us to tell which way the lion was walking. He ex-plained that if we wanted to survive we should continue our walk in the direction from which the lion came (or in a perpendicular direction), not in the same direc-

Great Software Debates. By Alan M. Davis
ISBN 0-471-649880 © 2004 Institute of Electrical and Electronics Engineers.

tion that the lion was walking. The smartest way to survive a lion encounter in the bush is to not have one. For a person living in the Kalahari (the westernized spelling of Kgalagadi), progress is increasing your chances of surviving in the bush. It is not gaining access to the Internet.

Progress is about finding ways to optimize your chances of survival in the environment in which you find yourself. Attempting to measure one society's progress using the yardsticks of another society makes no sense. Western man has the perception that Bushmen have somehow made less progress and that Western man needs to somehow assist them in evolving. However, Bushmen likely have exactly the opposite view; that Western man has made a serious turn backwards, and perhaps Bushmen should help Western man find a more positive evolutionary path.

PARALLELS TO THE ANIMAL KINGDOM

In most of the western world, man has destroyed all local predators, and we thus no longer need to be able to read animal tracks. In essence we have destroyed our environment to make our lives seem easier. As we destroy each layer of threat in our environment, we find ourselves with little to do other than to quench our thirst for new knowledge and new horizons and new pastimes using the Internet. Is this progress?

Over a similar period of years, the Bushmen of Africa have not destroyed the environment to reach their goals. Instead, their view of progress is to find ever more innovative ways to live in their environment without destroying it. So, instead of killing animals that could pose a threat to them, they learn from those predators, while avoiding confrontations with them. Every generation learns from earlier generations and from its members' own newly acquired knowledge, and in turn passes it all down to the next generation. Is this progress?

History has clearly shown that any population (human, other animal species, or even plants) that adapts to its environment survives. And any population that consumes resources that have no way to replace themselves will quickly die out ("quickly" in archeological time). If progress of one species entails the destruction of other species, or if progress entails the consumption of non-renewable resources (contrast our use of fossil fuels with the Bushmen's use of springbok), progress is not occurring. Instead, we are simply attaining a local positive slope in a steeply declining curve. Will Western man survive another ten thousand years? I doubt it. Will the Bushmen survive another ten thousand years? I would like to say yes. Unfortunately I cannot, because Western man is running out of its own resources to consume, and is quickly destroying the resources and environment of the Bushmen. How sad. Not only will we destroy ourselves, but we will be the downfall of others as well.

WHAT CAN I DO?

Before I came to the realization that our perception of progress is illusionary, I wondered how I as just one man could make a difference in sub-Saharan Africa. What could I do to help? Is the answer more capital? Is it improved K-12 education? Is it better college education? Is it more basic life-sustaining resources such as water and food? Or is the climate just so harsh that such development is just plain impossible? Then I thought of Phoenix, Arizona and Fargo, North Dakota (with apologies to the residents of these two cities who may consider their respective climates to be close to perfect). Their weather has not held them back at all (with apologies to the Phoeniphobes and Fargophobes who may think that progress in these cities has indeed been severely hampered).

I thought about my own career, so devoted to helping others develop skills and acquire knowledge. Can I somehow use my skills to assist these apparently less fortunate people?

We sit in the western world and lament that others have no access to the Internet. And the Bushmen stand in the Kalahari and lament that we westerners would not survive even a day in the desert. We sit in the western world and are critical of others because they have shorter life spans. And the Bushmen are likely critical of us: we may live longer, but do we even live at all? Is it better to live 50 years and know the world? Or to live 75 years and to have never experienced what life really is all about? Is it better to live 50 years and leave the Earth no worse than it was before being born? Or to live 75 years and to have contributed to the destruction of our species? The Earth of course will exist for millennia after the destruction of the habitat that man needs for its survival. And it will of course support other great empires such as dinosaurs and man. So man is not really destroying the Earth, it is just destroying those parts of the Earth that we need for our survival.

SUMMARY

I guess one thing to conclude from these observations is that each society makes progress in its own way. The Bushmen progress by learning new ways to survive in their environment, and Western men progress by learning new ways to survive in their environment. Members of either society should have the ability to acquire knowledge to survive in the other culture if they so desire. However, if I were forced to proclaim that one culture is more advanced than the other, I would have to select the Bushmen.

On the other hand, as we progress up Maslow's hierarchy of needs [MAS98], we also take longer-term perspectives. The "advancement" I describe above for the Bushmen is less destructive to the environment, but it is also extremely short term (i.e., survival for the next few hours). Bushmen do very little planning for the next few years. Meanwhile, the "advancement" I describe for Western man is more destructive of the environment, but it is oriented around planning for the next few years (or decades), but unfortunately not for millennia. This short-term vs. long-term orientation is also mirrored in the activities of poor vs. well-to-do people [MAH03]

We in the western world see the employment of software as a fundamental means to achieve our society's goals. The good news is that software by itself does not consume valuable natural resources. On the other hand, its ever presence in our lives continues to foster our blindness with respect to the really important issues facing mankind.

REFERENCES

[MAH03] Mahlangu, B., "Achievement Motivation among University Students," *Empowerment through Entrepreneurship Conference,* sponsored by *Entrepreneurship Policy Journal,* Cape Town, South Africa, November 2003.

[MAS98] Maslow, A., *Toward a Psychology of Being,* Third Edition, New York: John Wiley and Sons, 1998.

[NOR01] Norris, P., *Digital Divide: Civic Engagement, Information Poverty, and the Internet Worldwide,* Cambridge University Press, 2001.

SEEDS FOR DEBATE

1. Argue that Western man's view of technological progress is the only true progress.

2. Argue that Bushmen have a much better handle on true progress than Western man.

3. What is the relationship between climate and human progress?

THE FUTURE*

Many writers far more eloquent than me have noted that the software industry is in its infancy. What will occur during its next major life phase, adolescence? I do not pretend to be a soothsayer; I hold no magic, no supernatural insight. All I have are my opinions, my fears, and my excitement about the future, which is based on my (what seems to me to be a paltry) 30 years or so of exposure to the software industry. How quickly one moves from being a neophyte to being a geriatric case!

OVERALL

The software industry is ripping itself into segments, each going its own way. These segments are adopting standards and practices so diverse that I expect, by 2010, we will no longer consider "the software industry" to be an industry. The two predominant segments today are the "increasing control of process" (ICP) world and the "decreasing control of process" (DCP) world. Both believe they are on the path to conquering the inherent difficulty of software construction.

The ICP world is mostly on the path toward higher levels of CMM or some other process improvement path. They believe that by instituting more control on the development process, they'll have more control over the quality of the resulting product. The DCP world employs more and more powerful tools to unburden itself from the tedium and error-proneness of software development. Thus, they program in visual languages to create user interfaces and database applications; they are more interested in achieving higher productivity than measuring it.

SOFTWARE DEVELOPMENT METHODS

Like glaciers, the fads will continue to encroach and retreat, carving great canyons in our terrain. Each serves a valuable purpose in shaping industry practices, and each leaves a permanent mark when it departs. Since joining the industry, I have seen the rise and fall of the Fortran and Cobol eras; I have seen the rise and fall of the Structured era; I have seen the rise and fall of the CASE era; and we are all now witnessing

---

*Originally published as "Predictions and Farewell," in *IEEE Software*, 15, 4 (July/August 1998), pp. 6–9.

Great Software Debates. By Alan M. Davis
ISBN 0-471-649880 © 2004 Institute of Electrical and Electronics Engineers.

the fall of the Object era.* Just as happened in earlier eras, the Object era's terms will disappear like glacial ice, but the good ideas created during this era will, like glacially carved canyon walls, persist. I do not believe that such glaciers will cease their cycling for many more decades. The only real question is what name the next age will bear.

REQUIREMENTS

When I wrote *Software Requirements* (Prentice Hall, 1990, 1993) . . . , the world thought that requirements management was equivalent to model building. This has proven incorrect. As I discussed in "The Harmony in Rechoirments" on page 115, requirements management is about people, about communications, and about attempting to understand before attempting to be understood (*The Seven Habits of Highly Effective People,* Stephen Covey, Simon and Schuster, 1989). I guess I hold little hope in the near term for researchers in requirements management. This fatal proclivity to overlook communications, according to Tom DeMarco in his 1996 keynote at the *Second International Conference on Requirements Engineering,* is alive and well, and researchers will continue to solve the technically simple parts of hard problems (see "Requirements Researchers: Do We Practice What We Preach?" on page 199).

I have more hopes for practitioners. Over my 20+ years of requirements management consulting, I have seen a strong movement away from formal requirements modeling, and toward

- Communicating with customers,
- Writing requirements in natural language, and
- Storing requirements in a database where they can be annotated, traced, sorted, and filtered.

DESIGN

The lack of a design discipline in software engineering has made us the laughing-stock of other engineering disciplines. How pleased I was to see the influx of books over the past five years on the principles of software architecture (*Software Architecture,* Mary Shaw and Dave Garlan, Prentice Hall, 1996) and design patterns (*Design Patterns,* Erich Gamma, et al., Addison Wesley Longman, 1995). We are not there yet though, for several reasons:

- Practitioners still fail to analyze alternative architectures before selecting one.
- Students of software engineering are rarely exposed to *principles* of design (there are obviously some exceptions).

---

*The object-oriented analysis world has clearly fallen; the object-oriented design world still lives.

- The books just scratch the surface when compared to, say, residential or commercial building architecture.
- Most importantly, we have not yet produced a discipline of "beauty" and "elegance" in software architecture, let alone the concept of the interplay between form and function, between beauty and utility.

And yet we are clearly making major headway here. I suspect that these problems will go away in a decade or so (see my later comments on academe).

PROGRAMMING LANGUAGES

I predict an end to the language wars by 2020.* We are all too obsessed today with language. The visual languages and their associated environments are showing us that we need not select one language. Environments now allow us to program bits and pieces in whatever language makes the most sense for that piece. Those features that make Java relatively platform-independent will become available in most languages. User interfaces and database designs have already become orders of magnitude easier to construct than they were just ten years ago. These aspects will continue to progress. A few other aspects of programming will likely follow. The result will be less emphasis on algorithms and data structures and more emphasis on thinking at higher levels of abstraction. I recently started programming again after a 15-year hiatus, I am simply overwhelmed by how languages and programming environments have progressed I have now been freed from details and can think with abstractions from the application domain.

METRICS

The software industry will continue being obsessed with measurement for at least 10.375 more years. Measurement of software product and software process is important. It provides us with yet one more means to assess whether we are getting better or worse as we change. My problem is not that with measurement but what we do with the data: when we use data to drive decisions at the expense of common sense, we have gone too far. For example, although using a circular saw is 53.2 percent more likely to sever a finger than using a hand saw, that data should not be used to abandon circular saws! In an example closer to home, data indicates that inspections are far more effective at locating defects than is testing; that should be grounds for doing inspections, not for abandoning testing.

Measures should be used to verify the effectiveness of change, not to drive change. We could use a measure to verify that brainstorming was more effective

[*Hmmm. Perhaps I was too optimistic in 1998. I had not imagined the Microsoft-Sun wars over languages like Java and C#.]

than interviews for requirements elicitation, but trying to achieve better values for such a measure could lead to disastrous results. That is, select a process change that you believe in and monitor its effectiveness by data, but don't let the data drive process changes. In short, keep your brain in gear. There are only a few measurement pundits around today who appreciate the criticality of this difference. Until I see more measurement folks acknowledging this, I will remain pessimistic with respect to their potential for positive effect on industry practices.

ACADEME

I wish I could say I had high hopes for academe, but I do not. I expounded on my views that software engineering educators must have real experience in the real world before they attempt to teach the next generation.* We have a responsibility to transmit knowledge and facts that are based in reality, not lies and theories that we as academics have learned from earlier generations of inexperienced academics. Yes, there is a place for educating other researchers, but a degree program that purports to teach software engineers (not software engineering researchers) must have educators with extensive industrial experience. It is okay for medical researchers to teach other budding medical researchers. But physicians of tomorrow must be educated by physicians with real patient experience. If software engineering degree programs do not start learning from medical schools and architecture schools (thanks to Colin Potts for pointing out that local practicing architects are often invited into the classroom to comment on the beauty and utility of student designs), we will end up with a new generation of graduates with no ability to produce software.

Computer science programs are in even more danger than software engineering programs. Too much of the core of many computer science degrees hinges upon achieving efficiency of computing resources (time, memory, and so on) that are no longer in short supply, and on building things that most practitioners no longer build. Too little time is devoted to producing reliable, maintainable, quality software.

FAREWELL

This is my time to say good-bye. My goal was to share words with you that would help you realize that your profession is an honorable one, that you are fulfilling a cause, but most of all that you have a responsibility to be more than "just" software development personnel. You have a responsibility to [yourself to think rather than just follow, and to] your fellow humans—to make others lives more meaningful, enjoyable, or satisfying as a result of being touched by you and your wares.

[*See Essay 32.]

SEEDS FOR DEBATE

1. In the third paragraph of this essay, I describe the DCP world (of 1998) as one that "employs more and more powerful tools to unburden itself from the tedium and error-proneness of software development." Since 1998, the agile development folks have emerged. Clearly they are also part of the DCP world. Can they be characterized in the same way? Or should the description of DCP worlds be modified for today's context?

2. In the third paragraph of this essay, I also describe the DCP world (of 1998) as one that is "more interested in achieving higher productivity than measuring it." Since 1998, the agile development folks have emerged. Clearly they are also part of the DCP world. Can they be characterized in the same way? Or should the description of DCP worlds be modified for today's context?

3. The battle for supremacy between languages like C# and Java are not like the earlier language wars. What is at stake? Why is the battle being waged?

4. Put together an argument for why defect-removal data when doing inspection is so convincing that testing *should be* abandoned (you might want to investigate the "cleanroom engineering" movement).

Index*

---

*Bold entries refer to chapter titles; *italicized entries* refer to book titles.

Great Software Debates. By Alan M. Davis
ISBN 0-471-649880 © 2004 Institute of Electrical and Electronics Engineers.

CL

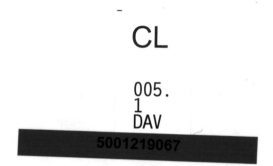